The Open
University

AA308
Thought and Experience:
Themes in the Philosophy of Mind

D1343515

BOOK 5

Consciousness

KEITH FRANKISH

This publication forms part of an Open University course AA308 *Thought and Experience: Themes in the Philosophy of Mind*. Details of this and other Open University courses can be obtained from the Course Information and Advice Centre, PO Box 724, The Open University, Milton Keynes MK7 6ZS, United Kingdom: tel. +44 (0)1908 653231, email general-enquiries@open.ac.uk

Alternatively, you may visit the Open University website at http://www.open.ac.uk where you can learn more about the wide range of courses and packs offered at all levels by The Open University.

To purchase a selection of Open University course materials visit the webshop at www.ouw.co.uk, or contact Open University Worldwide, Michael Young Building, Walton Hall, Milton Keynes MK7 6AA, United Kingdom for a brochure. tel. +44 (0) 1908 858785; fax +44 (0)1908 858787; email ouwenq@open.ac.uk

126

GIFT

The Open University
Walton Hall, Milton Keynes
MK7 6AA

First published 2005

Edited, designed and typeset by The Open University.

Printed and bound in the United Kingdom by Bath Press, Bath.

ISBN 0 7492 9645 3

1.1

207270b/aa308b5i1.1

CONTENTS

READINGS

Preface

O, what a world of unseen visions and heard silences, this insubstantial country of the mind! What ineffable essences, these touchless rememberings and unshowable reveries! And the privacy of it all! A secret theater of speechless monologue and prevenient counsel, an invisible mansion of all moods, musings, and mysteries, an infinite resort of disappointments and discoveries... An introcosm that is more myself than anything I can find in a mirror. This consciousness that is myself of selves, that is everything, and yet nothing at all – what is it?

And where did it come from?

And why?

(Jaynes 1976, 1)

What is the most intense physical pleasure you have ever experienced? Try to recall the occasion. Think of what it was like – the wonderful quality of the feeling, the way it spread through your body and overwhelmed your mind, blotting out all other thoughts and feelings. Next think of the most intense physical pain you have ever experienced. Again, try to recall it as vividly as you can. Now ask yourself this: *What exactly was happening on those occasions?* Various physical processes were taking place inside you – sensory receptors were being stimulated, nerve impulses travelling to your brain, clusters of brain cells undergoing electrochemical changes and so on. But how did all that produce the overwhelming sensations you felt? How could nerve impulses and electrochemical changes in brain cells produce *feelings* at all? This, in essence, is the problem of consciousness.

Few philosophical problems are as contentious as this one. Some philosophers regard it as one of the hardest problems there is; others deny that there is any special difficulty about it. Some argue that we shall never solve it; others that we have almost done so. Some claim that its solution will require a revolution in our view of reality; others that it merely requires some conceptual reorganization. The only thing on which there is any agreement is that the problem is an important one – if only for the misconceptions it generates. The problem of consciousness concerns the very essence of human life and has implications for our treatment of other living creatures and for the prospects of creating artificial life. It is, in short, a big problem – arguably one of the few really big problems left to solve.

All this makes consciousness an exciting topic to think about. And this is an exciting time to be thinking about it. After neglecting the topic for many years, philosophers and scientists have recently taken a renewed interest in consciousness, with the 1990s and early 2000s seeing a proliferation of articles, books, journals, websites and conferences devoted to the topic. Consciousness is now one of the hottest topics in philosophy of mind and looks set to continue so for some time.

This book is an introduction to the problem of consciousness. It will outline some of the key positions and arguments and guide you through some important readings from the contemporary literature. The book has five chapters. The first introduces consciousness and the so-called 'hard problem' it presents for a science of the mind. Chapters 2 and 3 are devoted to the question of whether consciousness is a physical phenomenon which can be explained by standard scientific methods – Chapter 2 setting out the arguments for a non-physicalist approach and Chapter 3 looking at some physicalist responses. Chapter 4 then goes on to examine some contemporary theories of consciousness which aim to explain it in broadly physical terms. Finally, Chapter 5 explores the idea that our view of consciousness involves some serious misconceptions and that we need to rethink our approach to the problem.

By the end of the book you should have a good understanding of the problem of consciousness and be in a position to decide where you stand on it. You will also, I hope, have discovered what a fascinating and challenging subject consciousness is and have experienced the intellectual excitement which its study can deliver. The problem of consciousness is a difficult one and – like all philosophical problems – it requires rigorous thinking and an open mind. But in return it offers the thrill of engaging with one of life's big unsolved mysteries.

In writing this book I have benefited greatly from the advice and support of my colleagues on the AA308 course team – in particular Alex Barber, Mike Beaney, Sean Crawford, Carolyn Price, Gerald Schmidt and Peter Wright. Thanks are also due to Gerry Bolton for overseeing the production process and to Peter Carruthers and Maria Kasmirli for their generous comments and advice.

CHAPTER 1

Introducing Consciousness

Consciousness: The having of perceptions, thoughts, and feelings; awareness. The term is impossible to define except in terms that are unintelligible without a grasp of what consciousness means. ... Consciousness is a fascinating but elusive phenomenon: it is impossible to specify what it is, what it does, or why it evolved. Nothing worth reading has been written about it.

(Sutherland 1995, 95)

Consciousness is at once the most important and most baffling aspect of the mind. It is the very heart of our existence – our 'self of selves' as Julian Jaynes puts it – yet it is extraordinarily difficult to describe and explain. This chapter is an introduction to this slippery phenomenon and the problems it presents. It is in three sections. The first explains what contemporary philosophers usually mean when they talk about consciousness; the second examines the phenomenon in more detail and highlights some of its puzzling features; and the third sets out the central philosophical problem surrounding consciousness – the so-called 'hard problem' of explaining how it arises and whether it is a physical phenomenon.

Defining consciousness

We use the words 'conscious' and 'consciousness' in a variety of ways. We talk of losing and regaining consciousness, of being conscious of one's appearance and of taking conscious decisions. We speak of self-consciousness and class-consciousness, of consciousness-raising activities and consciousness-enhancing drugs. Freudians contrast the conscious mind with the unconscious, gurus seek to promote world consciousness and mystics cultivate pure consciousness. These various uses reflect the history of the words. The original meaning of 'consciousness' was *awareness* or *knowledge*, either shared or private, and some of our modern uses reflect this. Self-consciousness is awareness of oneself as an individual; class-consciousness is awareness of belonging to a particular socio-economic group; to be conscious of one's appearance is to be very aware of it; and so on. In the seventeenth century, however, philosophers and other writers began to use the word in a more specific sense, to refer to our *inner* awareness of our own mental states – our perceptions, sensations, feelings and thoughts. As the philosopher John Locke (1632–1704) put it, 'Consciousness is the perception of what passes in a Man's own mind' (Locke 1961, vol. 1, 87). (Previously 'conscience' had been used in a similar way, but that word was coming to be used to refer to an inner moral sense.) Again, some of our modern uses reflect this philosophical usage. The conscious mind is the level of mental activity of which we are aware, in contrast to the repressed unconscious; consciousness-enhancing drugs are ones that alter our mental states in various ways; pure consciousness is mental awareness stripped of all particular content. When contemporary philosophers speak of 'the problem of consciousness' they too are using the term in broadly this sense, though with a subtle difference. In this section I shall explain in more detail what they have in mind.

What it's like

Suppose you have just had a dental procedure under general anaesthetic and are coming round. You are aware of a dazzling light above you and of a muffled voice echoing in your ears. There is sickness in your stomach and a sharp metallic taste in your mouth. You feel a moment of panic as you struggle to work out what has happened. Moving your head, you recognize the dentist's face and realize that he is speaking your name and asking if you want a glass of water. Your remember where you are, sit up shakily and take the glass.

Think about what happened as you regained consciousness. Various bodily processes resumed. Your sense organs started functioning again, registering stimuli and sending signals to your brain. Your brain also resumed its normal activity, processing these incoming signals and responding to them. Various brain centres became active, including ones devoted to visual processing, face recognition, emotion, memory, language and conceptualized thought. Signals flew back and forth from region to region and out to your organs and limbs. But this wasn't all that happened when you came round. You also started having *conscious experiences* – experiences with a certain *feel* to them. Imagine having the various experiences I described – seeing a dazzling light above you, hearing a muffled voice, having a metallic taste in your mouth, feeling a stab of panic and so on. Focus on what it is *like* to have those experiences – on what it feels like from the inside. Each of them, like every other experience, has its own character, which is instantly recognizable but very difficult to describe.

Philosophers use a variety of terms for this aspect of experience. You will find them speaking of an experience's 'qualitative feel', 'phenomenal feel', 'phenomenal character', 'phenomenal content', 'phenomenology' (in some contexts), 'subjective character', 'raw feel', 'what-it-is-likeness' and 'qualia' (a Latin plural meaning 'qualities'; the singular is 'quale'). Some of these terms – 'qualia' in particular – often carry theoretical overtones, but at bottom all refer to the same thing: what a given experience feels like from the inside. When contemporary philosophers speak of *consciousness* it is usually this to which they are referring.

Another way to home in on the phenomenon of consciousness is to contrast conscious mental states with non-conscious ones. Although some philosophers (Descartes for one) have rejected the idea, it is now widely accepted that we are not aware of all of our mental states and processes. This view has been popular among psychologists since at least the nineteenth century, and everyday life provides plenty of evidence for it. Consider driving, for example. One can drive a car, drawing upon one's knowledge of the rules of the road and of the car's controls, without giving any conscious thought to what one is doing. Or think of cases where the solution to a problem pops into one's head some time after one has given up thinking about it consciously. In these cases it seems, some quite complex mental activity must be going on below the surface.

Many writers also hold that non-conscious *perception* is possible. At first sight this may seem a bizarre claim. How could we *see* non-consciously? The idea is not as odd as it sounds, however. One way to illustrate this is to think about a robotic system. Consider Cog. Cog is a robot which is being built by the Humanoid Robotics Group at The Massachusetts Institute of Technology, under the direction of Rodney Brooks (Figure 1). Cog has a mechanical body (only the upper part so far), powered by electric motors and controlled by microprocessors similar to those found in personal computers. It also has a visual system, consisting of two head-mounted video cameras and a network of microprocessors for analysing their signals. (I say 'it' because the MIT team deny that Cog has a gender.) This gives Cog some basic visual abilities. It can identify faces and other interesting objects, follow moving objects with its eyes and use visual information to guide its hands. But though Cog has a form of vision, no one seriously thinks that it has conscious visual *experiences* of the sort we have when we look at the world around us. We might say that it has *non-conscious* vision: it sees things, but its sight does not have any felt quality to

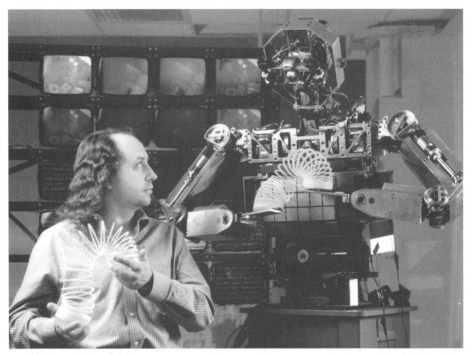

Figure 1 Rodney Brooks and his android robot Cog. Photo by Peter Menzel. Copyright ©
Peter Menzel/Science Photo Library.

it. The MIT team are also working to equip Cog with auditory and tactile
sensors, but again no one expects these to provide it with conscious
experiences of hearing and touch. (For more information about Cog, see
Adams et al. 2000; Brooks et al. 1998; Humanoid Robotics Group 2004,
online.)

There are times when we seem to perceive things in a Cog-like way.
Psychologists have shown that it is possible to influence a person's behaviour
by means of stimuli which are not consciously perceived (Dixon 1971). In a
typical experiment a word is displayed for a split second, so that the subject has
no conscious awareness of seeing it. In subsequent testing, however, the
subject makes word associations which are influenced by the word displayed –
revealing that they had in fact perceived it at some level. (This is known as
subliminal perception.) A similar phenomenon seems to occur frequently in
everyday life. When driving or walking along a busy street, we continually
fine-tune our movements in response to visual cues of which we are not
consciously aware – adjusting speed and direction to compensate for the
movements of those around us. We also respond in this way to signals from
our own bodies, shifting position to avoid cramp or to protect an injury, yet

without consciously noticing any discomfort. In these cases, it seems, our brains are registering information and using it to control our behaviour, yet without generating any conscious perceptions or sensations. There are also pathological conditions which seem to involve non-conscious perception. The most famous of these is *blindsight* (Weiskrantz 1986, 1997). People with this condition have normal eyes but have suffered damage to the visual processing areas of their brains, with the result that they seem to be blind in large areas of their visual field. They say – quite sincerely – that they see nothing in these areas. Yet if presented with an object in the blind area and asked to make a random guess as to its location or orientation, these people usually guess correctly – much to their own surprise when subsequently told the results. It seems that they are visually detecting the objects without any of the felt quality of normal vision.

(You may feel that it is twisting words to talk of non-conscious perceptions. Surely, *seeing* is by definition a conscious experience? This is really a terminological issue, however. If we use the term 'perception' in that way, then there are no non-conscious perceptions, just as there are no married bachelors. But it is compatible with this that there are non-conscious mental states which are very *like* perceptions in the role they play, and calling them 'non-conscious perceptions' is a way of emphasizing this. Some writers also talk of non-conscious sensations and experiences, and the same goes for those terms.)

These reflections on non-conscious mentality should help to clarify what philosophers mean when they talk about consciousness. Their focus is not on the nature of perceptions, sensations and thoughts as such, but rather on what is special about those perceptions, sensations and thoughts that have a feel to them. What exactly is this *feel* that conscious experiences have? How does it come about and what is its function? Whatever the answers, the phenomenon is surely tremendously important. As the American philosopher Thomas Nagel (b. 1937) puts it, to say that a creature has conscious experiences is to say that it is *like something* to be that creature – that it has an inner life (Nagel 1974). A non-conscious being such as Cog might be able to perform sophisticated tasks, guided by information from its sensors, but without conscious experience it would have no inner life. It might detect colours and sounds, but it would never know what it was like to see a brilliant blue sky or to hear leaves rustling in the breeze. It might register when it was damaged or running low on energy, and take appropriate action, but it would never feel real pain or hunger. It might act like us, but it would be dead inside, without any of the conscious experience that accompanies our activities. Life without consciousness would not be life at all as we know it. Indeed, the philosopher Colin McGinn (b. 1950) suggests that the emergence of consciousness was an event of cosmic significance, analogous to the Big Bang. Just as the Big Bang created the physical universe, so the emergence of consciousness – McGinn calls it the 'Soft Shudder' – created a new dimension of mental reality (McGinn 1999, 15).

ACTIVITY   Which of the following do you think have conscious experiences in the sense outlined above: apes, dogs, snakes, fish, insects, bacteria, plants, rocks?

DISCUSSION   Here is my answer. I find it hard to doubt that apes and dogs have conscious experiences very much like ours. I am not sure what to say about snakes and fish. I am fairly confident that insects do not have conscious experiences and I am certain that bacteria, plants and rocks do not.

Your intuitions may differ from mine of course. You may believe that all animals, even insects, are conscious. (Indeed, as we shall see, some philosophers think that even rocks have a *little bit* of consciousness!) You may be right, but I think you should at least consider the possibility that you are wrong. The fact that animals *behave* like us does not prove that they *feel* like us too. It would be fairly easy to program Cog to detect when it was damaged and issue sounds resembling cries of pain, but it still would not have any conscious pain sensations. And it is possible that animals are the same. In Chapter 4 we shall look at a theory of consciousness which may have the consequence that no non-human animals – except perhaps some apes – possess conscious experiences.

A note on terminology. We are going to need a standard term to refer to the feel of conscious experience. None of the options is unproblematic: 'feel' is ambiguous, 'qualia' has theoretical overtones, and 'what-it-is-likeness' is cumbersome. I shall use 'phenomenal character'. Although the term may sound technical, remember that it denotes something quite simple – the phenomenal character of an experience is *what it is like* to have it. I shall also occasionally speak of an experience's 'phenomenal properties'; this means the same.

Some distinctions

I now want to distinguish consciousness, in the sense outlined above, from some related phenomena. This should help to clarify the concept further and avoid potential confusion. What follows draws in part on distinctions and terminology introduced by the philosopher David Rosenthal (Rosenthal 1993).

The first distinction I want to make has already been introduced. When I described your experience at the dentist's I spoke both of *you* being conscious and of *your experiences* being conscious. These are different notions of consciousness, of course. When I spoke of you being conscious, I meant that you were awake, as opposed to being asleep or knocked out. When I spoke of your experiences being conscious I meant that they were of the sort that have a phenomenal character to them. These two sorts of consciousness are sometimes referred to as, respectively, *creature consciousness* and *state consciousness* ('state' here means 'mental state'). Of course, in us creature consciousness involves possession of state-conscious experiences, but perhaps in other creatures the comparable condition does not. When a stunned fish comes round, does it start having conscious experiences? I do not know.

As well as talking of creatures being simply *conscious*, we also talk of them being conscious *of* particular things – as when we say that someone was conscious of a face at the window. This is sometimes referred to as *transitive consciousness,* since it is directed at an object. To be conscious of something in this sense is to be *aware* of it – to be perceiving it or thinking about it. Again, for humans this usually involves having a conscious experience of it, but perhaps for other creatures it does not. Thus, we might say that Cog is conscious of the people around it, in virtue of the fact that it detects their presence and responds to them.

The second distinction is between consciousness, in the senses just mentioned, and *self*-consciousness. Self-consciousness is awareness of oneself as an individual. Fully developed, it involves the ability to think about oneself as a thinking, feeling creature, with a history, future and unique perspective on the world. This clearly requires some conceptual sophistication and it seems unlikely that many non-human animals are self-conscious in anything more than a rudimentary way, even if they are fully conscious in the other senses. Self-consciousness raises some important and difficult philosophical issues, but they are tangential to our main topic and I shall not be discussing them in this book.

A third, more contentious, distinction is between kinds of state consciousness. Here the philosopher Ned Block (b. 1942) has argued that we should distinguish between what he calls *phenomenal consciousness* and *access-consciousness* – *P-consciousness* and *A-consciousness* for short (Block 1995). Phenomenal consciousness is consciousness of the sort we have been discussing: a mental state is phenomenally conscious if it has a phenomenal character. Access-consciousness, on the other hand, is a rather different notion. A mental state is access-conscious if the information it carries is directly available to other mental processes, including reasoning, behavioural control and speech. Normally, of course, our experiences are access-conscious. If I see or hear something, then I am usually able to go on to think about it, tell others about it and decide how to react. But there are exceptions. Blindsighted people cannot draw on their blind-field perceptions in this way and can access them only indirectly, by making guesses. Similarly, subliminal perceptions are only partially available to other mental processes (we cannot report them or draw on them in our general reasoning).

Although phenomenal consciousness and access-consciousness typically go together, Block argues that they are distinct and could in principle come apart. As an example, he suggests that blindsighted people might be trained to make spontaneous guesses about what is present in their blind field, thereby improving their access to the visual information from that region. With enough training, they might find that the information popped into their heads automatically without the need for guessing. So when a red circle was shown in that area they would spontaneously think, 'There is a red circle there' and be able to report the fact and reason about it – even though they still could not *see* the circle in the normal sense. (Block calls this imaginary condition 'superblindsight'.) The information about the red circle would then be access-conscious without being phenomenally conscious. Whether Block is right about this is a matter of considerable dispute. As we shall see, some philosophers hold that phenomenal consciousness is at bottom just a kind of access-consciousness, and that we can explain the phenomenal character of a mental state in terms of its relations to other mental states and processes.

There is one final distinction I want to mention. One can have a phenomenally conscious experience without paying attention to it. For example, all day I have had a slight pain in my left leg. I have not thought about it much, but it has been there, in the background. Occasionally, however, we deliberately focus on our mental states and attend to their features. Now that I have mentioned the pain in my leg, I have started thinking about it and attending to its location, quality and intensity. This sort of inner attention is often referred to as *introspection*, and I shall say that mental states that are the object of it are *introspectively conscious*, whereas states that are conscious in the ordinary way are *non-introspectively conscious*. This distinction is particularly important when thinking about the mental life of non-human animals. It may be that the experiences of dogs, for example, are phenomenally conscious but not introspectively conscious – that dogs do not attend to their experiences in the way that we do.

The seventeenth-century notion of consciousness mentioned earlier ('perception of what passes in a man's mind') is close to that of introspective consciousness. In contemporary discussions, however, the focus is firmly on non-introspective phenomenal consciousness – on ordinary routine experience. What seems mysterious is how experience could have a phenomenal character at all. The fact that we can also deliberately attend to this character is a secondary matter. This is why I said that the modern notion of consciousness is subtly different from the older one.

At this point you may be feeling a bit confused. Surely, even non-introspective consciousness must involve inner awareness of some sort? How could a mental state *feel like* something if one isn't *aware* of its feel? Some philosophers would agree with this, arguing that even non-introspective consciousness involves inner awareness of some sort. We shall consider this view in a later chapter. But we should not prejudge the issue here. Many writers insist that the phenomenal character of an experience is not an object of awareness at all, but something that *accompanies* our awareness of other things. When we gaze at a beautiful sunset, they claim, we are aware only of the sunset, but our awareness of it has a certain phenomenal character. As Mark Rowlands puts it, what it is like to undergo an experience is not something *of* which we are aware, but something *with* which we are aware (Rowlands 2002, 159).

Here is an exercise to help you check your grasp of the distinctions mentioned above. Which meaning of 'consciousness' do the authors of the following quotations seem to have in mind? (Unless otherwise indicated, the quotations are taken from the *Oxford English Dictionary* entry on consciousness.)

ACTIVITY

1   It is only to the consciousness of these evils that knowledge and reflection awaken him (F.A. Kemble).

2   We class sensations along with emotions, and volitions, and thoughts, under the common head of *states of consciousness* (Thomas Huxley).

3   [Consciousness is] being aware of oneself as a distinct entity, separate from other people or things in one's environment (C. Evans, *Dictionary of the Mind, Brain and Behaviour*, quoted in Smith 1985, 129).

4   A state is conscious if it has experiential properties. The totality of the experiential properties of a state are 'what it is like' to have it (adapted from Block 1995, 230).

5   Consciousness is a word used by Philosophers, to signify that immediate knowledge which we have of our present thoughts and purposes, and, in general, of all the present operations of our minds (Thomas Reid).

6   When the fever left him, and consciousness returned, he awoke to find himself rich and free (Dickens).

7   Content is conscious in virtue of... reaching the Executive system, the system in charge of rational control of action and speech (adapted from Block 1995, 232).

8   [H]ow it is that anything so remarkable as a state of consciousness comes about as the result of irritating nervous tissue, is just as unaccountable as the appearance of Djin when Aladdin rubbed his lamp... (Thomas Huxley).

DISCUSSION   1   Transitive consciousness (note the 'of').

2   State consciousness (phenomenal, non-introspective?).

3   Self-consciousness.

4   Phenomenal consciousness (the original reads 'P-conscious').

5   Introspective consciousness.

6   Creature consciousness.

7   Access-consciousness (the original reads 'A-conscious').

8   Phenomenal consciousness.

These are the only distinctions I shall mention for now. But you should remember that the word 'consciousness' has other senses too, both in ordinary speech and in technical writing, and you should always check to see how it is being used. As I explained, our focus in this book will be on state consciousness of the ordinary non-introspective variety – phenomenal consciousness, in Block's terminology. I shall not keep spelling this out, however, and from now on, unless otherwise indicated, the words 'conscious' and 'consciousness' should always be understood in that way.

The elusiveness of consciousness

Consciousness is, in a sense, the most familiar thing in the world: our lives consist of a succession of conscious experiences. Yet consciousness can also seem elusive and mysterious, and this section contains some activities designed to highlight this. Here is a simple exercise to start us off.

ACTIVITY

Think about the different varieties of conscious experience you have and make a list of them. Include perceptual experiences (sight, hearing, etc.), bodily sensations (pain, for example) and any others you can think of. Then turn to Reading 1, which is an extract from the opening chapter of David Chalmers's book *The Conscious Mind* (Chalmers 1996), and compare your list with his. Do you find Chalmers's descriptions accurate? Are there are any points on which you disagree with him?

DISCUSSION

Chalmers notes that his catalogue is not intended to be exhaustive and you may have included items he omits. His list does, however, cover the main varieties of conscious experience, and it seems to me both evocative and, for the most part, accurate. There are only two points on which I would disagree with Chalmers. First, I think he misdescribes the feel of conscious thoughts (paragraphs 13–14). Such thoughts, he says, often have a distinctive qualitative feel, reflecting their subject matter: thoughts about lions, for example, have a 'whiff of leonine quality' about them. This does not reflect my own experience. I agree that occurrent thoughts often have a phenomenal character, but for me it is primarily the feel of *uttering* the thought to myself in inner speech – a feeling similar to that of saying it aloud, but muted. My thoughts are also sometimes associated with visual images and emotional feelings, though these tend to be vague and ill-defined. Secondly, I am not sure that Chalmers is right to claim that there is a distinct feel associated with the sense of self – a 'background hum', as he puts it, which accompanies our other more fleeting experiences (paragraph 17). For my part, I am not aware of such a feeling but only of specific experiences like those mentioned elsewhere in Chalmers's catalogue.

I suggest you refer back to your list and to Chalmers's catalogue as you work through this book. In philosophical discussions of consciousness it is common to focus on very simple experiences – usually visual ones – but it is important to keep in mind the range and variety of conscious experience, since theories of consciousness are intended to apply to all of them.

Chalmers concentrates on describing the feel of the various experiences he lists, but there is often more to an experience than its feel. Most experiences also carry information, or misinformation, about our environment (misinformation in the case of perceptual illusions, such as when a stick looks bent in water). So, visual experiences tell us about the colours, shapes and movements of things around us; auditory experiences tell us about the location and motion of objects; tastes and smells tell us about the substances present in our food and in the air; bodily sensations, such as pain and thirst, tell us about the condition of our bodies; and so on. States that carry information are known as *representational states* and the information they carry is known as their *representational content* (the terms 'intentional state' and 'intentional content' are also frequently used, with the same meaning). For example, suppose I have a visual experience as of seeing a blue circle in front of me. The experience has the representational content *that there is a blue circle ahead*. If there is indeed a blue circle there, then this content is true – the experience represents the world accurately. If there is not a blue circle there (if I am hallucinating, say), then the content is false – the experience represents the world inaccurately.

ACTIVITY

Do all conscious experiences have representational content? Can you think of any that do not? Does a headache carry information (about the state of blood vessels in the head, perhaps)? Does a buzz of excitement or a rush of euphoria? Does an orgasm?

DISCUSSION

This question is a controversial one. It is widely held that some bodily sensations and feelings lack representational content. Some philosophers, however, argue that representational content is the essence of consciousness and that all conscious experience possesses it. I am not going to discuss the issue here; we shall return to it in Chapter 4. For the moment, just bear the question in mind and see if your opinion changes as we go on.

I said that consciousness can seem elusive and mysterious and I want to use the rest of this section to illustrate some aspects of this.

Look back to Reading 1, especially paragraphs 1–7. Chalmers highlights two ways in which consciousness seems mysterious. What are they?

ACTIVITY

DISCUSSION

One point Chalmers mentions several times is that the phenomenal character of many conscious experiences seems *ineffable* – we cannot find words to describe it adequately. Another point he mentions is that, in many cases, the connection between a stimulus and the resulting experience appears *arbitrary* – there seems to be no reason why the experience should have the phenomenal character it does, rather than a different one.

Let us consider these claims in more detail, beginning with ineffability. Chalmers's point is that it is often hard to describe an experience in a way that really conveys what it is like and that would be informative to someone who had never had it. This is not just because experiences can be very complex. Indeed, complex experiences may be easier to describe than simple ones, since we can break them down into more basic components. For example, a wine critic may describe the bouquet of a wine by saying that it contains scents of peach, anti-freeze and grass clippings. But these more basic sensory experiences seem indescribable. How could we describe the smell of grass clippings? It is distinctive and easily recognizable but seemingly impossible to characterize. (Of course, we can describe it *indirectly* as 'the smell you get from grass clippings', but how could we describe what it is like *in itself*?)

It is worth dwelling on this point a little. Take a simple visual experience – looking at a blue surface, say. How could I set about conveying the quality of this experience to someone who had never had it? I might try comparing it to other experiences – saying, for example, that it is more like the experience of seeing green than it is like that of seeing yellow. But such descriptions would be of use only to someone who had already had those other experiences. What description could I give to someone who was congenitally blind? The only option, it seems, would to be make comparisons with non-visual experiences,

"It's a naïve domestic Burgundy without any breeding, but I think
you'll be amused by its presumption."

Figure 2 The difficulties of describing phenomenal properties. Cartoon by James Thurber.
Copyright © 1933, 1961 Rosemary A. Thurber. All rights reserved.

but it is hard to find informative ones. (A famous example, cited by John
Locke, is that of a blind man who had the idea that scarlet resembled the sound
of a trumpet (Locke 1961, vol. 2, 30). Although not bad as such comparisons
go, this still falls a long way short of capturing what it is like to see something
red.) The same goes for experiences involving other sense organs.

In this connection is it interesting to note that we do not have distinctive words
for phenomenal properties themselves. Take the experience a normally
sighted person has when looking at a ripe tomato. What term should we use for
the phenomenal character of this experience? We might loosely call it 'red' – in
everyday speech we do sometimes talk of having red sensations or red
afterimages. (An afterimage is the sensation ones gets after staring at a bright
light and then looking away.) But the *experience* – the mental state – is not
really red, at least not in the same sense the tomato is. The experience is not
coloured red. (It is true that if experiences are states of the brain, as many
philosophers believe, then the neural tissues involved will have colours. But
there is no reason to think they will be *red*. Your brain doesn't change colour
depending on what you are looking at!) To get round this difficulty some
writers coin special terms for phenomenal properties. The philosopher
Joseph Levine, for example, uses 'reddishness' for the property possessed by
experiences of red (Levine 2001). Thus Levine would say that red things
cause reddish experiences.

The claim that conscious experience is ineffable is closely related to another
claim often made about it – namely, that it is *subjective*. The phenomenal

character of an experience, it is claimed, can only be appreciated from the inside, from the first-person point of view. We might study the brain processes involved in a certain type of experience in the most minute detail, but we would not learn what the experience was really *like* unless we were to have it for ourselves. To emphasize the point, the phenomenal aspect of experience is often referred to as its *subjective character* – in contact to the objective, publicly observable features of the brain states involved (Nagel 1974).

Turn now to Chalmers's second point – the arbitrariness of phenomenal character. The idea here is that, in many cases, the connection between what an experience is *of* and the way it *feels* seems arbitrary. 'Why should *that* feel like *this*?' we are tempted to ask, reflecting on a stimulus and the experience it causes. Of course, as Chalmers notes, this is not true of all experiences. It is surely not arbitrary that the experience of seeing a cube and that of seeing a sphere should feel the way they do, rather than the other way round. But in many cases the connections do seem arbitrary. Colours, sounds and smells offer good examples. Why should the light reflected from a ripe tomato produce a reddish sensation (to use Levine's terminology) rather than a greenish one? Why do the sound waves produced by a telephone cause us to hear a ringing sound, rather than, say, a squeaky one? Why do the chemicals in newly mown grass produce the particular smell they do, rather than another?

Of course, there is much we do not know about the brain processes involved in sense perception. But even if we knew everything about them it is still not clear that this sense of arbitrariness would be removed. We might still be at a loss to know why particular brain processes give rise to the particular experiences they do – why nerve firings in a certain region of the visual cortex (the area of the brain associated with vision) give rise to a reddish sensation, rather than a greenish one, or why the stimulation of certain cells in the olfactory bulb (the brain region associated with smell) causes a smell of grass clippings, rather than, say, one of linseed oil.

The apparent arbitrariness of phenomenal character suggests a strange possibility. If the links between stimuli and the experiences they cause really are arbitrary, then perhaps the same stimuli do not produce the same experiences in everyone. Perhaps when other people look at blue objects they have an experience of the sort I have when I look at yellow ones – so that for them looking at a cloudless summer sky is like looking at a vast sandy desert. How would I know?

ACTIVITY

Could I tell by questioning other people if the phenomenal character of their blue and yellow experiences is inverted in this way? Pause and think for a few minutes.

DISCUSSION

It seems unlikely that I could. Asking them if the sky looks blue or yellow won't help. They will say it looks blue – since they have learned to call things that produce experiences with this phenomenal character 'blue'. The question is whether they associate the word 'blue' with the same phenomenal character I do. Nor will it help to ask them to describe the experience itself. For, as we have seen, it is very hard to describe simple experiences in a way that conveys their phenomenal character. Perhaps the best option would be to ask them to make comparisons between colours. If blue things produce yellowish experiences in them, then they will say that blue things look more similar to orange things than to green things, whereas if they produce bluish experiences, they will say it is the other way round. Even this would not be conclusive, however. For it might be that their other colour experiences are switched round too – so that, for example, the experiences they have when looking at orange things are like those I have when looking at green things and vice versa. If the whole range of their colour experiences was systematically inverted, then – arguably – all colour comparisons would be preserved and the inversion would be undetectable. This is referred to as the possibility of *interpersonal spectrum inversion* (Figure 3).

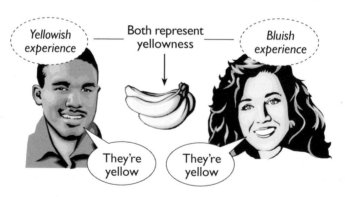

Figure 3 Spectrum inversion.

The possibility of spectrum inversion is sometimes said to show that the phenomenal character of an experience is independent of its representational content. The thought is that differences in phenomenal character need not make any difference to the way we classify objects and use colour words. You and I could agree on which things are yellow, even if these things produce different experiences in each of us. And the resulting experiences would represent the same thing – namely, the presence of something of the sort we both call 'yellow' – despite their difference in phenomenal character. We can imagine inversions in other sense organs, too. For example, patchouli might produce in you the smell sensation that almond oil produces in me. Again, however, both experiences could *represent* the same thing – the presence of patchouli. Considerations like these lead some people to say that the phenomenal character of an experience is an *intrinsic*, or *non-relational*, property of it – that is, one which it possesses in its own right, independently of its relations to other things. The representational properties of an experience, on the other hand, are not intrinsic, but determined by its relations to the object or property represented.

The conception of phenomenal properties just outlined – as ineffable, subjective and intrinsic – has been very influential in philosophical thinking about consciousness, and the claims just mentioned will crop up again throughout this book. Not everyone agrees that the conception is correct, however. Although consciousness can seem elusive when we reflect on it from the first-person point of view, many philosophers believe that our intuitions in this area should be treated with caution. Some writers deny that we are aware of intrinsic, non-representational features of our experiences and many believe that conscious experiences are states of the brain which are, in principle, publicly observable and describable in physical terms. We shall return to these issues in later chapters.

The problem of consciousness

Let us turn now to the problem of consciousness. What exactly is the issue here that so divides philosophers and is the focus of such vigorous debate? In broad terms, it is the question of the place of consciousness in the world – the question of how it arises and how it is related to processes in the brain. It is hard to deny that consciousness is closely dependent on the brain. Changes in the brain can affect consciousness (think of the effects of anaesthetics and psychedelic drugs) and damage to the brain can remove it permanently (think of blindsight, for example). But *how* does the brain generate consciousness? How *could* conscious experiences arise from the activity of brain cells –

individually not much different from any other cells? As Colin McGinn puts it, it seems like magic:

> How is it possible for conscious states to depend upon brain states? How can technicolour phenomenology arise from soggy grey matter? What makes the bodily organ we call the brain so radically different from other bodily organs, say the kidneys – the body parts without a trace of consciousness? How could the aggregation of millions of individually insentient neurons generate subjective awareness? We know that brains are the *de facto* causal basis of consciousness, but we have, it seems, no understanding whatever of how this can be so. It strikes us as miraculous, eerie, even faintly comic. Somehow, we feel, the water of the physical brain is turned into the wine of consciousness, but we draw a total blank on the nature of this conversion. Neural transmissions just seem like the wrong kind of materials with which to bring consciousness into the world, but it appears that in some way they perform this mysterious feat. The mind–body problem is the problem of understanding how the miracle is wrought, thus removing the sense of deep mystery. We want to take the magic out of the link between consciousness and the brain.
>
> (McGinn 1989, 349)

This is the problem of consciousness – the problem of taking the magic out of its link to the brain and, thereby, to the rest of the natural world. For many philosophers, solving this problem would involve giving a *reductive explanation* of consciousness, and I shall begin by saying something about explanations of this kind and the reasons for seeking them.

Naturalism and reductive explanation

There is a widespread commitment among contemporary philosophers and scientists to a *naturalistic* view of the world. In broad terms, naturalism is the view that everything is scientifically explicable – to put it crudely, that there are no miracles. (Note that I am using 'naturalism' here for a *metaphysical* position – a view about the nature of the world. It is also used for a *methodological* position – a view about how the world, or some aspect of it, should be studied. Indeed, the word has a variety of meanings and should be used with care.) Thus, naturalists deny the existence of supernatural entities and powers and assume that everything that happens is causally explicable by reference to scientific principles and laws. Some naturalists also make a further assumption. They assume that natural phenomena form a hierarchy and that higher-level ones can be explained by reference to more basic ones, right down to the level of chemistry and physics. *Reproduction*, for example, counts as a high-level phenomenon, which can be explained in terms of more basic genetic and cellular processes, which can themselves be explained in chemical and physical terms. This sort of explanation, where a phenomenon at one level is explained in terms of those at a lower level, is called *reductive explanation*. The notion of reductive explanation is a key one in the modern debate about consciousness and it is important to understand how reductive explanations work. An example may be useful.

Suppose that a person who has had no previous contact with modern civilization is shown a working television set, displaying images of events taking place many miles away. They are astonished by the device and declare that it must be magic. How would we convince them otherwise? The answer, of course, is by explaining how a television set works. We might begin by describing a television camera – explaining that it uses a lens to focus a moving image onto a light-sensitive plate, which then generates a stream of electronic pulses, corresponding to the pattern on the plate. We would then explain how this electronic signal is amplified and broadcast – explaining what radio waves are and how they can be used to carry an electronic signal. Finally, we would turn to the television set itself and explain that it detects radio waves via an antenna, decodes the signal and uses it to modulate the beam of a cathode ray tube, causing the tube to emit patterns of light which correspond to the images in the camera and which are perceived by the human eye as a moving picture. Of course, in order to make all this comprehensible we would have to provide a lot of further information about the underlying physical processes – about light, optics, electricity, radio waves and so on – but with time and access to reference books we could surely satisfy our hearer that there was nothing magical about the television.

In doing all this we would have *reductively explained* the television's power to display moving images of distant events. That is, we would have shown that this property follows from more basic, lower-level properties of the television – its possession of various mechanical and electronic components. These properties explain the television's power to display moving images of distant events because it is obvious that they are sufficient for it. Nothing more is needed in order for the television to have that power than for it to possess those properties. In a widely-used phrase, the lower-level properties *realize* the higher-level one: the television possesses the latter *in virtue* of the fact that it possesses the former.

It is important to distinguish reductive explanation from *reduction*. To say that a property can be *reduced* to a lower-level one is to say that it can be identified with it across the board – that they are in fact the same property, under different names. (Or at least that is one common meaning of 'reduction'.) For example, the property of being water reduces to that of having the molecular structure H_2O. Reductions like this are quite rare, however, since most properties can be realized in more than one way ('multiply realized'). Different kinds of television, for example, work in different ways and are made of different materials (some have plasma screens instead of cathode ray tubes, some receive the signal by cable instead of aerial, older models use vacuum tubes or transistors instead of integrated circuits and so on). So we cannot identify the property of being a television with that of having a particular set of components. *Any* components will do, provided they do the job. However, the fact that a phenomenon cannot be reduced to a lower-level one does not mean that it cannot be reductively explained in lower-level terms. Each *instance* of the phenomenon may be realized in lower-level properties and explicable in terms of them, even if these properties are not the same in every case.

Now as I said, many philosophers and scientists assume all that phenomena above the level of basic physics can, in principle, be reductively explained. They view the natural world as a unified structure, whose higher levels of organization emerge in a thoroughly comprehensible way from lower-level ones and ultimately from basic physical states and processes. I shall refer to this view as *strong naturalism*.

Strong naturalism has considerable plausibility. It is a remarkable fact that just about every phenomenon scientists have studied has turned out to yield to reductive explanation. Take life, for example. Until the middle of the nineteenth century it was common for biologists to maintain that life was not the product of more basic inorganic processes, but dependent on a special vital spirit or force – a view known as *vitalism*. It is easy to see why they thought this. Inanimate structures tend to decay steadily, whereas living things are able to sustain, repair and reproduce themselves. Given the undeveloped state of biological knowledge, it was not implausible to think that this amazing regenerative ability could not be the product of mere physical processes. In fact, of course, this was quite wrong. As biologists studied organic processes in more detail, they discovered that they were nothing more than complex chemical reactions, which could be replicated in the laboratory. With time, more and more biological phenomena yielded to reductive explanation, and today vitalism is wholly discredited. What is special about living things, it turned out, is not that they possess a non-physical ingredient but that they involve a unique and very complex *organization* of physical elements.

What proved true in biology has proved true in the other sciences, too. Almost everywhere scientists have been able to explain higher-level phenomena in terms of lower-level ones.

Can you think of any properties that seem unlikely to yield to reductive explanation? (Set aside mental ones for the moment.)

ACTIVITY

DISCUSSION

The most obvious candidates, I think, are moral and aesthetic properties. Can the rightness and wrongness of our actions be reductively explained by reference to their physical characteristics – when and where and in what manner they were performed? It seems unlikely: the very same action, physically characterized, might be disloyal, say, in one context but not in another. Similarly, can we explain why objects have the aesthetic properties they do – why they are graceful or elegant or ugly, for example – by reference to their physical properties – their colours and shapes and so on? Again, many would say no: we cannot read off an object's aesthetic properties from its physical ones.

It may be, then, that moral and aesthetic properties cannot be reductively explained. But even if this is so, there is no fatal objection here to strong naturalism. For defenders of the doctrine may simply deny that moral and aesthetic properties are real properties of actions and objects and claim instead that they are just projections of our own responses to them. Indeed, for some people, the very resistance of these properties to reductive explanation is a reason for denying their reality. If a phenomenon cannot be reductively explained – if we cannot see how it could arise from lower-level processes – then, these people would say, that is a good reason for thinking that it is not real or has at least been seriously mischaracterized.

(It is worth stressing at this point that a strong naturalist need not claim that reductive explanation is the only legitimate kind of explanation. A reductive explanation shows how a phenomenon is constituted, but there are other types of explanation with different functions. For example, much scientific explanation involves explaining processes at a high level of description without going into the details of how they are constituted. This is the case with explanations in the so-called *special sciences* – the sciences devoted to specific phenomena above the level of basic physics – biology, chemistry, psychology and so on. Strong naturalists need not deny the legitimacy or usefulness of these other types of explanation, though they will claim that there are reductive explanations of *why* they hold.)

Here is an activity to reinforce the points just made.

ACTIVITY Which of the following claims would strong naturalists endorse?

1   Everything that exists is natural.

2   Everything that happens can be scientifically explained.

3   Science can only deal with natural processes; supernatural ones are beyond it.

4   All phenomena above the level of basic physics can be explained in lower-level terms.

5   All phenomena can be reduced to physical ones.

6   Reductive explanation is the only legitimate kind of explanation.

DISCUSSION Strong naturalists would endorse (2) and (4). (1) is ambiguous. If 'natural' means 'not supernatural', then strong naturalists would endorse it. If it means 'not man-made' then of course they would not. Naturalism has nothing to do with the contrast between the natural and the man-made. (3) is a misunderstanding of the naturalist position, as I have characterized it. Naturalists do not claim that supernatural processes are beyond science; they claim that there *are no* supernatural processes. As for claims (5) and (6), I have already explained that strong naturalists need not endorse them. The strong naturalist need not maintain that higher-level phenomena can be reduced to physical ones, merely that they can be reductively explained in physical terms. Nor need they deny the legitimacy of other kinds of explanation.

The easy problems and the hard problem

What implications do naturalism and strong naturalism have for the study of the mind? There are two. First, naturalists will deny the existence of souls, spirits and other psychic phenomena and maintain that the mind is part of the natural world, subject to natural laws. This view is shared by most modern philosophers of mind. Secondly, *strong* naturalists will hold that mental phenomena can be reductively explained in terms of processes in the brain, which can themselves be explained in terms of lower-level processes at the chemical and physical level. Although not as widely accepted as the first, this view is also common among contemporary philosophers, and, indeed, there is a strong case for it. All other high-level phenomena seem to be reductively explicable; why should the mind be any different?

But how *could* brain processes give rise to minds and mental states? How could collections of neurons and synapses generate beliefs and desires, hopes and fears, pains and pleasures? Much of contemporary philosophy of mind has been devoted to trying to answer this question – to constructing a naturalistic theory of the mind – and though we are still a long way from fully understanding how the mind works, there are plenty of theories as to how mental states and processes might be realized in the brain.

An important development was the idea that many mental states and processes can be defined *functionally*, in terms of the causal role they play in the operation of the mind – the view known as *functionalism*. So, for example, a belief is a state which is generated by perception or inference, serves as a premise in reasoning and prompts actions that would be rational if it were true; a desire is a state which is caused by bodily needs, serves as a goal in reasoning and tends to produce behaviour which will satisfy it; perception is a process in which information about the environment is acquired through the receipt of sensory stimuli; and so on. If we think of mental states and processes in this way, then it not too difficult to see how a brain could support them. It would just have to possess states and mechanisms which play the appropriate causal roles.

Another source of inspiration was the development of computers, which provided models of how reasoning could be performed mechanically, through the manipulation of symbols. This suggested that the brain itself might be a biological computer operating on symbols in an internal language, and a new field of research opened up devoted to modelling mental processes in computational terms. Again, on this view it is not too difficult to see how brain tissue could support a mind; it would simply need to be organized in such a way as to implement the relevant computational processes. This approach may not be the right one (there are rivals to it) and many problems remain – in particular, that of explaining how symbols in the mental language get their meaning. But it does suggest that there is no obstacle *in principle* to providing reductive explanations of many mental phenomena.

When it comes to consciousness, however, the functional/computational approach runs into problems. Although some of the things we call 'consciousness' may be explicable in functional/computational terms (access-consciousness, for example), it is very hard to see how *phenomenal* consciousness could be. This problem has been recognized since the development of functional approaches to the mind in the late 1960s, but it was powerfully restated in the 1990s by the Australian philosopher David Chalmers (b. 1966), who has famously dubbed it the 'hard problem' of consciousness. I shall let Chalmers outline it himself, in an extract from one of his first papers on the topic.

ACTIVITY

Turn to Reading 2 and answer the following questions.

1   In paragraph 2 Chalmers lists various phenomena associated with the word 'consciousness'. Which of the terms introduced earlier ('creature consciousness', 'access-consciousness', 'transitive consciousness', etc.) corresponds best to each of the items in the list? (Note that in some cases the correspondence is not exact.)

2   What does Chalmers mean by 'experience'? (Paragraphs 5–6)

3   Why, according to Chalmers, are the easy problems easy? (Paragraphs 7–11)

4   Why is the hard problem hard? (Paragraphs 12–14)

DISCUSSION

1   The phenomena line up roughly as follows. The first (the ability to discriminate, categorize and react to stimuli) is a state of general awareness, so it falls under the heading of creature consciousness. The second, third and fourth items (the integration of information, reportability and internal access) involve the passing of information between internal systems, so they can be grouped under access-consciousness. The fourth phenomenon (attention) is a perceptual process, so it comes under the heading of transitive consciousness (awareness *of* something). A deliberate action is one performed with reflective awareness, so the fifth item (the deliberate control of behaviour) involves introspective consciousness (and perhaps also self-

consciousness). The last item (wakefulness) corresponds to creature consciousness again.

2   He means *phenomenal consciousness* – the subjective aspect of our experiences, *what it is like* to have them.

3   The easy problems are easy because the phenomena to be explained are functionally definable and we can explain how a system exhibits them by describing the mechanisms that perform the relevant functions. These mechanisms might be described either in neurological terms or in more abstract computational ones. (In the latter case, to give a full explanation we would also have to specify the neural mechanisms which implement the computational processes, but that would be just another 'easy' problem.) Thus, for example, if we can identify the brain mechanisms that give us the ability to make verbal reports of our beliefs and other mental states, then we shall have explained the phenomenon of reportablity.

4   The hard problem is hard because it goes *beyond* the performance of functions. Even when we have explained all the various functional processes that occur when we perceive things, we would still not have explained why these processes are accompanied by conscious experience – that is, why our perceptions have a phenomenal character. This looks like a much more difficult problem.

In this extract Chalmers is appealing to intuition rather than offering arguments, and you should not take his comments to be the final verdict on functionalism. But the intuition to which he appeals is certainly strong. Put simply, functionalism characterizes mental states by what they *do*, rather than by how they *feel*. And it seems that a brain state could play the functional role of an experience without having any phenomenal character to it. Take pain, for example. Pains have a distinctive functional role: they are caused by bodily damage and cause characteristic behavioural reactions. Yet, it seems, a brain state could play this role without actually *hurting*. Think about Cog again. Suppose that damage to Cog's body activates an internal subsystem which registers the location and extent of the damage and initiates appropriate action, such as protecting the damaged area, withdrawing from the source of the damage and emitting the word 'Ouch!' from a speech synthesizer. Then when this subsystem is activated, it would be appropriate to say that Cog is *in pain*, in the functional sense, even though it doesn't actually *feel* anything. Similarly for other perceptions and experiences. It seems that a brain state could play the functional role appropriate to a visual perception – say, of a bright blue light – without having the phenomenal character normally possessed by such a state, or indeed with a quite different phenomenal character. So, it seems, functionalism leaves the mystery of consciousness untouched: how do some brain states come to have phenomenal character?

We can look at the same problem from another perspective. Suppose the MIT team wanted to give Cog conscious experiences. What would they have to do? Would it involve new programming? Or new circuitry? Or what? There are many things they could do to improve Cog's visual system – increasing the sensitivity of its camera-eyes, boosting the power of its visual processors and upgrading their software – but it is not clear what they could do to give its visual processes phenomenal character. Where would they start? If we have no idea how nature produces conscious experiences, then how can we set about trying to produce them artificially? It is worth noting that practically all the research programmes currently being pursued by the MIT team and other roboticists are devoted to equipping robots with specific functional capacities – capacities to discriminate, categorize, learn, perform everyday tasks and so on. None is devoted directly to making it *conscious*. Indeed, the MIT say they try to avoid using the 'c-word' in their labs!

Let me repeat that you should not take this as the final verdict on functionalism. Many functionalists think that their approach *can* explain consciousness. When properly understood, these writers claim, the functional processes involved in experience do explain its phenomenal character. And, of course, even if functionalist explanations fail, a reductive explanation in other terms might still be possible. But it is undeniable that there is a serious problem here, and some people believe that consciousness is resistant *in principle* to reductive explanation. Here, they claim, strong naturalism reaches its limits.

Physicalism and the hard problem

I introduced the hard problem as an explanatory problem – the problem of explaining how consciousness arises. But it can also be presented as a metaphysical problem – the problem of saying what kind of phenomenon consciousness is, and, more specifically, whether it is a *physical* one. In this section I shall say something about this aspect of the hard problem and its relation to the explanatory one.

The terms 'physical' and 'physicalism' (the view that everything is physical) are used in a number of different senses and it is easy to become confused by them. Some writers who count as physicalists in one sense of the term count as anti-physicalists in another. (The same goes for 'materialism', which is sometimes used interchangeably with 'physicalism'.) I shall distinguish some important senses and give them labels, but you should note that other writers draw the distinctions in different ways and use the terminology differently.

In one form, physicalism is the view that everything in the universe is composed wholly of the basic entities and forces postulated by modern physics (electrons, protons, gravity, electromagnetism and so on). It is the view that, as John Haugeland puts it, 'if you took away all the atoms, nothing would be left behind' (Haugeland 1982, 96). I shall refer to this view as *substance physicalism*. (*Substance dualism*, on the other hand, is the view that the universe also contains other entities and forces in addition to the basic physical ones – immaterial souls or psychic energy, for example.) Now I am going to assume that substance physicalism is true. This reflects the prevailing view among contemporary philosophers of mind, including some who would describe themselves as being, in another sense, non-physicalists. The modern debate over physicalism focuses on other claims, not about *substances*, but about *properties*. (If you are sympathetic to substance dualism, you should not conclude that the rest of this book will be irrelevant to you; I shall explain why shortly.)

Suppose substance physicalism is true. Still, questions remain about the *properties* of things. Let me begin by introducing the notion of a *basic physical property*. By this I mean a property invoked by physicists, such as mass or electrical charge, or a property that can be defined in terms of the properties invoked by physicists, such as that of being composed of atoms of a certain kind. Now if physics describes the basic components of the world, then there is a sense in which the basic physical properties of things are the fundamental ones. But, of course, things possess many other properties in addition to their basic physical ones. Take me. I have various basic physical properties. For example, I have a certain mass, I am composed of millions of molecules arranged in elaborate structures, I am the site of numerous complex electro-chemical processes. But I also have many other properties: I am alive, I am human, I have a digestive system, I belong to blood group O, I like Bob Dylan, I currently have a slight headache and so on. Let us call these *high-level properties*. But how are these high-level properties related to my basic physical ones? The question could also be phrased in terms of facts. For each of my properties there is a corresponding fact – the fact that I possess the property. So another way of putting the question would be to ask how the high-level facts about me are related to the basic physical facts about me. Most modern debates about physicalism are about the answers to questions like these.

Property physicalism is the view that high-level properties are not fundamentally distinct from basic physical ones. They are not new features of the world, in addition to the basic physical ones, but just those same features under different guises. So, for example, my having a digestive system is not an extra property of mine, over and above the basic physical ones. Rather, it *consists in* my having certain basic physical properties – having certain basic physical components arranged in a certain way and performing certain functions. Similarly for all other high-level properties. Or, putting it in terms of facts, high-level facts are not extra facts, over and above the basic physical ones; rather, they are just redescriptions of the basic physical ones. There is, it is true, a sense in which high-level facts plainly are different from basic physical ones: the claim that I have a digestive system does not *mean the same* as the claim I have certain basic physical properties. But – the physicalist will say – there is just one underlying state of affairs which makes both claims true. This is sometimes expressed by saying that once God fixed the basic physical facts, he fixed all the facts; there was no more work for him to do (Kripke 1980). (The reference to God need not be taken literally – it is just a vivid way of making the point about the relation between the different properties.)

Property physicalism contrasts with *property dualism*. This is the view that some high-level properties *are* fundamentally distinct from basic physical ones – that they are additional features of the world, over and above the basic physical ones. Or, putting it in terms of facts, some high-level facts are extra facts, distinct from the basic physical ones. So when God fixed the basic physical facts, he still had more work to do: he still had some high-level facts to fix. If he had pleased, God could have created a world which was exactly like ours in all its basic physical details but which didn't have the same high-level properties. It is worth stressing that property dualists do not claim that *all* high-level properties are distinct from basic physical ones, but only that *some* are. Thus, while property physicalism is a general claim about all high-level properties, property dualism comes in different versions, each concerned with a different high-level property or group of high-level properties.

Consider the property of being alive.   ACTIVITY

1   What would a property dualist about life say about the relation between my basic physical properties and the fact that I am alive?

2   What would a property physicalist say?

DISCUSSION

1   The dualist about life would say that being alive is an extra property of mine over and my basic physical ones. God could have made a creature that was exactly like me in all its basic physical properties but was not alive.

2   The property physicalist would say that my being alive is not an extra property of mine, over and above my basic physical ones. Given that I have all the basic physical properties I do, I could not fail to be alive: there is nothing more to it.

Of course, the dualist about life may accept that there is a regular *correlation* between the presence of certain basic physical properties and the presence of life. After all, we don't find life in just any old physical structure but only in certain highly organized ones. The dualist may even say that it is a law of nature that when certain basic physical properties are present, then life is, too. But, they will say, it is a contingent fact that this law holds and it could have been different. (Compare the way that light has a certain speed in our universe but could have had a different one.) The physicalist, on the other hand, will deny that it is a contingent fact that certain basic physical properties are correlated with life. Rather, they will say, there is *nothing more* to being alive than having the right set of basic physical properties, and the latter could not occur without life.

There is one more distinction to make before we move on. Property physicalism is the view that high-level properties are not fundamentally distinct from basic physical ones, but there are stronger and weaker versions of this view. According to the stronger version, high-level properties *reduce* to basic physical ones. That is, each high-level property can be identified with a single basic physical property (or single set of such properties) in all its instances. This is sometimes expressed by saying that the two properties are *type-identical*. This strong form of property physicalism is not plausible. *Some* high-level properties reduce to basic physical ones; for example, having blood group O reduces to having blood of a certain molecular composition. But, as I mentioned earlier, most high-level properties can be constituted in more than one way. For example, the digestive system involves quite different structures in different animals. The same goes for mental properties, too. An alien might suffer from headaches and like Bob Dylan despite having a completely different brain chemistry from me. It does not follow, however, that these properties are fundamentally distinct from basic physical ones; it remains open that they are *realized in* basic physical properties. That is, every instance of these properties might be identical with an instance of some basic physical property – the nature of the latter varying from case to case. So a weaker and more plausible version of property physicalism holds that high-level properties *either* reduce to *or* are realized in basic physical ones.

This weak form of property physicalism is the most popular contemporary version of physicalism and the chances are that when you come across the

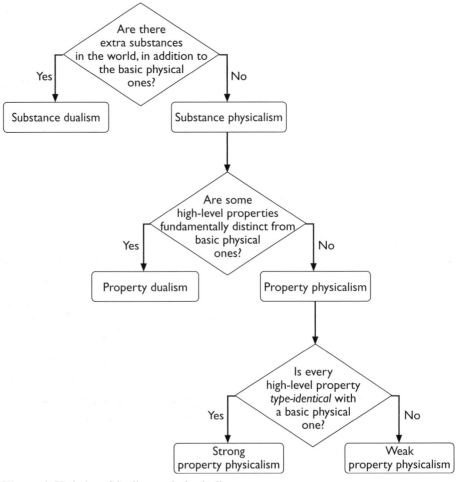

Figure 4 Varieties of dualism and physicalism.

word 'physicalism' (or 'materialism') in a contemporary book or article it is this weak form of property physicalism, or something very close to it, that is meant (though there will be exceptions and you should always check to make sure). For convenience, I too shall use the term 'physicalism', without qualification, to refer to this position. I shall also assume that physicalists in this sense endorse substance physicalism, though I shall not be discussing this aspect of their position. Two more terminological points. I shall use the term 'physical' in a broad sense to refer both to basic physical properties and also to high-level properties that are realized in basic physical ones. Likewise, I shall use the term 'physical facts' both for facts about basic physical properties and also for facts about high-level properties that are realized in basic physical ones. Thus, the physicalist, in the sense just defined, holds that all properties are physical properties and that all facts are physical facts.

Which of the following statements would be endorsed by a physicalist, in the sense just defined?   **ACTIVITY**

1   All high-level properties reduce to basic physical ones.

2   Each instance of a high-level property is identical with an instance of some basic physical property.

3   All high-level properties either reduce to, or are realized in, basic physical ones.

4   Only basic physical properties are real.

5   All objects are composed wholly of basic physical entities.

Physicalists would endorse (2), (3) and (5) (the first two of these say much the same thing). (1) is a stronger claim than the one physicalists make. Physicalists accept that many high-level properties can be multiply realized and so cannot be reduced to basic physical ones. Nor is there any reason for a physicalist to endorse (4). Physicalists do not hold that high-level properties are unreal – only that they are not the fundamental ones. Indeed, for a physicalist, showing that a high-level phenomenon is physically constituted amounts to a demonstration of its reality – proof that it is not illusory but firmly grounded in physical reality. Finally, (5) is a statement of substance physicalism, which we are assuming physicalists also endorse.   **DISCUSSION**

It is worth stressing that most writers accept that *many* phenomena are physical in the broad sense defined above. It is widely accepted, for example, that chemical, biological, neurological and functional properties are physical ones, and in the rest of this book I shall assume that this is the case. The question is whether consciousness is a further, non-physical property, over and above these.

I now want to link up this discussion of physicalism with the earlier discussion of reductive explanation. The crucial thing to note is that strong naturalists are committed to physicalism, in the sense just defined. For they hold that all high-level properties can ultimately be explained in basic physical terms. And such explanations will be possible only if high-level properties are not fundamentally distinct from basic physical ones. Recall how we explained the television's power to display moving images. The explanation worked because it was clear that the properties mentioned in the explanation were *sufficient* for the existence of the power. With those components, working in that way, the set simply *could not fail* to display moving pictures. There was nothing more to it. In short, the properties cited explained the power because they *realized* it.

For the same reason, if a high-level property *is* distinct from basic physical ones, then it will not be possible to explain it in basic physical terms. Suppose property dualism about life were true – that life was an extra property, over and above basic physical ones. Then it would not be possible to give a reductive explanation of life in basic physical terms. For even if we were to identify all the various chemical and physical processes associated with life, there would still remain a mystery: *Why* does life emerge when those properties are present? If life were something extra, over and above those properties, then identifying them would not fully explain its existence. (I should add that very few people are property dualists about life; as I mentioned earlier, it is widely accepted that organic processes can be reductively explained in terms of chemical and physical ones.)

To sum up: if you believe that all high-level phenomena can be reductively explained in basic physical terms, then you are committed to the view that high-level properties are not fundamentally distinct from basic physical ones – that is, you are committed to physicalism.

ACTIVITY What implications does the conclusion just reached have for the hard problem of consciousness?

If solving the hard problem involves reductively explaining consciousness in lower-level terms and ultimately in basic physical ones, then a solution will be possible only if consciousness is a physical phenomenon – that is, only if phenomenal properties are physical properties.

DISCUSSION

The converse also applies. If consciousness is a physical phenomenon, then it should be possible to reductively explain it by identifying the physical properties in which it is realized. When these properties are described in detail, it should be obvious that they are sufficient for the existence of consciousness – just as it was obvious that the various electrical and mechanical components of the television were sufficient for it to have the power to display images of distant events. The question of whether consciousness is a physical phenomenon and that of whether it can be reductively explained are thus two sides of the same coin: considerations for and against the one claim count equally for and against the other.

I shall close this section by addressing some worries that may have been raised by the preceding discussion. First, I mentioned that I was going to assume that substance physicalism was true. The question we shall be considering is whether the *property* of consciousness is a physical one, not whether the *substance* which possesses this property is. I shall assume that this substance is simply the brain. But what if you do not share this assumption? What if you believe that we have a non-physical soul as well as a brain? Won't you find the debate about properties irrelevant? I don't think you should. For it is quite possible to hold *both* that we have a non-physical soul *and* that consciousness is a property of the brain. *Some* mental properties may be physical, even if others are not. (And, as I noted earlier, it is hard to deny that consciousness is at least very closely related to the brain; we know that chemical changes in the brain can affect consciousness and that damage to the brain can remove it.) If, on the other hand, one of your reasons for believing in substance dualism is that you think that consciousness is *not* a physical phenomenon, then you will need to consider the arguments for the view that it is, and think about how you would respond to them. You might also want to consider whether you really need to endorse *substance* dualism, as opposed to the weaker property-based version.

Secondly, you may feel uncomfortable with the emphasis I have placed on a reductive, physicalist explanation of consciousness. Why should we bother to look for such an explanation? Isn't the whole approach dehumanizing?

Wouldn't it be better to turn to novelists and poets for an account of our inner lives, rather than to scientists? There is something in this. If we want descriptions of what consciousness is *like* – the subtle shades of perception, sensation, emotion and thought – then a reductive explanation is likely to leave us cold. This is true across the board. An account of how a phenomenon is constituted will not tell us much about how it affects us. If you want to know about the emotional impact of the *Mona Lisa*, then a chemical analysis of the paint will not satisfy you. But it would be a mistake to think that this is an objection to reductive explanation. High-level descriptions of a phenomenon are not made redundant by a reductive explanation of it. The two serve quite different purposes: one tells us how the phenomenon appears to us, the other how it is constituted. Indeed, the two approaches may be complementary; close observation of a phenomenon may provide hints as to how it is constituted, and learning how it is constituted may illuminate our observations of it. A chemical analysis of a painting may help us to see it in a new way – to see new relations between its colours and to understand why they have the effects they do. There is no need, then, to fear that a reductive explanation of consciousness will replace the descriptions of novelists and poets; indeed it may help to enrich them.

Thirdly, is physicalism really a coherent position? Some people object that it is not, since it is not clear what counts as a basic physical property. After all, physicists keep revising their catalogue of the basic physical entities and forces, and they will probably continue to do so for some time (Crane and Mellor 1990). This is a fair point, but not, I think, a fatal one. Physicalists can respond that their position involves an open-ended commitment – a commitment to regard as fundamental the properties posited by our current physics, whatever these happen to be. (Compare how being a law-abiding citizen involves an open-ended commitment to abide by the laws in force at the time, whatever these may be.) This means that physicalism is not a tightly defined doctrine, but in practice this does not matter too much, especially so far as philosophy of mind is concerned. For what is chiefly at issue in debates about the mind is whether mental properties are identical with, or realized in, *non-mental* ones. The exact nature of these non-mental properties is a secondary issue. So physicalists can live with some vagueness in their position (Papineau 1993, 2002). Of course, if physicists were to decide to include *mental* phenomena in their catalogue of the fundamental entities and forces, then it would be a different story. But in that case the whole debate would take on a completely new aspect and everyone would have to rethink their position.

The function of consciousness

There is another problem I want to mention briefly. What is the *function* of consciousness? What difference does it make to have phenomenally conscious experiences?

This may seem an odd question. Surely, the answer is obvious: the function of consciousness is to provide us with information about our environment – about colours, shapes, sounds and so on. But this is too swift. We do not need to have conscious experiences in order to acquire perceptual information about our environment. Cog's sensors provide it with information about colours and shapes and sounds, too – it is just that this information does not have a phenomenal character to it. What is added by supplementing this information with phenomenal character? We can put the same point in terms of the distinction between access-consciousness and phenomenal consciousness. It is obvious why it is useful for a creature's experiences to be access-consciousness – to be available to the processes controlling reasoning and behaviour. But why is it useful for them to be phenomenally conscious, too?

It might be suggested that the phenomenal character of an experience affects our *reaction* to it. Pain, for example, not only tells us that our body has been damaged, but also induces us to react to the damage in a certain way. If I touch something hot, then the pain moves me to withdraw my hand. Smells, tastes and colours also provoke characteristic reactions. Again, however, this is too swift. For a sensory state could cause a reaction without having any phenomenal character. As I mentioned earlier, it would be possible to program Cog to take avoiding action when it detects damage to itself – so that if someone pokes it in its eye, for example, it registers the fact, withdraws its head quickly and says 'Ouch!'. Yet it might still not actually *feel* anything – not have any conscious sensations of pain. So what is the point of consciousness? Provided Cog reacts to damage in the right way, why need it feel pain as well?

There is a general problem here. Whatever effects a conscious mental state has, it seems, a non-conscious one could also have. ('Conscious' here means 'phenomenally conscious' of course.) So why did evolution equip us with conscious experiences, rather than non-conscious ones? What survival advantage does phenomenal consciousness confer? Does it do anything at all? Or is it just a by-product of other processes, like the exhaust from a car's engine, which does not play any useful role?

This problem is closely connected with that of providing a reductive explanation of consciousness. Reductive explanations of mental phenomena typically exploit the fact that mental states can be characterized in functional terms – in terms of the role they play in mental processing and behavioural control. If a mental state can be characterized in this way, then we can identify it with whatever brain state plays the role in question. But if consciousness does not have a function, then this approach is a non-starter.

You may be feeling that something must have gone wrong here. Surely it is absurd to suggest that consciousness has no function – that the painfulness of a pain makes no difference to its effects. The suggestion is certainly counterintuitive; but we should not rule it out at this stage. Even our strongest intuitions can mislead us (it seemed obvious to our ancestors that the earth was flat and that the sun moved through the sky), and we may have to escape the confines of our familiar outlook if we are to understand consciousness. We shall be returning to the question of the function of consciousness throughout this book.

Conclusion and preview

This chapter has laid the groundwork for our study of consciousness. We have identified the phenomenon we are interested in, looked at some of its mysterious features and considered the problems it poses. The rest of the book will explore some responses to these problems. You may have been wondering exactly what philosophers have to contribute here. Isn't explaining consciousness a matter for scientists – requiring the formation and testing of empirical hypotheses, not conceptual analysis and a priori reasoning? There are at least three aspects to the answer, and the structure of the following chapters will reflect them.

First, in posing a challenge to strong naturalism and physicalism, consciousness raises questions that go *beyond* science. Can everything be reductively explained? Are we capable of understanding all natural phenomena? Is physicalism true? Can there be a science of consciousness? These are metaphysical and epistemological questions – questions about the fundamental nature of reality and about the limits of our knowledge – and as such fall squarely within the province of philosophy. Chapters 2 and 3 will focus on questions of this kind.

Secondly, even if a reductive explanation of consciousness is possible, there are some very general theoretical questions that need to be addressed at an early stage. What overall shape should the explanation take? What kind of mechanisms should it postulate? Could phenomenal consciousness be a form of access-consciousness? Does it involve inner awareness of some kind? These questions, too, are ones that philosophers are currently trying to answer. They see themselves as working in conjunction with scientists, helping to establish an outline theory of consciousness which will provide a framework for future empirical work. This does not require detailed scientific knowledge – though philosophers of mind do draw on empirical work. Rather, it involves thinking at a very general level about the facts of consciousness and how best to explain them. Chapter 4 will look at some recent work of this kind.

Thirdly, it may be necessary to rethink the very way we pose the problem of consciousness. Some philosophers believe that our commonsense view of consciousness involves serious misconceptions, which blight philosophical and scientific work on the subject, and that philosophers have a role to play in exposing these and developing a better conception of the phenomenon. Chapter 5 will look at some proposals along these lines.

Further reading

For a more advanced introduction to the topic of consciousness, which includes an historical survey of philosophical and psychological work on the topic and a survey of recent debates, see:

GÜZELDERE, G. (1997) 'The many faces of consciousness: a field guide', in N. Block, O. Flanagan & G. Güzeldere (eds), *The Nature of Consciousness: Philosophical Debates*, Cambridge, Mass., MIT Press, pp.1–67. (The collection in which this essay appears – henceforth referred to as 'Block et al. 1997' – is a useful one, which reprints many important papers on consciousness.)

The following chapters also contain useful introductions – though each reflects its author's own theoretical preoccupations and assumptions:

CARRUTHERS, P. (2000) *Phenomenal Consciousness: A Naturalistic Theory*, Cambridge, Cambridge University Press, Chapter 1. (Introduces some useful distinctions and concepts and provides a route map of contemporary theories of consciousness.)

CHALMERS, D. (1996) *The Conscious Mind: In Search of a Fundamental Theory*, New York, Oxford University Press, Chapters 1–2. (Chapter 1 is an accessible introduction to the problem of consciousness; Chapter 2 is technical but includes useful discussion of reductive explanation.)

DENNETT, D.C. (1991) *Consciousness Explained*, Boston, Little, Brown, Chapter 2. (Argues against substance dualist approaches to consciousness.)

MCGINN, C. (1999) *The Mysterious Flame*, New York, Basic Books, Chapter 1. (Emphasizes how strange and inexplicable consciousness can seem.)

TYE, M. (1995) *Ten Problems of Consciousness: A Representational Theory of the Phenomenal Mind*, Cambridge, Mass., MIT Press, Chapter 1. (Introduces phenomenal consciousness and outlines a number of problems surrounding it.)

Finally, a useful general resource, which you may like to explore at your leisure, is David Chalmers's website, at http://consc.net/chalmers/. This contains a wealth of material on consciousness, including a list of online papers, bibliographies of philosophical and scientific work and many of Chalmers's own papers.

CHAPTER 2

Property Dualism

We are, moreover, obliged to confess that perception *and that which depends on it* cannot be explained mechanically, *that is to say by figures and motions. Suppose that there were a machine so constructed as to produce thought, feeling, and perception, we could imagine it increased in size while retaining the same proportions, so that one could enter as one might a mill. On going inside we should only see the parts impinging upon one another; we should not see anything which would explain a perception.*

(Leibniz 1973, 181)

The previous chapter introduced the hard problem of consciousness. The rest of this book explores some responses to it. As we saw, the fundamental question is whether consciousness is a physical phenomenon, which can be reductively explained, or whether it is an extra feature of the brain over and above its physical ones. If consciousness is not physical, then it cannot be explained in standard ways and scientists will have to rethink their view of the mind. This chapter and the next will be devoted to this fundamental question. The present chapter will set out two of the most important anti-physicalist arguments and assess a property dualist view of consciousness. Then the following chapter will look at how physicalists have responded to these arguments.

The knowledge argument

One of the best-known arguments for the view that consciousness is not a physical phenomenon is what is known as the *knowledge argument*. In outline, the argument runs as follows. If physicalism is true, then the physical facts are all the facts there are. (I am using 'physical' here in the broad sense to include chemical, biological, neurological and functional facts, as well as basic physical ones.) Thus, if we knew all the physical facts about a person, then, according to the physicalist, we would know all the facts there are to know about them. Yet – the argument goes – we might know all the physical facts about a person without knowing what their experiences were *like* – what phenomenal properties they had. Hence, the phenomenal properties of experience are not physical ones and physicalism is false.

This argument has a long history. The German philosopher Gottfried Leibniz (1646–1716) outlined an early version of it in the passage quoted at the head of this chapter (Leibniz 1973, 181). Even if we could wander round a working brain and observe everything that goes on within it, Leibniz suggests, we would still not understand how it produces perceptions – which seems to indicate that perceptions are something over and above brain processes. In modern times, Thomas Nagel outlined a version of the argument in a famous paper titled 'What is it like to be a bat?' (Nagel 1974). He argues that there are facts about the experiences of other creatures – bats, in his example – which are essentially subjective and which we can never know. We cannot imagine what it is like to be a bat – sensing the world by echolocation rather than sight – and no scientific study of bat neurology will ever enlighten us. Nagel's paper has been very influential. For the definitive statement of the knowledge argument, however, we need to turn to a 1982 paper 'Epiphenomenal qualia' by the Australian philosopher Frank Jackson (b. 1943).

ACTIVITY

Reading 3 contains an extract from Jackson's paper. Turn to this now and read the first three paragraphs. Note that by 'purely physical information', Jackson means physical information in the broad sense – information about basic physical properties and about physically realized higher-level properties.

1   What does Jackson mean by the term 'qualia freak'? Which of the positions described in the previous chapter would a qualia freak endorse?

2   How is Jackson using the word 'qualia' here?

3   Is Jackson going to argue that qualia are not properties of the brain?

DISCUSSION

1   He means someone who believes that facts about the phenomenal properties of experience (the hurtfulness of pains, the itchiness of itches and so on) are not included among the physical facts in the broad sense. Qualia freaks are thus *property dualists* about consciousness – they think that phenomenal properties are extra features of the world, which are fundamentally distinct from the basic physical ones.

2   He is using 'qualia' to refer to phenomenal properties, but with the added implication that these properties are not physical ones. The word often carries this implication, which is why I have used the more neutral term 'phenomenal properties'. Physicalists deny the existence of qualia in

Jackson's sense, though few of them deny the existence of phenomenal properties.

3   No. He is going to argue that qualia are non-physical *features*, not that they are features of a non-physical *substance*. Again, it is property physicalism, not substance physicalism, that he is going to challenge.

Let us now look at the argument Jackson uses to support his qualia freakiness.

ACTIVITY

Read the rest Reading 3 and answer the following questions. Note that the 'cones' referred to in paragraph 7 are light-sensitive cells in the retina which detect colour. Humans with normal vision have three types of cone.

1   The examples of Fred and Mary are both designed to support the same core argument. What is this core argument? Try to set it out in the form of premises and a conclusion.

2   How do the examples support the core argument?

3   The argument involves claims about physical and non-physical *facts*. How do these claims relate to ones about physical and non-physical *properties*?

4   Jackson suggests that versions of the knowledge argument could be constructed for other forms of conscious experience as well as vision. Give your own example.

DISCUSSION

1   The core argument might be set out as follows:
      Premise 1   If physicalism is true, then any person who knows all the physical facts about colour vision knows everything there is to know about it.

      Premise 2   It is not true that any person who knows all the physical facts about colour vision knows everything there is to know about it.

      Conclusion   Physicalism is not true.

2   The examples of Fred and Mary are designed to support Premise 2. (Premise 1 follows from the definition of physicalism, which is the claim that the physical facts are all the facts there are.) We might know all the physical facts about Fred's visual system without knowing what it is like to see the colours he calls 'red$_1$' and 'red$_2$'. (Remember, these are not just shades of red, but two quite distinct colours. Fred can see an extra colour which other people cannot.) Similarly, Mary knows all the physical facts about human colour vision but does not know what it is like to see colours.

(We are meant to suppose, not just that she is currently confined to a black-and-white room, but that she has been brought up in one and has never seen colours.) In each case, it seems, the only way to acquire the missing knowledge is by actually having the relevant experiences – in the first case by modifying our visual systems so that they resemble Fred's; in the second by Mary leaving the black-and-white room and experiencing colour vision for herself.

3   Physical facts are facts about physical properties. To say that there are non-physical facts about X is to say that X has some non-physical properties.

4   Here is my example. Marie is a scientist specializing in the biology and neurology of sexual experience. She knows all the physical facts about the bodily and neurological processes involved in sexual arousal and orgasm. However, she herself has had very little sexual experience. For religious reasons she has taken a vow of chastity and has never experienced an orgasm. There is thus something that Marie does not know about sexual experience, and if she were to renounce her vow and lead a fulfilling sex life, then she would discover something new – namely what it is actually *like* to have an orgasm.

The knowledge argument has become a classic and a large literature has built up devoted to analysing and assessing it. In discussing the argument, philosophers have focused almost exclusively on Mary's case rather than Fred's – probably because it is more straightforward. Although people do vary in the sensitivity of their colour vision, there are no people like Fred who can see completely new colours (though some animals can detect ultra-violet and infra-red radiation that is invisible to us). Mary's case is simpler, since she has normal colour vision.

ACTIVITY   How could the knowledge argument be restated with specific reference to Mary?

DISCUSSION   Here is one way of setting it out:

Premise 1   If physicalism is true, then on leaving her room Mary will not learn any new facts about colour vision (since, by hypothesis, she already knows all the physical facts about it).

Premise 2   On leaving her room, Mary learns new facts about colour vision (namely, what it is like to see various colours).

Conclusion   Physicalism is not true.

Of course, Mary's case has its own implausibilities. How could Mary have avoided all experience of colour vision? Is her own skin and hair painted black and white? Has she never seen her own blood, or produced coloured sensations ('phosphenes') by touching her eyeball? Moreover, if she really had been deprived of all colour stimuli, then it is unlikely that she would be able to see colours properly after leaving her room. In order for the visual system to develop normally it needs to receive a variety of stimuli in early infancy. People with congenital eye defects do not develop the neural pathways needed for normal vision and if their eye defect is corrected in later life they do not suddenly recover normal vision. See Oliver Sacks's fascinating essay 'To see and not see' (in Sacks 1995). These implausibilities are not necessarily flaws in the argument, however. The issue is not whether a person really could be brought up in the way Mary is, but whether, *if this were somehow to happen*, the person would know all there is to know about colour vision. Likewise, it does not matter whether such a person really would develop a normal visual system, but whether, if they did, they would learn something on their first exposure to colours. All have we to do is imagine the situation and ask what would follow. Exercises of the imagination like this are known as *thought experiments* and it is generally accepted that they have an important role in many kinds of philosophical investigation.

We shall consider some physicalist responses to the knowledge argument in the next chapter. For the moment, I shall just add a few notes to help clarify the argument and avoid possible confusions. Some of the following points draw on a short follow-up paper by Jackson (Jackson 1986).

First, it is crucial to the argument that while in her room Mary learns *all* the physical facts about colour vision – not just all that are *currently* known, but all there *are* to know. Thus we should think of her as living in the future, when the sciences of physics, chemistry, biology and neuroscience have reached their final, definitive form. Note that this makes Mary's case harder to imagine than it might seem at first sight. Since the complete physical facts of vision are not available to us, and since we would probably be unable to hold them all in our minds even if they were, we cannot imagine Mary's case in any detail. We shall return to this point in the next chapter.

Secondly, what Mary is supposed to lack, while confined in her room, is not the ability to *imagine* what colour vision is like, but *knowledge* of what it is like. Perhaps she can imagine what it is like. That is not the issue. The point is that, until released, she will not *know* – even though she does know all the physical facts.

Thirdly, it is important to distinguish different facts that Mary learns on her release. It is accepted by everyone that she will learn things on leaving her room – for example, she will learn about the surrounding environment and the people who live there. What is at issue is whether she will learn something about her specialist subject, colour vision. Moreover, the question is whether she will learn something about colour vision *in general*, not just about the particular colour experiences that she herself has. Jackson explains:

> the knowledge Mary lacked which is of particular point for the knowledge argument against physicalism is *knowledge about the experiences of others*, not about her own. When she is let out, she has new experiences, color experiences she has never had before. It is not, therefore, an objection to physicalism that she learns *something* on being let out. Before she was let out, she could not have known facts about her experience of red, for there were no such facts to know. That physicalist and nonphysicalist alike can agree on. After she is let out, things change; and physicalism can happily admit that she learns this; after all, some physical things will change, for instance, her brain states and their functional roles. The trouble for physicalism is that, after Mary sees her first ripe tomato, she will realize how impoverished her conception of the mental life of *others* has been *all along*. She will realize that there was, all the time she was carrying out her laborious investigations into the neurophysiologies of others and into the functional roles of their internal states, something about these people she was quite unaware of. All along their experiences (or many of them, those got from tomatoes, the sky, …) had a feature conspicuous to them but until now hidden from her (in fact, not in logic). But she knew all the physical facts about them all along; hence, what she did not know until her release is not a physical fact about their experiences. But it is a fact about them. That is the trouble for physicalism.
>
> (Jackson 1986, 292–3)

Finally, as a point of interest, Jackson could have made Mary's case more realistic by making her a complete *achromat* – that is, a person who has a defect of the retina and is unable to see colours. Such people exist, and at least one, the Norwegian Knut Nordby, is a scientist of vision. Of course, Nordby does not have the *complete* knowledge of colour vision that Mary is supposed to possess (no one does), but he stresses that his knowledge of the existing science has not given him any understanding of the phenomenal character of vision:

> Although I have acquired a thorough theoretical knowledge of the physics of colours and the physiology of the colour receptor mechanisms, nothing of this can help me to understand the true nature of colours. From the history of art I have also learned about the meanings often attributed to colours and how colours have been used at different times, but this too does not give me an understanding of the essential character or quality of colours.
>
> (Nordby 1990, 305)

This completes our introduction to the knowledge argument. You may like to pause here and make a note of your immediate reactions to it. Did it convince you? If not, why not?

The conceivability argument

The second anti-physicalist argument I want to introduce is the *conceivability argument* (sometimes also known as the *modal argument* or, for reasons that will soon become clear, the *zombie argument*). This argument, too, has a long history. Descartes used a version of it to argue for substance dualism (see his *Meditations* II and VI) and several contemporary philosophers have employed it to attack various forms of physicalism. Perhaps the best-known modern version of the argument is in Saul Kripke's *Naming and Necessity* (1980). However, Kripke's presentation is complicated, and we shall consider a simpler, generic version of the argument outlined by David Chalmers.

The argument begins with the claim that it is conceivable that the facts about consciousness could vary without any change in the physical facts. A particularly vivid way of stating the argument appeals to the conceivability of *zombies* – creatures which are exact replicas of us in all their basic physical aspects but lack conscious experience. Here is how Chalmers sets out the argument:

Premise 1   It is conceivable that there be zombies.

Premise 2   If it is conceivable that there be zombies, it is metaphysically possible that there be zombies.

Premise 3   If it is metaphysically possible that there be zombies, then consciousness is nonphysical.

Conclusion   Consciousness is nonphysical.

(Based on Chalmers 2002a, 249)

The structure of the argument is straightforward. If Premises 1 and 2 are true, then it is metaphysically possible for there to be zombies (that is, zombies could exist). And that claim, together with Premise 3, entails the conclusion. Thus if all the premises are true, then the conclusion must be true too: the argument is valid. However, the premises need some explaining. I shall take them in turn.

The first thing is to say more about zombies. Zombies in the present sense are very different from those pictured in Hollywood movies, and it is important to understand exactly what they are supposed to be. Chalmers himself has done much to promote interest in zombies, and we can turn to him for a brief introduction to them. Before you begin reading, note that in this extract Chalmers uses the word 'psychological' in a technical sense. His use refers back to a distinction drawn in the earlier chapters of his book between the *phenomenal* and *psychological* concepts of mind. The phenomenal concept of mind is that of conscious experience, and the phenomenal concept of a mental state is that of a state with a certain phenomenal character. The psychological concept of mind, on the other hand, is that of a system for the control of behaviour, and the psychological concept of a mental state is that of a state which performs some function in such a system (for example, carrying information about the external world or about bodily damage). So Cog has a mind in the psychological sense – it has a behavioural control system and possesses internal states which perform various functions in this system. It is doubtful, however, that it has a mind in the phenomenal sense – that it has conscious experiences. Chalmers suggests that the two concepts correspond to different aspects of the mind and that everyday thinking about the mind incorporates both. For example, we think of pain both as a state with a certain feel and also as a state which plays a certain role in behavioural control (which registers bodily damage and causes appropriate behaviour).

ACTIVITY   Turn to Reading 4, read paragraphs 1–3 and answer the following questions. Note that not all of these questions are discussed in the extract – you will have to try to work out the answers on the basis of what is there.

1 Why does Chalmers say that his zombie twin will be *functionally* identical to him?

2 Why does Chalmers say that his zombie twin will be *psychologically* identical to him?

3 What is the difference between a psychological zombie and a phenomenal zombie?

4 Why would there be problems in the depiction of phenomenal zombies in a movie?

5 Can you be sure that the people around you are not phenomenal zombies?

1 Because he assumes that functional facts are realized in basic physical ones. He assumes that the function of a brain state within the mind–brain system is wholly determined by its basic physical properties, including its relations to other brain states and the outside world. For example, a brain state has the functional role of pain in virtue of the fact that it is triggered by signals from pain receptors in the skin and triggers behavioural and other reactions appropriate to injury. Since Chalmers's zombie twin is, by hypothesis, identical to Chalmers himself in all its basic physical aspects and inhabits an identical environment, it follows that it has brain states which perform exactly the same functions as his do. So, for example, if the zombie stubs its toe, it will enter a state which performs the functions associated with pain – causing the zombie to hop around, wince, cry 'Ouch!' and say 'I'm in pain'. The state will *do* exactly what Chalmers's pain states do, it will just *feel* differently – indeed, it will have no feel at all.

DISCUSSION

2 Because the psychological concept of mind (in Chalmers's sense) is simply that of a behavioural control system with various functionally defined components, and the zombie will have a system of this kind that is identical to Chalmers's own.

3 A psychological zombie differs *psychologically* from a normal person – its behavioural control system is impaired in various ways. It cannot report on its own mental states and cannot control its movements properly (and, judging from Hollywood movies, has an unusual and very limited range of interests). A phenomenal zombie, on the other hand, does not differ psychologically from a normal person; it can do all the things a normal person can and has the same mental states, in the psychological sense. It is just that its mental states do not have any phenomenal character to them.

4 Because they would be behaviourally indistinguishable from normal humans. (The only differences would be on the inside.)

5 Arguably, you can't, since zombies would talk and act just like normal people.

Figure 5 Group therapy for zombies. Cartoon by Mike Peters ('Mother Goose and Grimm' series). Copyright © Grimmy, Inc. Reprinted with special permission of King Features Syndicate.

Of course, Premise 1 of Chalmers's argument does not say that zombies actually exist or, indeed, that they could exist in the world as we know it. All it says is that they are *conceivable*. 'Conceivable' here means *imaginable*, or, more precisely, *clearly and coherently* imaginable. To say that a situation is conceivable is to say that we can form a coherent and detailed conception of it, free from contradictions. Chalmers defends the claim that zombies are conceivable in the remainder of Reading 4, and we shall consider what he has to say shortly. First, however, let us see how the conceivability of zombies is supposed to lead to the falsity of physicalism.

The second premise runs as follows:

> *Premise 2* If it is conceivable that there be zombies, it is metaphysically possible that there be zombies.

The crucial notion here is that of metaphysical possibility. The best way to come at this is by contrast with another sort of possibility, known as *natural possibility*. Something is naturally possible if it could happen, or could have happened, in the real world, consistently with the prevailing laws of nature. For example, it is naturally possible that most humans might have had red hair. It could have turned out that way, consistently with the laws of nature as they are. Metaphysical possibility, by contrast, is a broader kind of possibility which is not limited by the prevailing laws of nature. Something is metaphysically possible if it could happen in some alternative universe, or 'possible world', perhaps with quite different laws of nature. (This is sometimes put in terms of God's power. To say that something is metaphysically possible is to say that God – supposing he were to exist – could have brought it about.) Take telekinesis, for example – the ability to move objects simply by the power of one's mind. This is not naturally possible, but it is metaphysically possible. There could be a universe where the laws of nature are such that people have telekinetic powers. Although broader than natural possibility, metaphysical possibility still has limits. Some things could not happen, no matter how different the laws of nature were. There could be no universe where there are four-sided triangles or where I exist but Keith Frankish doesn't. (I *am* Keith Frankish, so how could I exist without him?)

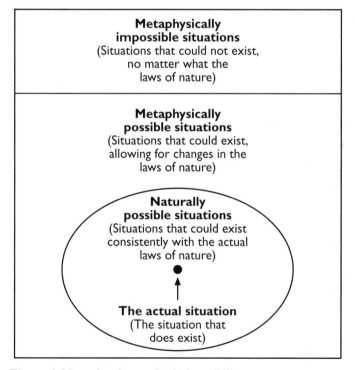

Figure 6 Natural and metaphysical possibility.

Say whether each of the following situations is metaphysically possible or metaphysically impossible, and, if it is metaphysically possible, whether it is naturally possible, too.

ACTIVITY

1   Humans can walk on water.

2   Pentagons do not have five sides.

3   Average human life-expectancy is 100 years.

4   Post-boxes are both red and green all over.

5   The Pope and the Dalai Lama will have a picnic on the moon within the next month.

1   Metaphysically possible but not naturally possible.

2   Metaphysically impossible.

3   Metaphysically possible and naturally possible.

4   Metaphysically impossible. (I cannot even imagine how something could be both red and green all over at the same time. What would it look like?)

5   Metaphysically possible and naturally possible – though very unlikely. (The example is borrowed, with a slight change, from one in Flanagan and Polger 1995, 314.)

Premise 2 of the conceivability argument amounts to the claim that if we can clearly and coherently imagine zombies, then they could exist, if not in this world, then in some alternative universe with different laws of nature. (It is important to stress, however, that the laws of *physics* are supposed to be the same in the zombies' universe – zombies are supposed to be exactly like us in all their basic physical aspects.) This premise is an instance of the general principle that if something is conceivable, then it is at least metaphysically possible. This principle is not uncontroversial and we shall consider a challenge to it in the next chapter, but it is certainly plausible. If we can form a clear, coherent and detailed conception of something, then, it seems, there could be a universe where it actually exists. (God could turn the conception into reality.)

Let us move on now to the final premise:

Premise 3   If it is metaphysically possible that there be zombies, then consciousness is nonphysical.

At first sight, this may seem outrageous. How can a claim about what is *possible* entail a claim about what is *actually* the case – that consciousness is non-physical? It is metaphysically possible that cats might understand quantum physics, but that does not show anything about their actual abilities. This is too hasty, however. In fact, this premise is the least controversial of the three and follows straightforwardly from what we mean by 'physical'. Let me explain.

To say that zombies are metaphysically possible is to say that it is metaphysically possible for a creature to have all the basic physical properties associated with consciousness without having consciousness itself. But if it is *possible* for basic physical properties and phenomenal properties to come apart in that way, then those properties must *actually* be distinct – even if they always go together. And to say that phenomenal properties are distinct from basic physical ones is to say that consciousness is non-physical.

We can put the same point in terms of facts. If zombies are metaphysically possible, then it is metaphysically possible for the facts of consciousness to vary while the basic physical facts stay the same. And if that is so, then the facts of consciousness must be *extra* facts over and above the basic physical ones – which is to say that they are not themselves physical facts, in the broad sense.

If this isn't clear, then suppose that the facts about consciousness were *not* extra facts about our world, over and above the basic physical ones. Then it would not be metaphysically possible for the basic physical facts to hold and the facts about consciousness not to. For the basic physical facts would *guarantee* the existence of the facts about consciousness – indeed, the latter would not be extra facts at all, but just redescriptions of the basic physical ones. The following exercise may help to make the point.

ACTIVITY

Consider a television set again – say, one that is currently displaying live images from a sports match. Could there be a duplicate of this television (a 'zombie television') which has exactly the same basic physical properties, receives exactly the same signal and is subject to exactly the same physical laws but does not display moving images of the match? Is such a thing metaphysically possible? (Assume for the moment that conceivability is a reliable guide to metaphysical possibility.)

DISCUSSION

It is not metaphysically possible: I certainly cannot form a clear conception of it. (If you think you can, then make sure you are not tacitly supposing that some change has occurred at the basic physical level – that the duplicate is damaged in some way, or the signal interrupted, or the laws of physics different.) The reason I cannot conceive of it is that the fact that the set displays images of the match is not a further fact about it, over and above its basic physical ones. There is really *nothing more* to the set's displaying images of the match than its having all the basic physical properties it does and receiving an appropriate signal from a camera at the venue.

To sum up: zombie television is not metaphysically possible because the facts about TV images are physical ones. Conversely, if zombie people *are* metaphysically possible, then the facts about consciousness must be non-physical ones – which is what Premise 3 asserts.

You should now have a good idea of how the conceivability argument works. I have set out the argument in a formal way, but it may help to summarize it more informally.

ACTIVITY

Sum up the conceivability argument in a short paragraph (no more than four sentences).

DISCUSSION

Here is my attempt.

'If consciousness were physical, then the facts about consciousness would not be further facts, over and above the basic physical ones. And in that case, it would not be metaphysically possible for the basic physical facts to hold and the facts of consciousness not to. But that *is* metaphysically possible, as we can see from the fact that zombies are conceivable. So consciousness is not physical.'

To complete our introduction to the conceivability argument I now want to go back to Premise 1 and see what Chalmers has to say in defence of the conceivability of zombies.

ACTIVITY

Read paragraphs 4–12 of Reading 4 and answer the questions below. (Some notes on terminology. First, in this extract Chalmers uses the term 'logically possible' instead of 'conceivable'. (This is in fact potentially confusing, since other writers use 'logically possible' to mean *metaphysically possible*.) Secondly, 'empirically impossible' (paragraph 6) means 'naturally impossible'. Thirdly, 'intensions' (paragraph 7) means, roughly, 'meanings'.)

1   Does Chalmers think that zombies are naturally/empirically possible (paragraphs 4–6)?

2   What point is Chalmers making in paragraph 7?

3   What does Chalmers mean by 'nonstandard realizations' of his functional organization (paragraph 9)?

4   How does reflection on nonstandard realizations support the claim that zombies are conceivable?

5   What is the objection that Chalmers is addressing in paragraph 12? What is his response to it?

1   No – he thinks that zombies are probably not naturally possible. That is to say, he doubts that they could exist in our world, consistently with the prevailing laws of nature. (We shall see why he thinks this later in this chapter.)

2   Chalmers is suggesting that it is up to his opponents to provide reasons to think that zombies are *not* conceivable rather than up to him to provide reasons to think they are. Unless someone can point to a contradiction in the description of a zombie, the default assumption should be that there are no such reasons.

3   He means replicas of his brain constructed out of non-biological materials. The thought is that what the brain is *made of* is not essential to what it *does*. We could imagine replacing Chalmers's brain cells with millions of tiny silicon chips to make a 'silicon isomorph' of him. Provided the chips did the same jobs as the cells they replaced and were linked up in the same way to each other and to the rest of Chalmers's body, the overall operation of the system would be unaffected. We could even imagine replacing the cells with millions of *people*, passing signals to each other like brain cells. If they all did their jobs properly and quickly enough, they would collectively form a single giant brain.

4   The point is that it is quite coherent to suppose that these non-standard realizations would not have any conscious experiences, even though they had the same functional organization as Chalmers's brain. Thus, functional replicas without conscious experience are conceivable. But then zombies must be conceivable, too. For we could imagine taking Chalmers's silicon isomorph and replacing all the silicon chips with brain cells again, yet without thereby making it conscious. (Again, why should what it is made of make a difference?) And what we have thereby imagined is precisely a zombie. (It is worth stressing that Chalmers is not claiming

that functional replicas without consciousness are *naturally* possible – just that they are conceivable and hence that zombies are, too.)

5   The objection is that we cannot really form a detailed conception of a zombie. In order to do so, we would have to imagine a working human brain which does not support conscious experience, and the sheer complexity of the brain means that we cannot do this in any detail. Chalmers responds that it is not necessary to imagine all the low-level brain mechanisms. What matters is what these mechanisms *do* – the functions they perform. We just have to imagine all the normal brain functions occurring but without consciousness.

Although zombies provide a particularly vivid way of formulating the conceivability argument, it is worth noting that the argument could be restated without appeal to them. Instead of a physical duplicate with *no* conscious experiences, it is sufficient to imagine one with *different* conscious experiences. Consider, for example, a visual *invert* – a creature which is physically identical to you but has inverted colour experiences (red things look green, yellow things look blue, etc.). If such a being is metaphysically possible, then, again, the facts of consciousness must be distinct from the basic physical facts, contrary to physicalism.

This completes our introduction to the conceivability argument. Again, you may like to pause here and make a note of your first thoughts about it. We shall consider some physicalist replies to the argument in the next chapter.

ACTIVITY As a final exercise, think about the relation between the knowledge argument (pp.42–3) and the conceivability argument (pp.45–6). Are there similarities between them?

DISCUSSION Both arguments aim to show that the phenomenal facts about us are extra facts, over and above the physical ones. The first works by reflection on our ability to *know* those facts; the second by reflection on the *modal* relations between them ('modal' means 'concerning possibility'). The underlying structure of the arguments is similar: if the phenomenal facts were *not* extra facts, then something would be true which is not in fact true – in the first case, that one could not know the physical facts and remain ignorant of the phenomenal ones; in the second, that it would not be metaphysically possible for the physical facts to hold and the phenomenal ones not to. In each case, a thought experiment is employed to establish that the relevant claim is indeed false.

Assessing property dualism

We have looked at two arguments for a property dualist view of consciousness. In the rest of this chapter we shall see how this view can be developed and consider a problem facing it.

Naturalistic dualism

If phenomenal properties are fundamentally distinct from physical ones, then it follows that consciousness cannot be reductively explained in the standard ways. A reductive explanation works by showing how lower-level processes give rise to the phenomenon being explained. A description of the electrical and mechanical processes inside a television set explains its power to display images of distant events since we can see that those processes are sufficient for the existence of the power. But if Jackson and Chalmers are right, consciousness cannot be explained in this way. Consciousness is something over and above physical processes in the brain and no account of those processes will ever explain its existence.

Some people find this conclusion deeply unattractive. The property dualist seems to be rejecting the naturalistic outlook of science and accepting the existence of an irreducible mystery in the world. Indeed, property dualists are sometimes disparagingly referred to as 'mysterians'. Now the property dualist may respond that the attractiveness of their view is neither here nor there. The question is whether it is *true*. If their arguments are sound, then, like it or not, consciousness cannot be explained by the physical sciences. This is, I think, a perfectly good response, so far as it goes. But all the same, it is legitimate to press the dualist for more. Science seems on course to develop an integrated and elegant picture of the world, with each level of organization explicable in terms of processes at a lower level and ultimately in terms of a few fundamental particles and forces. Does consciousness have no place at all in this picture? Must we regard it as a unique and inexplicable anomaly?

Chalmers, in particular, has risen to this challenge and sought to show how a dualist view of consciousness is compatible with a broadly naturalistic view of the world. Science, he argues, must *expand* to incorporate a view of consciousness as a non-physical phenomenon. He calls this view 'naturalistic dualism', and we are going to look at a short extract in which he outlines it. Before we start, however, I need to introduce a notion which figures prominently in the extract and is widely employed in modern philosophy of mind.

The notion is that of *supervenience*. Supervenience is a relation between properties of different types. To say that properties of type A supervene on properties of type B is to say that an object's B properties *determine* its A properties. Thus, an object's A properties cannot vary without some change to its B properties, and any two objects which have the same B properties will also have the same A properties. For example, a person's physical health supervenes on the condition of their organs and other body parts. The condition of their organs and body parts determines their state of physical health, and their physical health cannot change without some change to the condition of their organs and body parts.

Now, we can distinguish different types of supervenience, corresponding to the different types of possibility mentioned earlier. First there is *natural supervenience*. To say that A properties supervene naturally on B properties is to say that in the real world it is a law of nature that B properties determine A properties: as a matter of fact a thing's A properties never vary without some change in its B properties, though we could imagine a world in which they did. Natural supervenience contrasts with metaphysical supervenience, which is a much stronger notion. To say that A properties supervene metaphysically on B properties is to say that a thing's B properties determine its A properties in all possible situations, including ones that are not naturally possible. If A properties supervene metaphysically on B properties, then not even God could make a thing's A properties vary without change to its B properties.

ACTIVITY

1   What will a physicalist say about the relation between phenomenal properties and basic physical properties? Will they say that the former supervene on the latter, and if so, will they say that they do so metaphysically or only naturally?

2   What do the anti-physicalist arguments considered earlier imply about the supervenience relations between phenomenal properties and basic physical ones?

1   A physicalist will say that phenomenal properties do supervene on basic physical ones and that they do so *metaphysically*. Physicalists hold that phenomenal properties are not fundamentally distinct from basic physical ones, and if this is so, then it will not be even metaphysically possible for the former to vary without change to the latter.

2   The arguments imply that phenomenal properties do not supervene metaphysically on basic physical ones. If phenomenal properties are fundamentally distinct from basic physical ones, then there is no reason to think that they cannot vary independently of them. Indeed, the conceivability argument could easily be recast as an argument for the failure of consciousness to supervene metaphysically on basic physics. If zombies are metaphysically possible, then the facts of consciousness can vary independently of the basic physical ones – which is precisely to say they do not supervene metaphysically on them.

One further note before we start the reading. In this extract Chalmers talks of logical supervenience rather metaphysical supervenience. Logical supervenience is an even stronger notion: to say that A properties supervene logically on B properties is to say that it is not even *conceivable* that a thing's A properties could vary without change to its B properties. Chalmers talks this way since he holds that conceivability and metaphysical possibility amount to the same thing – a situation is metaphysically possible if and only if it is conceivable. As we shall see in the next chapter, some philosophers would dispute this. For present purposes, however, it will not do too much harm to read 'logical supervenience' as 'metaphysical supervenience' in this extract. What matters is the contrast with merely *natural* supervenience.

Turn now to Reading 5, which is another extract from Chalmers's book, *The Conscious Mind*. The Reading divides into two parts. The first clarifies Chalmers's position and distinguishes it from others; the second discusses the prospects for a dualist science of consciousness. Start by reading the first part, from paragraphs 1 to 6. Note that when Chalmers speaks of 'physical properties' he means *basic* physical ones.

1   What is Chalmers's view of the relation between phenomenal properties and basic physical ones?

2   Are zombies naturally possible in Chalmers's view?

3   What point is Chalmers making in paragraphs 3 and 4?

4   What is the purpose of paragraph 6?

DISCUSSION

1   On Chalmers's view, phenomenal properties supervene naturally on basic physical ones. In our universe there are laws of nature which dictate that whenever such-and-such basic physical properties are present, then such-and-such phenomenal properties are present, too. However, it is a contingent fact that these laws hold and it could have been otherwise. The two kinds of properties remain fundamentally distinct, despite their systematic correlation.

2   No. If phenomenal properties supervene naturally on basic physical ones, then in our universe, or in any other with the same laws of nature, a physical duplicate of me would have the same conscious experiences as me. Zombies could exist only in a universe where the laws linking basic physical properties with phenomenal ones do not hold. (It is important to stress that the same *physical* laws are assumed to hold in the zombies' universe – from a physical point of view their world is supposed to be just like ours. The difference lies in the absence of the *extra* laws, linking the physical with the phenomenal.)

3   He is pointing out that he is not committed to substance dualism, of the sort advocated by Descartes, but only to a form of property dualism.

4   It responds to the objection that Chalmers's position should be regarded as a form of physicalism ('materialism'), since it assumes that phenomenal facts depend on basic physical ones.

ACTIVITY

Now read the second part of Reading 5, paragraphs 7–14.

1   Summarize the argument in paragraphs 7–8.

2   Chalmers argues that we need to recognize the existence of new fundamental properties. What does he think these properties might be?

3   What does Chalmers think the new fundamental laws will be like? What does he mean by saying that they will not *interfere* with physical laws?

4   Why does Chalmers think that a fundamental theory of consciousness must exist?

5   Summarize the claims in paragraphs 12–14.

1   Physics is a *fundamental* theory, which posits properties and laws that cannot themselves be explained. This fundamental theory explains *almost* all other phenomena. It cannot explain consciousness, however, and in order to do so we must posit new fundamental properties and laws, in addition to those of physics.

2   Chalmers makes two suggestions. One is to take phenomenal properties themselves as fundamental properties, the other is to suppose that phenomenal properties supervene logically/metaphysically on more basic 'protophenomenal' properties which are related to them in the same way that basic physical properties are related to higher-level physical ones. If we take the latter view, then consciousness will be reductively explicable in terms of the underlying protophenomenal properties.

3   They will specify how phenomenal properties are correlated with basic physical ones. In saying that these laws will not interfere with physical laws, Chalmers means that they will not specify that phenomenal properties have effects in the physical world – Chalmers assumes that all physical events can be fully explained by reference to basic physical properties and laws. (We shall return to this point in the next section.)

4   Because there seems to be a regular correlation between consciousness and physical processes. Such a correlation implies the existence of laws connecting the two.

5   The proposed view of consciousness is perfectly compatible with the scientific worldview. There are precedents for positing new fundamental properties and laws, and the new theory will supplement existing physical theories rather than overturning them.

DISCUSSION

The causal role of consciousness

I want to turn now to a problem for the property dualist. This concerns the causal role of consciousness – the effects it has in the physical world. It seems obvious that the phenomenal properties of experience make a difference to our behaviour. In explaining a person's actions we often refer to the character of their experiences. Why did Jack make an emergency appointment with the dentist? Because his toothache was unbearably painful. Why did Jill accept a second helping of chocolate pudding? Because it tasted so good. Why did Bob close the window? Because the sound of the traffic was bothering him. Yet, if consciousness is non-physical, then we may have to accept that this is an illusion and these explanations misguided.

Let me set out the line of thought. Note that, in what follows, when I speak of *explanation* I shall mean *causal explanation* – the explanation of events in terms of preceding ones. This should not be confused with *reductive explanation*, which is the explanation of how phenomena are constituted. We might think of causal explanation as *horizontal* – explaining why things change their properties, whereas reductive explanation is *vertical*, explaining how their properties are constituted.

The starting point for the argument is a claim about basic physical events. There is very strong evidence that all events at the basic physical level – all changes in atoms, molecules and so on – can be completely explained at that level, in terms of the effects of basic physical forces, operating in accordance with basic physical laws. This is often summed up by saying that the basic physical realm is *causally closed*, or that basic physics is *complete*: we need never appeal to anything outside the basic physical realm in order to explain events within it. (Possible exceptions are so-called *quantum events*. I shall say more about these later.)

Now if basic physics is causally closed, then it follows that the movements of our bodies can also be explained in basic physical terms. For our bodies are just collections of basic physical particles, and their movements could, in principle, be redescribed in terms of the motions of their constituent particles. And if causal closure holds at the basic physical level, then these motions will have sufficient causal explanations in basic physical terms. For example, suppose that I bang my shin against the table and let out a cry of pain. My crying out is a basic physical event involving contractions in the muscle fibres in my diaphragm, throat and mouth. And if basic physics is causally closed, then there will be a complete explanation of the event in basic physical terms. Very crudely, it might go like this. The contractions in my muscle fibres were caused by electrical impulses in my nerves, which were in turn the product of complex electro–chemical processes in various regions of my brain. This brain activity was itself triggered by electrical impulses in the nerves from my leg, which were in turn caused by the impact of my leg on the table. A similar explanation will be possible for every action we perform. More generally, any change in physical properties, in the broad sense, will be explicable in basic physical terms. For any such event will be redescribable in basic physical terms and will thus have a complete explanation at the basic physical level. To put it in terms of properties: the only properties we need to mention, in order to give a complete explanation of changes in the physical world are basic physical ones.

What about high-level properties, including mental ones? Does this mean that they have no causal influence on the physical world? Not necessarily. Suppose that high-level properties are *themselves* physical ones in the broad sense, as physicalists maintain. That is, suppose that each instance of a high-level property is identical with an instance of some basic physical property – some complex arrangement of basic physical particles. Then these properties *will* have a causal influence. For they will *inherit* the causal powers of the basic physical properties in which they are realized. Indeed, on this view high-level phenomena simply *are* basic physical ones under different descriptions. Take the case where I bang my shin and cry out. It would be natural to explain this in mental terms – to say that I cried out because of the pain I felt. And physicalists can endorse this explanation. For according to them there is *nothing more* to an experience of pain than the occurrence of certain basic physical processes. Thus, on their view, the mental explanation does not conflict with the basic physical one; it refers to the same thing under a different guise.

In short, a high-level property can have a causal influence in the physical world in virtue of being realized in basic physical ones. Thus we can rephrase causal closure as a claim about physical phenomena in the broad sense, to the effect that only physical properties can have effects in the physical world.

How does this generate a problem for property dualists about consciousness?

Property dualists hold that consciousness is *not* physical – that phenomenal properties are fundamentally distinct from basic physical ones. So if they accept that the physical world is causally closed, then it seems they must accept that consciousness has no causal influence within it.

We can put the problem for dualists in terms of an inconsistent triad of claims. One can endorse any two of the following claims but not, it seems, all three:

1 *Property dualism* Consciousness is non-physical.

2 *Efficacy of consciousness* Consciousness has effects in the physical world.

3 *Closure of the physical* Only physical phenomena have effects in the physical world.

Pause for a moment and think which of these three claims you would drop. You might give each a score out of ten – 1 meaning 'definitely not true' and 10 'certainly true' – and drop the one with the lowest score. See if your views change as we go on.

How should property dualists respond? They cannot give up 1, and it is hard to deny that 2 is true. The obvious choice, then, would be to reject 3 and deny that the physical world is causally closed. Let us consider that option first.

Interactionism

If the brain does have non-physical properties, then why not suppose that these properties influence the physical processes that occur within it – that there is interaction between the two? After all, we do not fully understand how the brain works. Who is to say that there are no non-physical influences there? The view that there are such influences is known as *interactionist dualism*, or *interactionism* for short, and it involves denying the causal closure of the physical. (Note that what we are concerned with here is the claim that there is *phenomenal-to-physical* interaction – that consciousness exerts a causal influence on the physical. The converse claim, that the physical causally influences consciousness is, in this context, less controversial, and it is generally accepted by property dualists. (It is hard to deny that physical events in our sense-organs play a role in generating our conscious experiences.) The important point to note is that physical-to-phenomenal causation would not violate the causal closure of the physical, as phenomenal-to-physical causation would. Causal closure denies that physical events have non-physical *causes*, not that they have non-physical *effects*.)

The suggestion here, then, is that new causal powers arise in the brains of conscious creatures – powers which go beyond those of the brain's basic physical components and exert a 'downward' influence on the behaviour of those components. If this is true, then the behaviour of conscious creatures cannot be explained in the same way as that of inanimate things, since there will be new causal powers at work in the former. This view is a form of *emergentism* – the idea that new causal powers emerge as matter is organized in increasingly complex ways. Emergentism was popular in the early twentieth century – its best-known advocate being the Cambridge philosopher C.D. Broad (1887–1971) – and it still has defenders. It has, however, come under extreme pressure from empirical research. There are two aspects to this. First, physics has undermined the idea that complexity generates new causal powers. The general tendency of research since the mid-nineteenth century has been to show that all changes in physical systems, from the simplest to the most complex, can be explained as the product of a few fundamental forces, which operate universally. (Modern physics postulates just four of these – the strong nuclear force, the weak nuclear force, electromagnetism and gravity, though it is widely believed that the first three of these are manifestations of a single, more fundamental force.) There is simply no room in this picture for the emergence of new causal powers in the brains of living creatures. The second source of pressure has come from physiology and, in particular, neurophysiology. If consciousness does exhibit a causal influence, then it is in the brain that we should expect to detect it. We should expect to find processes occurring there – brain cells firing or neurotransmitters being released – without adequate physical causes. And there is no evidence of this at all. It is true that we are still a long way from fully understanding how the brain works. However, scientists do understand its *low-level* functioning very well. They understand how brain cells work, what makes them fire and how their firing affects neighbouring cells. And, so far, there is absolutely no evidence of any non-physical interventions in these processes.

The evidence from physics and neurophysiology, then, strongly suggests that there are no non-physical influences on our behaviour. This is not the end of the story, however. For there is an area of physics which seems positively to encourage the idea that the physical world is not causally closed. This is quantum mechanics. Quantum mechanics is a theory of processes at the atomic and subatomic levels. Its details are highly complex and its interpretation a matter of controversy, but the important point for us is that it seems to entail that some basic physical events are not completely determined by basic physical causes. These so-called 'quantum events' seem to be genuinely unpredictable and some dualists suggest that this leaves an opening for consciousness to intervene in the physical world. If consciousness determines the outcome of quantum events in the brain and if the results are somehow amplified to produce large-scale neurological changes, then consciousness could have significant effects on our behaviour.

It is difficult to assess this suggestion – partly because quantum mechanics is such a complex and contentious subject, partly because, to date, dualists have not developed detailed theories of how quantum events could significantly influence our behaviour. But there is reason to be sceptical of the proposal. The main worry is that, according to quantum theory, basic physical factors still fully determine the *probabilities* of events at the quantum level. It is a bit like throwing a die: each of the possible outcomes has a certain predetermined probability, although the choice between them is random.

ACTIVITY

Why does the claim that basic physical factors fix the probability of outcomes at the quantum level create a problem for quantum-level interactionism?

DISCUSSION

If consciousness exerted an influence on quantum events, then the probabilities of these events would not be fully determined by basic physical factors. For consciousness would also affect the chances of one outcome occurring rather than another. So quantum theory, in its current form, rules out a role for consciousness here.

To sum up: the current scientific evidence comes down fairly heavily in favour of causal closure and against interactionism. This is not the last word on the matter, of course. Scientists are continually revising their theories and opinion may change. Perhaps neurologists will discover brain processes which have no physical causes. Perhaps the probabilities of quantum events are not completely fixed. But I think it is fair to say that most scientists consider these things extremely unlikely.

Epiphenomenalism

If the physical world is causally closed, then, it seems, property dualists must deny the efficacy of consciousness and accept that the phenomenal properties of experience – 'the hurtfulness of pains, the itchiness of itches, pangs of jealousy', to quote Jackson – have no effects on behaviour. On this view, consciousness is merely a by-product of brain activity, like the exhaust from an engine, which has no effects on the brain or the behaviour it produces (or, indeed, on anything else in the physical world). Such properties are described as being *epiphenomenal* and the view that phenomenal properties are of this kind is a form of *epiphenomenalism*.

It is important to stress that the view we are considering is not that experiences *themselves* have no causal influence – only that certain *properties* of them do not. The epiphenomenalist can accept that experiences are states of the brain and that they have an important role in guiding our behaviour. The claim is merely how these states *feel* – their phenomenal character – makes no causal difference. So, for example, when I bang my shin, my brain enters a certain state – a pain state – which causes me to say 'Ouch!', hop about, rub my shin and so on. But the *feel* of this state – the *painfulness* of the pain – makes no difference at all.

This view is counter-intuitive, but it may be the most stable one for property dualists to adopt and some of them do adopt it. Jackson is an example. In the paper in which he introduces the knowledge argument (which is titled 'Epiphenomenal qualia'), he goes on to discuss the causal role of qualia and to defend the view that they are epiphenomenal. Let us look at what he has to say.

ACTIVITY

Turn now to Reading 6. Summarize the three objections to epiphenomenalism listed by Jackson and his responses to them. The reference to Hume in paragraph 3 is to his claim that there is no *necessary connection* between causes and their effects, and that, for all we can tell by a priori reasoning, anything can cause anything.

DISCUSSION

The first objection is that it is just obvious that there is a causal connection between qualia and behaviour. The second is that if qualia were epiphenomenal, then they would not have evolved, since evolution only selects for characteristics that have some effect on an organism's survival chances, and epiphenomenal properties would have none. The third objection is that if qualia had no effect on behaviour, then we would have no reason to think that other people possess them. We cannot see into other people's minds and must infer their mental properties from their behaviour.

To the first objection Jackson responds that even apparently obvious causal claims can be overturned by wider theoretical considerations. The point is that we infer a causal connection after noticing a repeated sequence in events and may abandon the inference if we come up with a better overall explanation of what is happening. Jackson suggests that, in the light of the arguments for property dualism, we should cease to think of qualia as causes of actions and regard both qualia and actions as effects of brain states. Jackson responds to the second objection by pointing out that qualia may be a by-product of a characteristic that was conducive to survival – namely, the complex brain processes involved in perception and sensation. In response to the third objection Jackson points out that if qualia are caused by brain states, then we can infer their presence in others by a two-step manoeuvre. We can infer the presence of the relevant brain states from their effects on behaviour and infer the presence of qualia from that of the brain states.

There may be no knock-down arguments against epiphenomenalism, but it cannot be denied that it is an extremely counter-intuitive view, and I now want to turn to a short reading from Chalmers which vividly illustrates this. It involves reflection on our *claims* about our conscious experiences.

ACTIVITY   Turn to Reading 7. Note that 'judgements' (paragraph 2) is Chalmers's technical term for functional states which are exactly like beliefs except that they lack phenomenal properties. Judgements are physical states, and our zombie twins possess judgements which mirror our own beliefs. *Phenomenal* judgements are judgements about one's own conscious experiences.

1   Why will the explanation of the zombie twin's behaviour apply equally to Chalmers's own behaviour?

2   Is the zombie twin *lying* when it claims to have conscious experiences?

3   Why does the zombie judge that it has conscious experiences?

DISCUSSION   1   Because the zombie is physically identical to Chalmers himself. So if there is a complete physical explanation of its behaviour, then the very same explanation will apply equally to Chalmers himself (remember that our zombie twins, as Chalmers conceives of them, are behaviourally identical to us). Thus if zombies are metaphysically possible, then consciousness in the real world must be explanatorily irrelevant. The very conceivability of zombies seems to entail that consciousness is epiphenomenal.

2   No. The zombie will *judge* that it has conscious experiences, and its claims will reflect this. These claims will, of course, be *false*, but they will be sincere! (Elsewhere Chalmers suggests that the *content* of his zombie twin's judgements about its conscious experiences may differ subtly from that of his own corresponding beliefs, since direct acquaintance with consciousness may be needed in order to possess the full-blown concept of consciousness. He accepts, however, that the zombie's judgements will have the same functional roles as his own beliefs.)

3   For the same reason Chalmers believes he does. Chalmers's beliefs are functional states of his brain (albeit ones with additional non-physical phenomenal properties) and there will be some physical explanation of their origin in terms of past events in his life. Exactly the same explanation will apply to his zombie twin's judgements.

In short, consciousness is irrelevant even to those actions which ought to manifest its presence most directly – our reports about it. Chalmers refers to this as the 'paradox of phenomenal judgement' and describes it as 'at once delightful and disturbing' (1996, 181). Again, the existence of the paradox does not refute epiphenomenalism, but it does highlight how counter-intuitive the position is.

Panprotopsychism

We have considered the two obvious options for the property dualist – denying causal closure and embracing epiphenomenalism – but there are other more subtle moves they might make to defuse the tension.

One option is to maintain that, although our actions do have sufficient physical causes, they also have *additional* conscious ones. (Events which have more than one sufficient cause are said to be *overdetermined*.) This view gives consciousness a causal role, though not an *explanatory* one. It would still be unnecessary to refer to consciousness in order to explain our actions, since they would have occurred anyway, due to the accompanying physical causes. This view cannot be ruled out, but it is not a popular one.

Another option, proposed by Chalmers, involves some bold metaphysical speculation. We saw that one way to reconcile the efficacy of consciousness with the causal closure of the physical world is to maintain that conscious states are realized in basic physical ones. But, Chalmers suggests, we could also take the opposite view and hold that basic physical states are realized in conscious ones – that phenomenal properties, or rudimentary versions of them, are found at the fundamental level of physical reality, in the basic physical particles themselves. If so, then consciousness will be closely integrated with the physical world and the causal processes that occur there. This view, which Chalmers calls *panprotopsychism*, is an intriguing one, and I want to round off this chapter by looking at it in a little more detail.

ACTIVITY

In Reading 8 Chalmers briefly introduces the panprotopsychist position. Turn to this and answer the following questions. Note that *panpsychism* (paragraph 6) is the view that everything has mental properties. By the 'microphysical' (paragraphs 4, 7 and 9), Chalmers means the basic physical level – the level of atoms and suchlike.

1   Briefly summarize the suggestion in paragraphs 1–4.

2   How does the proposed view resolve the problem of the causal role of consciousness?

3   Two problems for panprotopsycism are mentioned in paragraphs 7–10. What are they?

DISCUSSION

1   Physics characterizes basic physical particles in terms of their relations and dispositions – the way they interact with other particles and their tendencies to produce certain effects – and does not say anything about their *intrinsic* properties. Yet they must have some intrinsic properties. The suggestion is that these properties are in fact phenomenal ones, or more basic, 'protophenomenal' ones. To put it crudely, subatomic particles are little sparks of consciousness or proto-consciousness. The physical and phenomenal worlds we know emerge from these particles – the former from their activity and the latter from their intrinsic properties.

2   The view does not contradict anything in physics and is compatible with causal closure. Yet it also gives consciousness a causal role, since it treats

phenomenal, or protophenomenal, properties as essential features of the entities mentioned in the causal explanations given by physics.

3   The first problem is that the view sounds strange. If the intrinsic properties are phenomenal ones, then we have to suppose that it is *like something* to be an electron – which is very counterintuitive. (Of course, Chalmers is not suggesting that electrons have rich phenomenal lives or that they engage in conscious thought, just that they have a tiny spark of consciousness. But even that is highly counterintuitive.) If, on the other hand, the intrinsic properties are protophenomenal ones, then we have no idea what they might be like. The second objection is that it is unclear how human consciousness could arise from the phenomenal properties of basic particles. How could billions of little bits of consciousness combine to produce the unified consciousness we each experience?

Chalmers declares himself attracted to the panprotopsychist position, though he does not formally endorse it and leaves open the other options of epiphenomenalism and quantum-level interactionism. (Elsewhere, he ranks these options in the following order of preference: panprotopsychism, epiphenomenalism and quantum-level interactionism (Chalmers 1999, 493).)

Conclusion

In this chapter we have looked at two arguments for property dualism, seen how the view can be developed and examined a problem for it. You should now be beginning to get a feel for where you stand on the debate. Here is a final exercise to help crystallize your views.

Earlier I asked you to rate the following three claims for plausibility: (i)   **ACTIVITY** property dualism, (ii) efficacy of consciousness and (iii) closure of the physical. We can now add a fourth claim: (iv) non-sentience of the basic physical. This is the view that basic physical particles do not possess phenomenal or protophenomenal properties. Again, these claims are jointly incompatible: one cannot hold on to all of them. (For simplicity I have set aside the possibility that our actions are causally overdetermined.) Now that we have looked at (ii) and (iii) in more detail, has your assessment of these claims changed? And how do you rate (iv) on the same scale? Which gets the lowest score? What do these scores say about your position on the problem of consciousness?

Your position on the problem is determined by which of the claims you rate least likely and are therefore most disposed to drop. If you gave (i) the lowest score, then you are a physicalist. If you gave (ii) the lowest score, then you are an epiphenomenalist. If you gave (iii) the lowest score, then you are an interactionist. If you gave (iv) the lowest score, then you are a panprotopsychist. (See Figure 7.)

Compatible with?	Property dualism	Efficacy of consciousness	Closure of the physical	Non-sentience of the basic physical
Physicalism	✗	✓	✓	✓
Epiphenomenalism	✓	✗	✓	✓
Interactionism	✓	✓	✗	✓
Panprotopsychism	✓	✓	✓	✗

Figure 7 Positions on the causal role of consciousness.

Many philosophers of mind give (i) the lowest score and adopt physicalism as their preferred position. In the next chapter we shall look at this position and see how physicalists have responded to the arguments we have been considering.

Further reading

Various writers have anticipated the knowledge argument. By far the most important and influential paper to appear before Jackson's is

NAGEL, T. (1974) 'What is it like to be a bat?', *Philosophical Review*, 83, 435–50. Reprinted in Block et al. 1997.

Jackson himself has produced a short follow-up paper on the knowledge argument, clarifying the details and responding to some objections:

JACKSON, F. (1986) 'What Mary didn't know', *The Journal of Philosophy*, 83, 291–5. Also in Block et al. 1997.

Knut Nordby (the real-life Mary) has written a fascinating memoir of his experiences:

NORDBY, K. (1990) 'Vision in a complete achromat: A personal account', in R. Hess, L. Sharpe & K. Nordby (eds), *Night Vision: Basic, Clinical, and Applied Aspects*, Cambridge, Cambridge University Press, pp.290–315.

Early versions of the conceivability argument can be found in

CAMPBELL, K.K. (1970) *Body and Mind*, London, Macmillan, Chapter 5.

KIRK, R. (1974) 'Zombies vs materialists', *Proceedings of the Aristotelian Society (Supplementary Volume)*, 48, 135–52. (One of the first discussions of zombies.)

KRIPKE, S.A. (1980) *Naming and Necessity*, Oxford, Blackwell, Lecture III. Extract reprinted in Block et al. 1997. (A demanding but brilliant work, which deals with fundamental issues in metaphysics and philosophy of language.)

There is a lot of material about zombies available on the internet, some of it serious, some less so. For a useful series of links, see David Chalmers's website at http://consc.net/chalmers/.

For Chalmers's detailed presentation of the anti-physicalist case, naturalistic dualism and the paradox of phenomenal judgement, see Chapters 3, 4 and 5 of his book *The Conscious Mind: In Search of a Fundamental Theory* (1996). Some of this material is difficult, but Chalmers helpfully highlights the more technical sections, so that first-time readers can skip them.

For an excellent historical account of the reasons that led most twentieth-century scientists to accept that the physical is casually closed, see the Appendix to

PAPINEAU, D. (2002) *Thinking About Consciousness*, Oxford, Oxford University Press.

CHAPTER 3

Physicalism

> [I]ntrospection... fails to make us aware of any great complexity in the phenomenal qualities, and further fails to make us aware of an identity of these qualities with complex physical properties. But it is clearly invalid to argue from lack of awareness of the complex physical nature of mental processes and phenomenal properties to the conclusion that we are aware that these processes and qualities lack this complex physical nature. The move from 'I am not aware that p' to 'I am aware that not-p' is an illegitimate shifting of the negation sign.
>
> (Armstrong 1981, 50–1)

This chapter continues the discussion of the metaphysics of consciousness by considering the case for a physicalist view. It looks at how physicalists have responded to the arguments for property dualism set out in the previous chapter and also assesses the prospects for a physicalist explanation of consciousness.

The general case for a physicalist view of consciousness has already been outlined. As we have seen, the central problem for property dualism concerns the causal role of consciousness. For many people none of the options here – epiphenomenalism, interactionism and panpsychism – is credible, and physicalism wins by default. Many people also find the property dualist's picture of the world inelegant and counter-intuitive. The posited laws correlating phenomenal properties with physical ones look like awkward appendages to the network of causal laws – 'nomological danglers' in Herbert Feigl's phrase (Feigl 1958). ('Nomological' means 'relating to laws'; the term 'nomological dangler' is also used to refer to phenomenal properties themselves, as in the quote below.) Moreover, as the English-Australian philosopher J.J.C. Smart noted some years ago, the correlation laws will be very unusual ones – linking highly complex physical properties with simple phenomenal ones:

> It is not often realised how odd would be the laws whereby these nomological danglers would dangle. It is sometimes asked, 'Why can't there be psycho-physical laws which are of a novel sort, just as the laws of electricity and magnetism were novelties from the standpoint of Newtonian mechanics?' Certainly we are pretty sure in the future to come across new ultimate laws of a

novel type, but I expect them to relate simple constituents: for example, whatever ultimate particles are then in vogue. I cannot believe that ultimate laws of nature could relate simple constituents to configurations consisting of perhaps billions of neurons (and goodness knows how many billion billions of ultimate particles)... Such ultimate laws would be like nothing so far known in science. They have a queer 'smell' to them. I am just unable to believe in the nomological danglers themselves, or in the laws whereby they would dangle. If any philosophical arguments seemed to compel us to believe in such things, I would suspect a catch in the argument.

(Smart 1959, 142–3)

I suspect that, like Smart, many philosophers would be inclined to dismiss the anti-physicalist arguments on general metaphysical grounds, even if they could not put their finger on the flaw in them. But, of course, if their metaphysical intuitions are sound, then there must be some flaw in the arguments and physicalists will greatly strengthen their case if they can identify them. Let us look, then, at some physicalist responses to the arguments, beginning with the knowledge argument.

Responses to the knowledge argument

Recall how the knowledge argument goes. The argument aims to show that the physical picture of the world leaves something out – namely, information about the phenomenal properties of experience. The best-known version of the argument focuses on Mary, the colour scientist confined to a back-and-white room. It can be set out as follows.

> *Premise 1*   If physicalism is true, then on leaving her room Mary will not learn any new facts about colour vision.
> *Premise 2*   On leaving her room, Mary learns new facts about colour vision (namely, what it is like to see various colours).
> *Conclusion*   Physicalism is not true.

Premise 1 follows from the definition of physicalism ('the physical facts are all the facts there are') and the hypothesis that Mary knows all the physical facts before leaving her room. Premise 2 is supposed to be intuitively obvious.

Physicalists have developed several lines of response to this argument. We shall look at three of the most influential ones.

The no-learning view

The first response I want to consider involves denying Premise 2 – that Mary learns something about colour vision on first experiencing it for herself. This response – the *no-learning view*, as I shall call it – has a powerful advocate in the person of the distinguished American philosopher Daniel Dennett (b. 1942).

According to Dennett, we have no good reason to think that Mary could not work out what it is like to see colours from the physical information available to her in her room. It is true that we have a strong intuition that she could not. We imagine Mary leaving her room and being surprised and amazed at the world of colours awaiting her. But, Dennett argues, this intuition is unsound and the thought experiment which generates it misleading.

Dennett has a general suspicion of thought experiments, which he refers to as 'intuition pumps'. The function of an intuition pump is, he says

> to entrain a family of imaginative reflections in the reader that ultimately yields not a formal conclusion but a dictate of 'intuition'. Intuition pumps are cunningly designed to focus the reader's attention on the 'the important' features, and to deflect the reader from bogging down in hard-to-follow details.

(Dennett 1984, 12)

Although Dennett accepts that intuition pumps can play a useful role in highlighting theoretically important aspects of complex situations, he maintains that they can also be seriously misleading – most often because they encourage us to imagine a scenario which is actually much simpler than the one they officially describe. Precisely this fault, he claims, is to be found in the Mary example.

Reading 9 is a short extract from Dennett's 1991 book *Consciousness Explained*.   **ACTIVITY**
Turn to this now and answer the following questions.

1   Why, according to Dennett, is the Mary example misleading?

2   How could Mary pass the blue banana test?

3   Is Dennett denying that one can learn something about the nature of colour experience as a result of undergoing it oneself?

1   Because it is very hard to imagine what it would be like for Mary if she   **DISCUSSION**
    knew *all* the physical information about colour vision. Instead we just
    imagine her knowing a *lot* – say, all that is currently known.

2   By hypothesis, Mary already knows what physical effects different colours would have on her nervous system, including what thoughts they would evoke in her. So she could tell which colour experiences she is having by noting these effects.

3   No. He explains that in any realistic version of the scenario Mary would learn something about colour vision on first experiencing it for herself. For in any realistic version she would not know all the physical facts about it.

It might be objected that Dennett's counterexample misses the point (see Jacquette 1995; Robinson 1993). Jackson does not deny that Mary would be able to work out what colour experiences she is having, just that she would know what they would be *like*. And it is compatible with Dennett's story that this might still be a revelation to her. Presented with the blue banana, she might say, 'I can tell from my reactions that I must be seeing something blue here. So this is what it's like to see blue, eh? Gosh, I had no idea.'

Now, strictly speaking, this is not incompatible with what Dennett says. As he makes clear in paragraph 4, the point of his counterexample is not to show that Mary does not learn anything, but to undermine Jackson's case for thinking that she does. We think she will learn something, Dennett suggests, because we imagine her being surprised when she leaves her room and vulnerable to tricks like that described. Since we are wrong to imagine this, the case proves nothing either way. However, I think it is clear from the Reading (and certainly from his wider work) that Dennett does believe that Mary would not learn anything.

ACTIVITY   Look again at paragraph 5 of Reading 9. What would Dennett say is involved in knowing what it is like to see colours? How could Mary acquire this knowledge?

DISCUSSION   He would say that it involves knowing how one would react to colours and being able to detect these reactions when they occur. Most of us acquire this knowledge in a practical way, by observing the reactions in ourselves, but Mary could acquire it theoretically by calculating what neurophysiological effects different colours would have on her and devising ways of recognizing these effects 'from the inside'.

Dennett's warnings about thought experiments are salutary, but does he really succeed in showing that Jackson's example is unreliable? He is certainly right that we cannot imagine Mary's situation in all its detail. We do not have access to the complete physical facts about vision and probably could not master them all even if we did. But does that really compromise the example? For we already have an idea of the *sort* of information Mary will have. It will be information about neurological mechanisms, the functions they perform and the reactions they produce. And, it might be argued, information of this kind, no matter how detailed, can never entail facts about consciousness. On the other hand, can we be sure that the details do *not* matter? Perhaps the reason we feel that consciousness is something over and above physical processes in the brain is just that we have such a crude understanding of the latter, and perhaps as we learn more and more about them – about the fine-grained discriminations that are made in the visual cortex and the complex behavioural, cognitive and emotional reactions they generate – our intuitions will change. Can we be sure they won't? After all, in the past many scientists had similar intuitions about life – holding that no amount of physical information would ever explain organic processes such as healing and reproduction.

Moreover, it is not too difficult to see how a person who had never had colour experience might begin to get some understanding of it. Take the experience of seeing red. The person might learn that red is experienced as having a location in relation to other colours – close to yellow but duller, closer still to orange, opposite to green and blue and so on. They might also learn that red experiences have certain characteristic links to non-visual experiences: red is felt as being warm, 'advancing', vibrant, exciting and sometimes discomforting (people tend to feel uneasy in red rooms). So if Mary knew all the facts of this kind and all about the psychological and physiological effects different colours produce, then perhaps she would be able to recognize colours straight off. And if she could do that, then wouldn't it be true to say that she knew what colour vision was like?

You will have to make up your own mind here. The no-learning view deserves to be taken seriously – and has, as we shall see, received endorsement from an unexpected quarter. None the less, it is not a popular view even among physicalists, many of whom feel that it is possible to adopt a more conciliatory line. We can deny that Mary learns new non-physical facts, they argue, without denying that she learns *something*. Let us look at a proposal of this type.

The ability hypothesis

A second response to the knowledge argument concedes that Mary gains new knowledge on leaving her room, but denies that she learns new *facts*. The response turns on a distinction between two kinds of knowledge: knowledge of facts (propositional knowledge) and knowledge of how to do something (practical knowledge). Take swimming, for example. A swimming manual will teach you lots of facts about swimming – which movements to make, when to breathe and so on. But knowing these facts is not the same as knowing *how* to swim – actually being able to do it. For that, you will need to put the manual aside and get into the water. Now, according to the response we are considering, knowing what it is like to see colours is knowledge of the second kind, not the first. It is a matter of possessing abilities, rather than grasping facts. This is known as the *ability hypothesis*.

The chief advocates of the ability hypothesis are Laurence Nemirow and David Lewis (Lewis 1983, 1990; Nemirow 1980, 1990). We shall look at Lewis's presentation of it, in an extract from a paper published in 1990. A note on terminology: Lewis talks of information 'eliminating possibilities'. The idea is that in gaining information we narrow down the possibilities as to how things are. For example, if you learn that a certain store is in central London, then you narrow down the possibilities as to where it is (you know that it's not in Birmingham or Glasgow, for example). If you learn that it is in the West End, then you narrow down the possibilities still further. And if you learn that it is at 363 Oxford Street, then you narrow down the possibilities to just one – the actual location. In these terms, physicalism is the thesis that the complete physical information about the world narrows down the possibilities as to how things are to just one: it specifies exactly how the world is in every detail. Property dualism, on the other hand, is the view that the physical information still leaves some possibilities open, since it does not specify what phenomenal properties experiences have. Thus according to the property dualist, there is extra, phenomenal, information to be had, in addition to the physical information.

Turn to Reading 10. (Note that Vegemite is a spread similar to Marmite.)

ACTIVITY

1   According to Lewis, what abilities are involved in knowing what it's like to taste Vegemite?

2   Could someone who has never tasted Vegemite acquire these abilities?

3   According to Lewis, why do we think that knowing what an experience is like involves acquiring new information? (Paragraph 7)

DISCUSSION

1   The abilities to remember, to imagine and to recognize the taste of Vegemite.

2   Not in practice. Perhaps future neurosurgery could do the trick, by bringing about the same subtle changes to your brain as the experience itself would. But lessons about Vegemite won't do it.

3   Because when we acquire an ability we usually acquire some information at the same time – knowledge-how and knowledge-that usually go together. For example, in learning how to swim we also learn facts about good swimming technique. And we tend to think that the same is true when we learn what an experience is like. Lewis claims that this is a mistake, however, since this case is a pure one, in which we gain an ability without gaining any information at all.

If sound, the ability hypothesis disarms the knowledge argument. According to Lewis, Mary does indeed acquire new knowledge on her release – knowledge she could not have gleaned from the physical information previously available to her. But it is know-how that she acquires – the ability to remember, imagine and recognize colour experiences – not factual knowledge. Premise 2 of the argument

Premise 2   On leaving her room, Mary learns new facts about colour vision (namely, what it is like to see various colours).

is thus false and the conclusion does not follow.

The ability hypothesis has other attractions, too. In particular, it offers an explanation of the *ineffability* of experience. If knowing what an experience is like is pure know-how, with no element of knowledge-that, then it is not surprising that we find it impossible to put it into words. In general, it is very hard to describe an ability in propositional terms. An expert swimmer may be completely unable to *describe* how to swim – they just know how to *do* it.

Is the ability hypothesis correct? Note that the issue is not whether knowing what an experience is like usually involves acquiring the abilities Lewis describes. Most people accept that. The question is whether that is *all* that it involves – whether knowing what an experience is like is a pure case of know-how, without any knowledge-that. I shall mention two objections to the view that it is.

The first objection is that the view does not reflect the language we use. In general, when we talk of *knowing what* X *is like*, we mean knowing *that* X has certain properties (Lycan 1996, 92–4). Knowing what Paris is like involves knowing (say) that it is a beautiful leafy city with wide boulevards and elegant architecture. Knowing what Mahatma Ghandi was like involves knowing that he was a modest and gentle man with great moral courage. And so on. By analogy, knowing what an experience is like should involve knowing that it has certain characteristic properties.

The second objection is that learning what an experience is like seems to bring with it, not just the ability to remember, imagine and recognize the experience, but also the ability to think new *thoughts* about it (Papineau 2002, 61; Tye 2000, 15). When Mary sees a banana for the first time, she will be able to think, 'So *this* is what the experience of yellow is like', '*This* is what I shall experience when I see lemons and primroses' and so on. A new range of thoughts will be available to her, which she could not previously think. But if so, then learning what an experience is like involves more than just acquiring the ability to remember, imagine and recognize it.

These two objections suggest that possessing the abilities Lewis describes is not *sufficient* for knowing what an experience is like. There is also reason to question whether it is *necessary*. For experience has a richness which outstrips our capacity to remember, imagine and recognize it (Tye 2000, 11–13). Look at a coloured surface near you. Now, will you be able to remember and recognize that colour later? To a degree, yes. You will be able to remember that it was, say, a light yellowish-green. But will you be able to remember and recognize the *precise shade* – accurately enough to distinguish it from other similar shades in a paint catalogue? Probably not. I certainly do not have that sort of visual memory. There will be similar difficulties in trying to imagine the shade. Yet in looking at the colour you knew *what it was like* to see that precise shade. Therefore, knowing what it is like to have a colour experience is not the same as being able to remember, imagine and recognize it. (If you are visually impaired, you can try the same experiment with other kinds of experience, such as taste or smell. Again, I suspect, the richness of the experiences will outstrip your capacity to remember, imagine and recognize them.)

You should not assume that these objections are fatal to the ability hypothesis. You may be able to think of rejoinders to them yourself. However, many physicalists feel that the ability hypothesis is inadequate and that Mary does acquire a kind of knowledge-that. Let us turn to another response, which aims to do justice to this intuition.

The perspectivalist view

The third response I want to introduce is what has come to be known as the *perspectivalist view*. This concedes that Mary does acquire some factual knowledge, but maintains that this knowledge is of a kind that poses no threat to physicalism: what she learns are not new non-physical facts, but familiar physical facts conceptualized in a new way – from a different perspective. This view has been advocated by a number of writers and is currently the most popular physicalist response to the knowledge argument. We shall focus on a presentation of the view by the British philosopher Michael Tye.

The perspectivalist view turns on considerations about concepts, and I want to begin by outlining the view of concepts Tye has in mind. Concepts, then, in the relevant sense, are mental representations. They are constituents of thoughts, in the way that words are constituents of sentences, and are defined in part by their functional role – by how they are formed and activated, and by the effects their activation has. So, for example, thinking about kangaroos involves the activation of the concept *kangaroo* – a mental representation which was acquired in a certain way (through seeing kangaroos, say, or being told about them) and which has certain characteristic effects on one's thought processes (perhaps tending to activate the concepts *marsupial* and *Australian*).

Now concepts represent, or refer to, things. For example, the concept *water* represents water. But they do not represent things, as it were, *transparently*. Rather, they represent them in a particular way – under some *mode of presentation* or *representation*. For example, the concepts *water* and H_2O represent the same substance, but do so under different modes of presentation. They are acquired in different ways, activated in different contexts and have different associations (the latter, for example, has direct links with the concepts *hydrogen* and *oxygen*, which the former does not). Some writers identify a concept's mode of presentation with an associated description, which identifies the thing referred to (which 'fixes the reference' of the concept). So, for example, the concept *water* can be thought of as associated with the description 'the colourless, odourless, drinkable liquid found in the oceans and lakes'. This view is sometimes referred to as *descriptivism*.

It is our ability to conceptualize one and the same thing in different ways that is the key to the perspectivalist view. Because of it, we can adopt different mental attitudes to the same state of affairs, depending on the concepts we use to represent it. A person may believe that there is water in the glass before them without believing that there is H_2O in the glass, even though there is a sense in which both beliefs amount to the same thing. As a consequence, Tye argues, there is an ambiguity in the knowledge argument, centring on the term 'fact'.

ACTIVITY

Turn to Reading 11, read the first seven paragraphs and answer the following questions. Two explanatory notes. By an 'indexical concept' (paragraph 2) Tye means one whose reference changes depending on the context in which it is applied – when, where, by whom, with what gestures and so on. Examples are *now, here, there, I, you, this, that one*. By 'functional concepts' and 'lower-level physical concepts' (paragraph 4), he means concepts that are associated with functional and lower-level physical descriptions respectively. For example, *telephone* is a functional concept ('device for receiving and transmitting the human voice') and *proton* is a lower-level physical concept ('positively charged particle forming part of the nucleus of an atom'). When we apply such concepts to an object, we represent the object as fitting the associated description.

1   Summarize the difference between coarse-grained facts and fine-grained facts, giving your own example.

2   Why is the existence of non-physical fine-grained facts compatible with physicalism?

3   Why does Tye say that the concept *I* is not a functional or lower-level physical one?

4   What bearing does the distinction between fine-grained facts and coarse-grained facts have on the knowledge argument (paragraph 7)?

1   A coarse-grained fact is an objective state of affairs – for example, the state of affairs that consists in the man William Shakespeare having written the play *Macbeth*. A fine-grained fact is a conceptual representation of a worldly state of affairs – some way of thinking of it. The following fine-grained facts all correspond to the single coarse-grained fact just mentioned: the fact that the Swan of Avon wrote the Scottish Play; the fact that Ann Hathaway's husband wrote Abraham Lincoln's favourite play (apparently this was *Macbeth*); the fact that *that man* wrote the play I saw last night (a fact appreciated by someone who has seen *Macbeth* the previous evening and is currently looking at a picture of William Shakespeare). (Not everyone would agree that what Tye calls 'fine-grained facts' really deserve to be called 'facts'. Some people prefer to reserve that term for objective states of affairs and to talk of *modes of presentation* of those states of affairs, rather than of fine-grained facts. You should bear this in mind, but Tye's usage is a convenient shorthand.)

2   Because physicalism is a claim about objective states of affairs. It says that there are no non-physical states of affairs – that all objects and properties are physical ones, in the broad sense. It does not deny that these states of affairs can be thought of under non-physical concepts.

3   Because it is not associated with a functional or lower-level physical description. When you think of yourself as *I*, you do not thereby think of yourself as a functional system or physical mechanism. A disembodied spirit (supposing them to exist) might think of itself as *I*. It is compatible with this, however, that you *are* a functional system or a physical mechanism.

4   For the argument to work, 'facts' in Premises 1 and 2 must mean 'coarse-grained facts' – physicalism is a claim about the world, not about how we conceptualize it. The issue, then, is whether Mary learns any new coarse-grained facts on leaving her room – whether she encounters any new 'real, non-conceptual items' as Tye puts it. If all she learns are fine-grained facts – new ways of conceptualizing coarse-grained facts she already knew – then the argument does not work.

So does Mary learn any new coarse-grained physical facts? Tye argues not. Learning what an experience is like, he argues, is simply a matter of coming to conceptualize it in a certain way, by applying what he calls *phenomenal concepts*. These concepts are special in that they are *perspectival* – in the normal course of things, they can be acquired only by someone who has undergone the experiences they represent. Here is how Tye explains the notion:

> Phenomenal concepts, I maintain, are conceptually irreducible concepts that function in the right sort of way. To possess the phenomenal concept *red*, for example, is to possess a simple concept that has been acquired by undergoing experiences of red (barring neurosurgery to induce the state or a miracle) and that not only disposes one to form a visual image of red in response to a range of cognitive tasks pertaining to red but also is brought to bear in discriminating the experience of red from other color experiences in a direct and immediate manner via introspection. The functional role that the concept plays is what makes it perspectival. A person who is blind from birth or who is always restricted to an environment of things with achromatic colors cannot possess a concept with the requisite role and hence cannot possess the phenomenal concept *red*.
>
> (Tye 2000, 27)

ACTIVITY

1 According to Tye, what functional role does the phenomenal concept *red* have?

2 Give an example of a thought that involves one or more phenomenal concepts.

3 Are physical concepts, such as neurological ones, perspectival?

DISCUSSION

1 Tye mentions three aspects. The concept (i) is acquired as a result of undergoing experiences of red, (ii) tends to trigger visual images of red and (iii) is applied when we inwardly attend to ('introspect') our own experiences and distinguish them from one another.

2 An example is the thought that experiences of red are warmer and more vibrant than experiences of blue.

3 No. We can grasp neurological concepts without having been in the corresponding neurological states. (Otherwise neurology would be a very difficult subject to study!)

Tye claims that we can also represent our experiences under indexical concepts, applied introspectively (Tye 1995, 167–8). We can mentally point to an experience, while we are having it, and think of it as *this* experience, without applying any general concept. (Tye suggests that we sometimes conceptualize simple moods in this way.) We can also combine indexical concepts with general phenomenal ones – for example, in the thought that we are having an experience of *this* shade of red. This allows us to represent subtle features of experience for which we have no general concepts (think of the thousands of shades of red you can perceive).

Now, property dualists can agree with most of what Tye says about phenomenal concepts. They will add, however, that these concepts represent *non-physical* properties. But, as Tye points out, we do not have to agree with that.

ACTIVITY

Read paragraph 8 of Reading 11 and summarize the position outlined there. You will see that Tye speaks of 'phenomenal content' rather than 'phenomenal character'. This reflects his wider views about consciousness, which we shall consider in the next chapter. For the present, the two terms can be taken as equivalent.

DISCUSSION

Because Mary has not had colour experiences herself, she cannot represent these experiences under appropriate phenomenal concepts – either general or indexical. There are thus fine-grained facts about them which she does not know. It is compatible with this, however, that colour experiences are physical states and that Mary knows all the *coarse-grained* facts about them, conceptualized under neurological or functional concepts. If so, she will not learn any new coarse-grained facts about colour experience when she is released, and there is no threat to physicalism.

In short, introspection does not reveal new features of the world that could not be described in physical terms, but simply allows us to characterize certain physical features in new ways. Thus, on this view Mary learns only fine-grained facts about colour vision and Premise 2 of the knowledge argument is true only if the word 'facts' is taken in that sense. But, as we saw, for the argument to work, 'facts' in Premises 1 and 2 must mean 'coarse-grained facts'. So the argument fails.

This, then, is the perspectivalist response. Unlike the ability hypothesis, it allows that Mary gains new knowledge-that on her release (albeit only of a fine-grained kind) and that she becomes able to think new thoughts. It also explains how we can know what experiences are like while we are having them even if we cannot later remember and recognize them. For knowing what an experience is like can involve conceptualizing it in an indexical way – thinking of it as, say, *this* shade of red – which we can do while we are actually having the experience, even if we are subsequently unable to recall its precise character.

As I mentioned, the perspectivalist view is currently the most popular response to the knowledge argument and it is the focus of intense debate – much of it highly technical. Here I shall focus on just one objection, first set out by Michael Lockwood (Lockwood 1989, 134–7; see also Chalmers 1996, 1999, 2004).

Lockwood argues that the fact that Mary lacks phenomenal concepts is a red herring. For even if she did possess these concepts, she would still be unable to work out what another person's experiences were like simply on the basis of physical information about them. To make the point, he describes the case of Harriet, who currently has a throbbing headache. We might know all the physical facts about Harriet, Lockwood claims, *and* possess the phenomenal concept *throbbing headache*, yet still be unable to work out that Harriet is experiencing a throbbing headache.

Now perspectivalists can reply that this is not a problem. They can say that the property of having a throbbing headache is a physical one – that of being in brain state X, let us say – and that in the case described we would know that Harriet has this physical property. It is just that we would not know this same fact under its phenomenal mode of presentation, as the (fine-grained) fact that she is having a throbbing headache.

Lockwood isn't finished yet, however. For he claims that the following principle is true:

> [If] one knows a fact under one mode of presentation... but does not know it under another... *then one's not knowing that it is the same fact that corresponds to each mode of presentation... must be attributable to one's failure to know some further substantive fact or facts, under any mode of presentation.*
>
> (Lockwood 1989, 136; italics in the original)

By a 'substantive fact' Lockwood means a fact about the world, rather than about our concepts. He gives an example. (Sir Percy Blakeney is a character in Baroness Orzcy's 1905 novel *The Scarlet Pimpernel*. Disguised as the eponymous hero, Blakeney rescues French aristocrats from the Terror.)

> [T]he only way one can know the fact that a certain person is in Paris, under the mode of presentation 'the Scarlet Pimpernel is in Paris', but fail to know it under the mode of presentation 'Sir Percy Blakeney is in Paris', is by failing to know,

under any (appropriate) mode of presentation, such facts as that one and the same person combines the attributes of being an English aristocrat and so forth, and of carrying out brilliant and daring rescues of people condemned to the guillotine.

(Ibid., 137)

The line of thought is this. The concepts *Sir Percy Blakeney* and *the Scarlet Pimpernel* each involve a different mode of presentation of the same person. These modes of presentation take the form of descriptions, which identify the person referred to *indirectly*, by way of some distinctive property or properties – in one case that being an English aristocrat and so on, in the other that of carrying out brilliant and daring rescues. The reason a person can know that the Scarlet Pimpernel is in Paris without knowing that Sir Percy Blakeney is in Paris is that it is possible to be ignorant of the fact that these descriptions identify the same man. But then anyone in this position will be ignorant of a coarse-grained fact about the world – namely that there is a single person who possesses the properties mentioned in both descriptions. To put it the other way round, if one knew all the coarse-grained facts about the man Sir Percy Blakeney, then one would be able to work out that he fitted the descriptions associated with both concepts and thus that both referred to him. According to Lockwood, a similar conclusion follows in all cases where one knows a coarse-grained fact under one mode of presentation but not under another: in each case one will be ignorant of some further coarse-grained fact linking the two modes of presentation.

ACTIVITY

1   Suppose I know the (coarse-grained) fact that a certain liquid is necessary for life under the mode of presentation 'water is necessary for life', but not under the mode of presentation 'H_2O is necessary for life'. If Lockwood is right, then it follows that I am ignorant of some coarse-grained fact. What is this?

2   If Lockwood's principle is correct, what would follow in the Harriet case?

3   Why is this a problem for the perspectivalist?

DISCUSSION

1   It is (something like) the fact that the colourless, odourless, drinkable liquid found in the oceans and lakes (the mode of presentation associated with the concept *water*) is made out of H_2O molecules (the mode of presentation associated with the concept H_2O).

2   It would follow that we are ignorant of some further coarse-grained fact about Harriet.

3   Because we are assuming that we already know all the coarse-grained *physical* facts about Harriet. Hence the coarse-grained fact of which we are ignorant must be a *non-physical* one. Thus, the perspectivalist response does not save physicalism after all.

Putting it the other way round, if the concepts *throbbing headache* and *brain state X* really did refer to the same thing, then we would be able to work out that they that both applied to Harriet. If we cannot do this, then the perspectivalist view must be mistaken.

Is Lockwood's argument successful? Again, the issues are complex, but there are responses open to the perspectivalist. The important thing to note is that the argument depends on a *descriptivist* view of concept reference – it assumes that concepts are associated with descriptions, which identify their referents by way of some characteristic property or properties. But what if phenomenal concepts don't work in this way? What if they latch on to their referents *directly*, rather than by way of description? Then the argument would not go through.

How might this view be defended? One option would be to reject descriptivism as a general account of concept reference and to argue that no (or few) concepts refer by way of associated properties in the way described. A less radical option, and the one I want to focus on, is to concede that many concepts refer by description, but argue that phenomenal concepts are different. One way of developing this idea is to claim that phenomenal concepts are *direct recognitional* ones. This view was initially proposed by Brian Loar, but it has been taken up by others, including Tye (Loar 1997, 1999; Carruthers 2000; Tye 2000).

A recognitional concept is one which is linked to a simple recognitional capacity. For example, suppose that while travelling in a foreign country I come across a flower I have never seen before and learn to recognize it by sight, yet without memorizing a description of it. I would then have a *recognitional concept* for the flower. I could think of it as a flower of *that* kind – pointing to one or imagining one. (Contrast this with someone who has a descriptive concept for this type of flower, acquired through reading botanical textbooks.) Now, even recognitional concepts do, typically, have a descriptive element. When I think of the flower I think of it as one that has a certain appearance – that causes visual experiences of a certain kind. But Loar suggests that phenomenal concepts are *direct* recognitional ones, which are not mediated in this way. Take pain, for example. When we think of a mental state as a *pain* we do not conceive of it indirectly, by way of the experiences or reactions it causes, but directly, by its essential phenomenal quality. Here is Tye again:

> [Phenomenal] concepts are simple. They are also, in part, *direct recognitional* concepts. For it is part of their characteristic functional role, *qua* phenomenal concepts, that they enable us to discriminate phenomenal qualities and states *directly* on the basis of introspection. In having the phenomenal concept *pain*, for example, I have a simple way of classifying pain that enables me to recognize it via introspection without the use of any associated reference-fixing intermediaries. Thus, it is guaranteed by the fact that the concept I am applying is phenomenal that I do not know introspectively that I am in pain *by* knowing something else connected to pain. My knowledge is direct and immediate.
>
> (Tye 2000, 28)

The claim that we have recognitional concepts for experiences has attractions. For example, it may help to explain why the feel of experiences seems ineffable and arbitrary. Compare the flower. I cannot describe it, except to say that it is one of *that* kind – indicating one. Similarly, I cannot give any account of *why* it looks the way it does. That's just how it is. And, in addition, the idea that phenomenal concepts are direct recognitional ones gives the perspectivalist a reply to Lockwood's objection – offering an explanation of how we could fail to know physical facts about Harriet under phenomenal modes of presentation without being ignorant of any further facts about her. If phenomenal concepts do not represent their referents as fitting some physical description, then it will not be possible to work out that they apply to a person on the basis of physical information about them, no matter how extensive. Thus, I might know all the physical facts about Harriet without realizing that her brain state is of the sort to which my recognitional concept *throbbing headache* applies. Nor could I work this out from the physical description: nothing in the description would entail that her brain state is one that would evoke my recognitional concept *pain*, if it were to occur in me. Compare the flower again. I might study a detailed description of a certain kind of flower without realizing that it is *that* flower – the one I have learned to recognize by sight. This seems to disarm Lockwood's objection. (It is worth stressing that property dualists can also endorse the idea that phenomenal concepts are recognitional ones, though they will say that what we recognize are non-physical properties and may want to argue that the idea does not really rebut Lockwood's objection.)

This is not the end of the story, of course. Property dualists have responses to this counter-argument and the debate continues. However the position just outlined – which combines the perspectivalist view with the claim that phenomenal concepts are recognitional ones – is regarded by many as the most promising physicalist response to the knowledge argument.

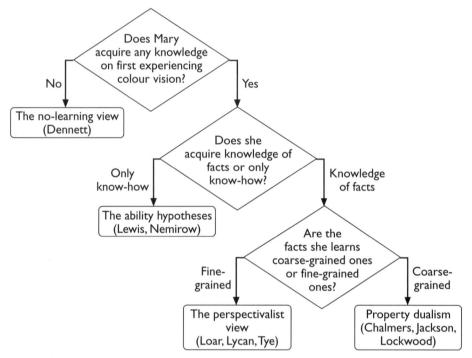

Figure 8 Responses to the knowledge argument.

A postscript on Jackson

As a postscript to our discussion of the knowledge argument, I want to say a little about Frank Jackson's current views. Here there is something rather surprising to report: Jackson, the author of the knowledge argument, no longer believes it and has rejected property dualism in favour of physicalism.

Jackson announced his change of mind in a short 'Postscript' to his original paper, published in 1998 (Jackson 1998, ch.7; see also his 2003). He explains that he now accepts that the best theory of sensory experience is that the facts about it can, in principle, be deduced from physical ones. (His reasons for changing his mind are rather subtle and we shall not explore them here.) Jackson now endorses a *representationalist* theory of consciousness: he holds that the phenomenal character of an experience is a matter of what it represents – the information it carries about the world around us or the state of our bodies. This information, he holds, is entirely physical in character and there is nothing in our colour experience which could not, in principle, be known to Mary while still in her room. Thus Jackson now holds that Mary learns nothing on her release – or, at most, acquires a sort of know-how. The challenge posed by the knowledge argument, he goes on, is to explain why we have such a strong intuition to the contrary.

His answer is that sensory experience involves a systematic illusion. The physical information conveyed by colour experience, Jackson argues, is of a highly complex kind – information about subtle optical similarities and differences between things. Relational information like this is normally hard to acquire and since vision presents it to us in a very quick and easy way, we are misled as to its nature – taking it to be information about simple intrinsic properties of the experiences themselves. This illusion, Jackson holds, is the source of the intuition which supports the knowledge argument.

(Do not worry if you found the previous paragraphs hard to follow. We shall be looking at representational theories of consciousness in detail in the next chapter. The important thing to note is that Jackson no longer believes that knowing what it is like to have an experience involves acquiring information about non-physical properties and that he now agrees with Dennett that the Mary thought experiment is misleading.)

Responses to the conceivability argument

We shall now move on to look at some physicalist responses to the conceivability argument. Let us begin by reminding ourselves of the argument:

Premise 1   It is conceivable that there be zombies.

Premise 2   If it is conceivable that there be zombies, it is metaphysically possible that there be zombies.

Premise 3   If it is metaphysically possible that there be zombies, then consciousness is nonphysical.

Conclusion   Consciousness is nonphysical.

(Based on Chalmers 2002a, 249)

This argument is valid, and, as we saw in the previous chapter, Premise 3 follows from the definition of physicalism. Thus the issue turns on the truth of Premises 1 and 2. We shall consider them in turn.

Are zombies conceivable?

The first option for the physicalist is to deny that zombies are conceivable. 'Conceivable' here, you may recall, means 'clearly and coherently conceivable' – conceivable in a way that involves no conceptual confusion or latent contradictions. As we saw in the previous chapter, Chalmers holds that zombies are conceivable in this sense. Not everyone agrees, however. The notion of a zombie, some claim, does not stand up to scrutiny. Dennett is one of the chief proponents of this view.

According to Dennett, the zombie thought experiment is just another misleading intuition pump. The important point, he stresses, is that zombies are supposed to behave *exactly* as we do and to possess mental states that are functionally identical to our own. (Perhaps we should not apply our mental-state terms to zombies, but we can say that they have zombie analogues of our mental states – beliefs^Z, desires^Z, etc. – which function exactly like them and generate the same behaviour.) The supposition that zombies are behaviourally indistinguishable from us is, of course, crucial to the thought experiment. If our zombie twins behaved differently, then they would not be physically identical to us. Dennett notes, however, that it is easy to slip into thinking of zombies as behaviourally impoverished in some way – as not being upset by memories of pain, not engaging in sexual fantasies, not speculating about consciousness and so on. It is this tendency to mis–imagine zombies, he argues, that gives the zombie thought experiment its plausibility. As a corrective, he asks us to imagine more sophisticated zombies – he calls them 'zimboes' – which really do have all the complex information-processing capacities required to support behaviour like ours. When we do this, he claims, it becomes harder to sustain the intuition that zombies are any different from us at all.

We can get a flavour of Dennett's approach from an extract from his provocatively titled paper 'The unimagined preposterousness of zombies' (Dennett 1995). This is in part a response to an earlier paper by Owen Flanagan and Thomas Polger (Flanagan and Polger 1995), which was devoted to the discussion of 'conscious inessentialism' – the view that any intelligent activity we perform *with* consciousness could, in principle, be performed without it. Flanagan and Polger defend the view but argue that it leaves us with a puzzle as to why we have conscious experiences. If consciousness is not essential for any intelligent activity, then it does not confer any adaptive advantage. Why, then, did we develop it? Why are we not zombies? Note that the Turing Test, mentioned in paragraph 1 of the Reading, is a proposed test for determining whether a machine has intelligence. It involves interrogating the machine via a remote link and seeing whether its responses can be distinguished from those of a normal human being. The terms 'informationally sensitive' and 'experientially sensitive' (paragraph 3) were coined by Flanagan. To be informationally sensitive to a stimulus is to be able to detect it and respond to it; to be experientially sensitive to a stimulus is to have a phenomenally conscious experience of it.

Turn now to Reading 12 and answer the following questions.   **ACTIVITY**

1   What distinguishes zimboes from other zombies?

2   Why is it important to distinguish zimboes from simpler zombies?

3   How, according to Dennett, does reflection on zimboes reveal that his opponents' concept of consciousness is 'subtly self-contradictory'?

4   Why does Dennett think that it is a mistake to ask what the adaptive advantage of consciousness is?

5   What is the challenge Dennett poses in the final two paragraphs of the extract?

1   Zimboes are zombies that are able to reflect on, and report, their own   DISCUSSION
    mental states. Zimboes not only possess thoughts and feelings (in the functional zombie sense) but also believe that they possess them, talk about them, recall them, anticipate them, speculate about their nature and so on.

2   Because only zimboes would be capable of displaying the same behaviour as us. Thus, when a philosopher asks us to imagine our zombie twin, it is a zimbo we should imagine.

3   Because his opponents must either accept that zimboes are conscious or admit that their concept of consciousness is different from the commonsense one – not being linked to any of the behavioural responses we normally associate with consciousness.

4   Because on his view consciousness is not a distinct feature, over and above the proper working of the various information-processing systems which control our behaviour. A properly functioning brain could no more exist without consciousness than a properly functioning body could exist without health. There is thus no separate question about the adaptive advantage of consciousness.

5   The challenge is to imagine a being which (a) is not conscious and (b) does not lack any of the informational sensitivity that we possess.

The moral of Dennett's discussion is that we cannot clearly imagine subtracting consciousness from a normal human being while leaving their behaviour unaffected. It follows that zombies, of the sort relevant to the conceivability argument, are not conceivable after all.

I am going to leave you to assess Dennett's view for yourself. It has similarities to his response to the knowledge argument and similar considerations apply. You may also find it helpful to look back to what Chalmers says in Reading 7. Chalmers believes he can rise to the challenge of imagining a non-conscious zimbo. Does his description of his qualia-obsessed zombie twin convince you – or just reinforce Dennett's claim that there is no real difference between such sophisticated zombies and ourselves?

Does conceivability entail possibility?

Even if we concede that zombies are conceivable, we can still block the conceivability argument by denying its second premise – the claim that if zombies are conceivable then they are metaphysically possible. (I shall not keep the repeating the word 'metaphysical'; in the rest of this section 'possibility' always means 'metaphysical possibility'.) This premise is an instance of the general thesis that conceivability entails possibility – call it the 'CP thesis' for short. As we saw, the thesis is plausible; if we can form a clear conception of a situation then it is reasonable to think that it could have existed – at least given appropriate changes to the laws of nature. However, some physicalists argue that there are counterexamples to the thesis and that zombies are one of them.

At first sight, there may seem to be obvious counterexamples to the CP thesis. For example, it seems possible to imagine measuring the internal angles of a triangle and finding that they add up to 170 degrees, even though it is not possible for them to be anything other 180 degrees (not, at least, in Euclidian geometry). Such cases can easily be ruled out, however. For the sort of conceivability that is relevant to the CP thesis is a clear and coherent sort, free from confusion. And the imagined scenario is not of this kind. If we were to think it through in detail – for example, imagining ourselves extending the base of the triangle, drawing a line though its apex parallel to its base, and thinking about the relations between the angles so formed and those of the triangle – then we would soon see that there was a contradiction latent in the scenario. (Dennett can be seen as making a similar point about zombies. He concedes that we can conceive of zombies in a casual way but denies that we can do so in the clear and coherent way required by the argument.)

So are there any counterexamples to the CP thesis that do not involve confusion? Arguably there are. They concern cases where we have discovered through empirical investigation that two properties are identical. Take water, for example. We now know that water is H_2O. But suppose it had turned out that it was something else – XYZ, say. Can you imagine that? I can. Is there any lurking contradiction in the scenario? I do not think so. After all, prior to the discovery of the chemical composition of water, chemists entertained a variety of hypotheses as to its nature, without thereby running into any *conceptual* confusion, like that involved in the triangle case. So we can conceive of water being something other than H_2O. Yet it is not *possible* for water to be something other than H_2O, since water *is* H_2O and there is no way H_2O could be anything other than itself. Cases like this are known as *a posteriori necessities*. It is necessary that water is H_2O, but we discover this from empirical investigation of the world (a posteriori), rather than from abstract reasoning (a priori).

Now, the physicalist may say that the same goes for consciousness. Take pain, for example. Perhaps pain is in fact a physical state – C-fibre stimulation, say. (C-fibres are long thin filaments which transmit pain signals to the central nervous system.) And perhaps the fact that we can imagine C-fibre stimulation without pain no more shows that it is possible for one to exist without the other than the fact that we can imagine water being XYZ shows that it is possible for water to exist without H_2O. Again, there may be an a posteriori necessity here. (The identification of pain with C-fibre stimulation is a traditional philosophical example, not a serious scientific hypothesis. In fact, it is unlikely that pain can be identified with a particular neurological state; it is more likely to be a higher-level functional state which can realized in a variety of different neurological states.)

ACTIVITY   The objection just outlined is similar to the perspectivalist response to the knowledge argument. Can you see how?

DISCUSSION   Like the perspectivalist view, the objection appeals to the fact that we can think of the same thing in different ways – under different modes of presentation. According to the objector, the reason we can conceive of pain not being C-fibre stimulation, even though the two are the same thing, is that the concepts *pain* and *C-fibre stimulation* have distinct modes of presentation. There is thus no conceptual confusion involved in supposing that one could exist without the other, even though this is not in fact possible.

There is a powerful line of reply to this objection, developed by Saul Kripke and later elaborated by Chalmers, among others (Kripke 1980, Chapter 3; Chalmers 1996, 56–65, 131–4). Both Kripke and Chalmers present the reply in the context of wider semantic theories, but for our purposes I shall summarize it in a simplified form.

The reply goes as follows. The concept *water* is associated with a description, which identifies the substance referred to by its superficial features. This might be along the lines of 'the clear drinkable liquid found in oceans and lakes'. In the real world this description picks out H_2O, so the concept refers to H_2O. However, we can imagine a world in which the same description picks out something else. That is, we can imagine a world in which the clear drinkable liquid in the oceans and lakes is some other chemical compound. And, the reply goes, this is what we are imagining when we imagine that water is not H_2O. We are not really imagining *water* – the substance itself – not being H_2O. Rather, we are imagining something with the superficial features of water – *watery stuff* – not being H_2O. And there is thus no counterexample here to the CP thesis. For it *is* possible for there to be watery stuff that is not H_2O. Similarly (and this is a closer parallel to the zombie case), we can imagine a world where H_2O does not possess the superficial properties by which we normally identify it – where it is not clear, drinkable and so on (suppose that in this world we have a different physiology, so that we see clear things as blue and find H_2O poisonous). But again there is no counterexample to the CP thesis, since such a world is possible. In short, conceivability misleads in these cases only because we misdescribe the situation we are imagining – confusing the property of being water with that of possessing the various superficial features by which we identify water.

We now know that heat is molecular motion. To heat something is to increase the speed at which its constituent molecules move. Suppose I claim to be able to imagine molecular motion existing without heat. What would a defender of the reply just outlined say about this claim?

They would say that I am misdescribing the imagined scenario. What I am really imagining, they would say, is molecular motion existing without the property by which we *identify* heat – that is, without it producing heat sensations in us. They would deny that I can imagine *heat itself* existing without molecular motion, since that is what heat is.

Why is this a problem for physicalists? Can't they argue that we fall prey to a similar confusion when we imagine zombies? Perhaps pain is C-fibre stimulation and when we imagine C-fibre stimulation existing in the absence of pain, as in zombies, what we are really imagining is C-fibre stimulation existing in the absence of the superficial property by which we normally identify pain. And physicalists can concede that *this* is possible. There is a snag however. For what would the identifying property for pain be? Surely it would be that of *feeling painful*. How else do we identify pain but by the way it feels? So in imagining C-fibre stimulation existing without this identifying property we are imagining it existing without feeling painful. But wait a minute! How could there be a pain that doesn't feel painful? Feeling painful is not a superficial property of pain, as being clear and drinkable is a superficial property of H_2O; rather it is essential to it. The physicalist might bite the bullet and claim that zombies *do* have pains, albeit ones that do not *feel* painful. But then the property dualist can simply focus on the *feeling* of pain and run exactly the same argument with regard to that.

The upshot of this is that the analogy with the water–H_2O case does not hold. We do not identify pain by its associated properties, but directly, by the way it feels. And, consequently, there is no reason to think that we are misdescribing things when we speak of imagining C-fibre stimulation without pain. What goes for pain goes for other conscious states, too. In each case we pick out the state directly, by its essential phenomenal character, rather than by associated properties.

Let's review the state of play. The question is whether the conceivability of zombies entails their possibility. The property dualist argues that it does – that conceivability always entails possibility. The physicalist points to the water–H_2O case as an example of how conceivability can be misleading. The property dualist responds by arguing that the water–H_2O case involves misdescription of the imagined scenario and that the same does not go for the zombie case.

Are there are any further counterexamples to CP thesis? That is, are there any cases which do not involve confusion or misdescription, but where conceivability still misleads us? Some writers argue that there are. What we find conceivable, they argue, is determined by the nature of the concepts we possess and the information available to us, and it is not an infallible guide to what is independently possible. As Joseph Levine puts it:

> The point is, how can I tell, merely from facts about my own cognitive situation, including facts about various conceptual relations among my representations, that what one representation refers to is distinct from what another one refers to?... The bottom line is that my representations seem to present me with two distinct properties. But the possibility that distinct representations really refer to the same thing must always be an open one.
>
> (Levine 2001, 91)

To illustrate this point in more detail, I want to introduce a short reading from the British philosopher David Papineau.

ACTIVITY Turn to Reading 13. Begin by reading the first two paragraphs. These summarize the logic of the debate so far and you should check that you understand them, referring back if necessary to the discussion above. (Note that by 'contingent descriptions' Papineau means ones that identify an object or substance by its non–essential properties, such as, in the case of water, being drinkable and found in the oceans. Note, too, that the symbol '≠' means 'is not the same thing as'.)

Now read paragraphs 3–5 of the reading and answer the questions below. The Cicero–Tully example to which Papineau refers is one he has introduced earlier. It concerns Jane, who has picked up the names 'Cicero' and 'Tully' without realizing that they refer to the same person (namely, the Roman orator and philosopher Marcus Tullius Cicero) and without possessing any specific beliefs about Cicero or Tully. Papineau suggests that Jane might then entertain the thought that Cicero is not Tully, despite the fact that this is an 'impossible thought', which does not correspond to a real possibility.

1 Why does Jane's case provide support for rejection of the CP thesis? (Paragraph 3)

2 What, according to Papineau, will a defender of the CP thesis say about Jane? (Paragraph 4)

3 What point is Papineau making in paragraph 5?

DISCUSSION

1 Because Jane finds it conceivable that Cicero is not Tully, even though there is no corresponding possibility.

2 They will say that she is not really entertaining the thought that Cicero is not Tully, since she does not possess genuine concepts for Cicero and Tully. The only way Jane could really entertain the thought that Cicero is not Tully, they will maintain, is if she associates descriptions with the concepts. The apparent exception to the CP thesis could then be explained by saying that she is imagining a situation in which the associated descriptions pick out two distinct people – for example, one in which the Roman statesman who prosecuted Catiline was not the same person as the Roman philosopher who wrote the philosophical treatise *On Duties*.

3 He is claiming that it is not necessary to have specific ideas about an object in order to possess a concept for it. The fact that Jane has learned the terms 'Cicero' and 'Tully' from competent users and intends to use them as they do is sufficient for her to count as being a competent user of them – and thus as possessing the concepts *Cicero* and *Tully*. (Papineau is here referring to the so-called *causal theory of names*, according to which a name refers to the person it does because it was originally conferred on them and has been passed on from speaker to speaker in an unbroken chain down to the present time. On this view, 'Cicero' would still refer to Marcus Tullius Cicero even if the person using it knew nothing about Cicero, or had completely mistaken ideas about him.)

ACTIVITY

Now read the final two paragraphs of Reading 13 and answer the following questions. Note that by 'directly referring terms' Papineau means ones that do not refer by description, such as the names 'Cicero' and 'Tully', as used by Jane. The symbol '→', used in paragraph 6, means 'entails'.

1   What is the 'transparency thesis'? (Paragraphs 6–7)

2   Why are defenders of the CP thesis committed to the transparency thesis? (Paragraph 6)

3   Why does Papineau reject the transparency thesis? (Paragraph 7)

4   Sum up in one sentence Papineau's case against the CP thesis.

DISCUSSION

1   The transparency thesis is the claim that if two directly referring terms refer to the same thing, then it must be a priori knowable that they do so. In other words, we must be able to tell that they refer to the same thing simply by thinking about it and without needing to go and check.

2   Because we can tell a priori whether or not it is *conceivable* that two things are distinct and, in the case of directly referring terms, the CP thesis dictates that conceivability is an infallible guide to possibility.

3   Because he thinks that it offers an implausible view of the nature of direct reference. It assumes that when we use a directly referring term we have an immediate mental grasp of the thing referred to, which leaves no room for confusion as to its identity. Against this, Papineau claims that what a term refers to may depend on external factors about which we can be mistaken. (Papineau seems to have in mind both the causal theory of names, mentioned earlier, and also work on mental representation, according to which concept meaning is determined by causal or evolutionary factors of which the thinker may be completely unaware.)

4   The CP thesis should be rejected because it imposes implausibly strict requirements for concept possession – at least in the case of concepts that refer directly rather than by description.

The moral of this for consciousness is clear. As we have seen, phenomenal concepts refer directly, rather than by way of contingent descriptions. That is something on which both sides can agree. Initially this fact seemed to support the property dualist's position, since it meant that we could not explain away the conceivability of zombies as we could explain away the conceivability of water without H_2O. But it may tell equally in favour of the physicalist. For, if Papineau is right, the CP thesis is not reliable when directly referring terms are involved. Perhaps our ability to imagine C-fibre stimulation without pain is on a par with Jane's ability to imagine Cicero not being Tully.

Further support for this view comes from another argument, set out by Peter Carruthers (Carruthers 2000). The argument appeals to the idea, introduced earlier, that phenomenal concepts are recognitional ones. Since such concepts are not associated with beliefs about the nature of the things to which they refer, Carruthers argues, it would not be surprising if we could use them to frame thoughts that do not correspond to real possibilities. I shall round off this section by looking briefly at what Carruthers has to say.

Turn to Reading 14. Note that chicken-sexing is the art of determining the sex of new-born chicks – a difficult task, since to the untrained eye males and females are identical.

ACTIVITY

1   Summarize the claim made in paragraph 2. (You may find it helpful to look at paragraph 6 too.)

2   Why does Mary find it conceivable that the facts about A-hood may vary independently of the physical facts?

3   What is the objection raised in paragraph 5?

4   How does Carruthers respond to the objection?

DISCUSSION

1   The fact that we can conceive of the feel of an experience (i.e. its phenomenal character) varying without any change in its physical or functional properties reveals something about how we conceptualize experiences, but nothing about their nature. It shows that our concepts of feel are independent of physical and functional concepts, but not that feels themselves are independent of physical and functional properties.

2   Because her concept of A-hood does not involve beliefs about the physical basis of the property. All she knows about A-hood is that some chicks have it and some don't. She can thus imagine two physically identical chicks, one possessing A-hood, the other not.

3   The objection is that Mary probably will have some beliefs about the nature of A-hood – that is, her concept of A-hood will not be a *purely* recognitional one. If she thinks about how she detects A-hood, she will probably conclude that it has a causal effect upon her sense-organs and that in order to have such an effect it must be a physical property. She will thus discount the possibility that the facts about A-hood might vary independently of the physical facts.

4   He responds that we do not have beliefs about the processes by which we detect our own conscious experiences. We do not assume that introspection is a causal process and do not believe that it is sensitive only to physical properties. That is why we are able to construct plausible thought experiments involving zombies and suchlike.

Again, this is not the end of the story. Chalmers in particular has defended the CP thesis vigorously (Chalmers 1999, 2002b). However, the thesis is widely distrusted and the most common response to the conceivability argument is to reject it.

The 'explanatory gap'

Even if the arguments we have been considering do not refute physicalism, they may still establish a weaker conclusion. In particular, they may show that the physical sciences cannot *explain* consciousness. This view has been defended by Joseph Levine (1983, 1993, 2001), and I want to complete this chapter by looking briefly at his views and some responses to them.

Levine's argument

Levine rejects property dualism. He argues that the anti-physicalist arguments are not compelling and that reflection on the causal role of consciousness strongly supports a physicalist position. Physicalist theories of mind, Levine concludes, do not leave anything out in a metaphysical sense – there are no mental objects, events or properties that cannot be described in physical terms. He argues, however, that physicalist theories are inadequate in another way, in that they cannot *explain* the existence of conscious states and properties. Physicalist theories, he concludes, 'leave something out' in an epistemological sense, though not in a metaphysical one (Levine 1993, 127–8).

Suppose that scientists develop a theory of consciousness which identifies conscious experiences with physical states. For example, suppose they discover that people experience pain when, and only when, their brains enter a certain complex physical state. This might be a neurological state or, more likely, a functional state, which can be supported by different neurological ones. And suppose that this physical state has exactly the same causes and effects that pain has – that it is produced by nerve impulses from pain sensors in the skin and that it generates the behavioural, emotional and cognitive reactions typically associated with pain. On this basis, scientists conclude that the two states are identical – that pain just is this complex neurological or functional state. Still, Levine argues, this discovery would not *explain* the nature of pain, in the way that, for example, the discovery that water is H_2O explains the nature of water. There would remain an *explanatory gap* between consciousness and the physical.

Turn to Reading 15, which is a short extract from one of Levine's papers. Note that in this paper Levine sometimes uses 'physical' in a narrow sense to refer to low-level physical properties, such as neurological ones.

ACTIVITY

1 What is required for a reductive theory of some phenomenon to provide a successful explanation of it, according to Levine?

2 Why, according to Levine, is there an explanatory gap in the case of consciousness but not in that of water?

3 Set out Levine's argument in the form of premises and a conclusion.

DISCUSSION

1 The facts about the phenomenon should *follow from* the facts cited in the reductive theory – the former should be 'epistemologically necessitated' by the latter. In Levine's view, this means that it should be *inconceivable* that the facts about the phenomenon should fail to hold, given the facts cited in the theory. (The thought is that if it was conceivable that the former might not have held, given the latter, then there would remain a question of why they *do* hold, and they would not have been properly explained.)

2 In the case of water, the familiar facts about the phenomenon are epistemologically necessitated by the facts about H_2O. Given enough information about H_2O molecules, it is inconceivable that a collection of H_2O molecules would not have the surface properties of water – for example, that of boiling at 212°F. In the case of consciousness, on the other hand, the familiar phenomenal facts would not be epistemologically necessitated by the facts cited in any neurological or functional theory. This is shown by the fact that zombies and inverts are conceivable.

3   The argument can be set out like this:

Premise 1   For a physicalist theory to explain consciousness, it would have to be inconceivable that the facts of consciousness could vary independently of the physical facts cited in the theory (i.e. the former would have to be epistemologically necessitated by the latter).

Premise 2   Whatever physicalist theory is proposed, it will always be conceivable that the facts of consciousness could vary independently of the physical facts cited in the theory.

Conclusion   No physicalist theory can explain consciousness.

"I THINK YOU SHOULD BE MORE EXPLICIT HERE IN STEP TWO."

Figure 9 The explanatory gap. Cartoon by Sidney Harris. Copyright © Sidney Harris.

It important to stress that Levine does not think that it really is possible – even metaphysically – for the facts of consciousness to vary independently of the physical ones. He thinks it likely that conscious states are physical ones, in the broad sense. What he is denying is that we can understand *how* they could be physical states.

Papineau on the explanatory gap

How might physicalists respond to Levine? They could, of course, cut the knot by denying that zombies and inverts are conceivable, perhaps appealing to arguments like those used by Dennett. But suppose they accept the conceivability claim, as many physicalists do. What can they say then?

One approach, which has been defended by David Papineau among others, involves denying the need for the sort of explanation Levine seeks (Papineau 1995; 2002, Chapter 5). Papineau argues that it is misguided to ask why physical states give rise to conscious experiences:

> [It is] like asking *why* was Cicero the same man as Tully, or *why* is water the same stuff as H$_2$O? You cannot *explain* why the two terms of a true identity coincide, since the truth of the identity means there is only one item in reality, and so no possibility of 'them' diverging. Similarly with the identification of conscious states with physical ones. If physicalists are right to assert such identities... then there is no further question of why their two terms are always found together. Such an equation refers to a single state, and so there is nothing further to explain.
>
> (Papineau 1995, 264)

We might compare Mary the chicken-sexer. Suppose Mary is reliably informed that A-hood – the property she has been trained to detect – is in fact maleness. She will simply have to accept that as a brute fact. There is no sense in her asking *why* it is maleness. That's just what it is.

It may be objected that this does not explain the special *perplexity* we feel over phenomenal–physical identity claims. Here is Levine again:

> I am told that my concept of reddishness is really about a neurophysiological or functional property. I then wonder, as I ostend the reddishness of my visual experience, how could a functional or physiological state be *that*? In this case, even if one is convinced by the identity claim, one wouldn't be mystified as to what it is I'm wondering about. There does seem to be substantive content to my puzzlement.
>
> (Levine 2001, 81–3)

Papineau acknowledges the existence of this sense of puzzlement but argues that it arises from a special feature of phenomenal concepts and that it does not point to any real explanatory gap. When we apply a phenomenal concept, Papineau notes, we typically *undergo* a version of the experience it represents – either because we are applying the concept to an experience we are currently having or because the concept triggers in us an image, or 'faint copy', of the experience itself:

> When you think imaginatively about a pain, or about seeing something red – or even more, when you think introspectively about these experiences while having them – versions of these experiences themselves will be present in you, and because of this the activity of thinking phenomenally *about* pain or seeing something red will strike you introspectively as *involving* the feeling of these experiences themselves.
>
> (Papineau 2002, 170)

(Compare Tye's claim that the phenomenal concept *red* is apt to trigger in us a visual image of red.) But, of course, nothing like this happens when we think about neurological or functional states. Thinking about the stimulation of C-fibres or about processing activity in the visual cortex doesn't cause feelings of pain or sensations of red. Thus in a sense physical concepts leave something out:

> [T]here is an intuitive sense in which exercises of material concepts 'leave out' the experience at issue. They 'leave out' the pain and the technicolour phenomenology, in the sense that they don't activate or involve these experiences.
>
> (Ibid.)

This, Papineau argues, leads us to think – mistakenly – that physical concepts do not *refer to* the same things as phenomenal ones and thus that conscious states are distinct from physical ones. And it is this 'intuition of distinctness', he maintains, that is the real source of the feeling that there is an explanatory gap. This diagnosis is confirmed, he suggests, by the language we use to characterize the problem:

> The problem is often posed as that of explaining how brain processes can 'generate', or 'cause', or 'give rise to', or 'yield', or 'be correlated with', or 'be accompanied by' conscious feelings. These phrases may seem innocuous, but they all implicitly presuppose that conscious feelings are some extra feature of reality, distinct from any material properties. And once we slip in this dualist way of thinking, then it is unsurprising that we find ourselves with unanswerable explanatory puzzles.
>
> (Ibid., 146)

If we are not misled by the intuition of distinctness, Papineau concludes, we shall no longer be troubled by the sense that there is an explanatory gap.

Carruthers on the explanatory gap

Papineau's approach to the problem of the explanatory gap is what we may call *deflationary* – he denies that there is a gap to be filled. To some writers, however, such an approach smacks of defeatism. Peter Carruthers, in particular, has argued that we can and should expect more from a theory of consciousness than a catalogue of phenomenal–physical identities (Carruthers 2004). Unless we can explain why conscious experiences have the distinctive properties they do, he argues, we shall simply not have provided a reductive explanation of phenomenal consciousness.

Carruthers's own response to the explanatory gap problem draws again on the claim that phenomenal concepts are recognitional ones (Carruthers 2000, 2004). Carruthers accepts that physical or functional claims will not *entail* claims about consciousness, as we ordinarily express them. But this, he argues, is simply because of the nature of our phenomenal concepts. Since these concepts are direct recognitional ones, with no associated descriptions, it will not be possible to deduce claims involving them from claims couched in physical or functional terms. So, for example, we shall not be able to deduce that a certain neurological or functional state will evoke an introspective application of our concept *pain*, any more than Mary the chicken-sexer will be able to deduce that male chicks will evoke her recognitional concept *A-hood*. To this extent, reductive theories of consciousness will always seem to leave something out.

Carruthers argues, however, that it does not follow that such theories will in fact leave out anything substantive. For there may be *other* ways of conceptualizing our conscious experiences under which thoroughly satisfying explanations can be given. The right way to proceed, Carruthers suggests, is to characterize conscious experiences in a third-person way – as, say, internal states which can be recognized introspectively and which seem to possess ineffable subjective feels. We may then be able to develop reductive theories which *do* entail the facts about these states, characterized in this third-person way.

> [The] mistake is to assume that a given property or state can only be successfully reductively explained if the proposed mechanisms are what we might call *immediately cognitively satisfying*, in the sense that they mesh with the manner in which those states are conceptualised. While the 'explanatory gap' is of some *cognitive* significance, revealing something about the manner in which we

conceptualise our experiences, it shows nothing about the nature of those experiences themselves...

Admittedly, it will still remain possible, by *employing* our recognitional concepts of experience, to imagine [zombies]. But that will be revealed as *not* posing any additional explanatory problem. It will not be something about the nature of conscious experience which makes [zombies] conceivable, but merely something about the way in which we (can) *conceptualise* those experiences.

(Carruthers 2000, 67–8)

In other words, the (coarse-grained) facts about consciousness cannot be explained under all modes of presentation – and not, in particular, under phenomenal ones. It remains possible, however, that they can be explained under *some* modes of presentation – and that is all that is required.

ACTIVITY What would Carruthers say about Levine's argument, as set out earlier? (You may find it helpful to use Tye's distinction between coarse-grained and fine-grained facts.)

DISCUSSION He would say that it depends on what the word 'facts' means in the premises and conclusion. If it means 'fine-grained facts', then, he would say, the argument is sound but does not reveal anything about consciousness itself, as opposed to our ways of conceptualizing it. If it means 'coarse-grained facts', then, Carruthers would say, there is no reason to believe Premise 2, since we may be able to develop a physicalist theory of consciousness which entails the coarse-grained facts about it, conceptualized in a third-person way. And if so, then it will not be conceivable that the facts about consciousness, so conceptualized, could vary independently of the physical facts cited in the theory.

Conclusion

We have looked at various responses to the two main anti-physicalist arguments and to the problem of the explanatory gap. There is a pattern to them. In each case we can distinguish what we may call *radical* and *conservative* responses. The radical responses deny the intuitions on which the arguments depend – that Mary learns something, or that zombies are conceivable. The conservative responses accept these intuitions but seek to show that they are compatible with physicalism. A key idea is that the intuitions reveal more about the way we conceptualize conscious experiences than about the experiences themselves. They do not establish that experiences have special phenomenal *properties*, distinct from their neurological or functional ones, but they do reveal that we have special phenomenal *concepts* for experiences, which are quite unlike neurological or functional ones.

Of course, even if the responses considered are successful, it does not follow that physicalism is true. Disarming an objection to a thesis isn't the same as showing that the thesis is true. But many philosophers feel that if there are no knock-down arguments against physicalism, then wider considerations, including the attractions of strong naturalism and the problems facing property dualism, dictate its acceptance. In the next chapter we shall look at some attempts to explain consciousness from a physicalist perspective.

Further reading

'Someday there will be no more articles written about the "Knowledge Argument"', writes William Lycan, 'That is beyond dispute. What is less certain is, how much sooner that day will come than the heat death of the universe' (Lycan 2003, 385). The literature is indeed large and continually growing. A useful annotated bibliography of work on the argument has been compiled by Torin Alter. This is currently (2004) available on-line at:

>   http://host.uniroma3.it/progetti/kant/field/kabiblio.htm

(If it has moved, try a web search.)

The following paper provides a useful summary of different responses to the knowledge argument, as well as some discussion of the explanatory gap problem:

VAN GULICK, R. (1997) 'Understanding the phenomenal mind: are we all just armadillos? Part I: Phenomenal knowledge and explanatory gaps', in Block et al. 1997, 559–66.

At the time of writing two important collections of papers on the knowledge argument are going to press, which should provide a good overview of the current state of the debate:

ALTER, T. & WALTER, S. (eds) (2005) *Phenomenal Concepts and Phenomenal Knowledge: New Essays on Consciousness and Physicalism*, Oxford, Oxford University Press. (Includes new essays by, among others, Chalmers, Jackson, Levine, Nemirow, Papineau and Knut Nordby – the real-life Mary. It also includes an essay by Dennett introducing the character of RoboMary.)

LUDLOW, P., NAGASAWA, Y. & STOLJAR, D. (eds) (2004) *There's Something About Mary: Essays on Phenomenal Consciousness and Frank Jackson's Knowledge Argument*, Cambridge, Mass., MIT Press. (Contains essays by Chalmers, Churchland, Dennett, Jackson, Lewis, Loar and Tye, among others.)

From the vast earlier literature, I recommend:

LEWIS, D. (1990) 'What experience teaches', in W. Lycan (ed.), *Mind and Cognition*, Oxford, Blackwell, pp.499–518. Reprinted in Block et al. 1997. (The definitive statement of the ability hypothesis.)

LOAR, B. (1997) 'Phenomenal states', in Block et al. 1997, 597–616. (A difficult but important paper, which defends the view that phenomenal concepts are direct recognitional ones.)

LYCAN, W.G. (2003) 'Perspectival representation and the knowledge argument', in Q. Smith & A. Jokic (eds), *Consciousness: New Philosophical Perspectives*, Oxford, Oxford University Press, pp.384–95. (A lively statement of the case for the perspectivalist view.)

The literature on the conceivability argument is also large. Much of it is, moreover, highly technical. Three suggested papers are:

CHALMERS, D.J. (2002b) 'Does conceivability entail possibility?', in T.S. Gendler & J. Hawthorne (eds), *Conceivability and Possibility*, Oxford, Oxford University Press, pp.145–200. (The most sustained and detailed defence of the CP thesis to date. A technical and demanding paper, so be prepared to skip the difficult bits!)

COTTRELL, A. (1999) 'Sniffing the camembert: on the conceivability of zombies', *Journal of Consciousness Studies*, 6 (1), 4–12. (A lively and accessible attack on the view that zombies are conceivable.)

HILL, C.S. (1997) 'Imaginability, conceivability and the mind–body problem', *Philosophical Studies*, 87, 61–85. Reprinted in part in Chalmers 2002c. (Attacks the CP thesis.)

Three recommended papers on the explanatory gap problem are:

CARRUTHERS, P. (1994). 'Reductive explanation and the "explanatory gap"', *Canadian Journal of Philosophy*, 34, 153–74. (Sets out Carruthers's response in full.)

LEVINE, J. (1993) 'On leaving out what it's like', in M. Davies & G.W. Humphreys (eds), *Consciousness: Psychological and Philosophical Essays*, Oxford, Blackwell, pp.121–36. Reprinted in Block et al. 1997. (Presents Levine's argument for the existence of an explanatory gap.)

MCGINN, C. (1989) 'Can we solve the mind–body problem?', *Mind*, 98 349–66. Reprinted in Block et al. 1997. (Presents a different argument for the existence of an explanatory gap.)

A final recommendation is:

PAPINEAU, D. (2001) *Thinking About Consciousness*, Oxford, Oxford University Press, Chapters 2, 3 and 5. (A clearly written physicalist treatment of all three arguments considered in this chapter.)

CHAPTER 4

Representationalism

Standing on the beach in Santa Barbara a number of summers ago on a bright sunny day, I found myself transfixed by the intense blue of the Pacific Ocean. Was I not here delighting in the phenomenal aspects of my visual experience? And if I was, doesn't this show that there are visual Qualia?

I am not convinced... I experienced blue as a property of the ocean not as a property of my experience. My experience itself certainly wasn't blue. Rather it was an experience that represented the ocean as blue. What I was really delighting in, then, was a quality *represented* by the experience, not a quality *of* the experience. It was the color, blue, not anything else, that was immediately accessible to my consciousness that I found so pleasing.

(Tye 2002, 448)

In this chapter we shall look at what many consider the most promising strategy for reductively explaining phenomenal consciousness. This draws on two notions introduced in Chapter 1 – those of *representational content* and *access-consciousness*. To say that a mental state has representational content is to say that it carries information, or misinformation, about the world. (Some writers use the term 'intentional content' instead of 'representational content'; for our purposes the two terms can be taken as equivalent.) To say that a mental state is access-conscious is to say that the information it carries is available to other mental faculties, such as reasoning, decision-making and speech. It is widely agreed that our experiences often have representational content and that they are usually access-conscious. And there is reason to hope that these features can be reductively explained. Access-consciousness is a functional property, explaining which is among Chalmers 'easy problems', and many philosophers believe that representational content can also be explained in broadly functional terms. However, as we saw, conscious experiences also seem to have an ineffable *feel* or *phenomenal character*, which appears to be much more difficult to explain. In recent years, however, a number of philosophers have argued that phenomenal character can itself be explained in terms of representational content and access relations. At bottom, they argue, phenomenally conscious experiences are simply representational states that are linked in appropriate ways to other mental states and processes.

Views of this kind are known as *representational* theories of consciousness and they will be our focus in this chapter.

Representational theories divide into two broad kinds. Those of the first kind are the more straightforward. According to these, for an experience to have a phenomenal character is simply for it to have a certain sort of representational content, available in the right way to other mental processes (the theories differ as to the details). So, for example, having a conscious experience of a blue circle involves possessing a mental state which represents a blue circle in a certain way and has a certain role in mental processing. The second group of theories introduce a further element. In order for an experience to have a phenomenal character, they claim, it must *itself* be represented within the mind – it must be accompanied by a further thought or experience *about* it (or, on some versions, must be available to processes that can generate a thought about it). Thus, on this view, having a conscious experience of a blue circle involves *two* representational states – one which represents the presence of a blue circle and another which represents the presence of this experience of a blue circle. The latter is said to be a *higher-order representation* – a representation of a representation – and theories of this kind are known as *higher-order representational theories* ('HOR theories' for short). Theories of the first kind, on the other hand, which do not involve higher-order representations, are known as *first-order representational theories* ('FOR theories'). One of the questions we shall be considering in the chapter is whether a representational theory of consciousness should take a first-order or a higher-order form.

Whichever form they take, representational theories hold out the promise of a reductive explanation of consciousness. If phenomenal character can be explained in terms of representational content and access relations, and if these features can themselves be explained in lower-level terms, and ultimately in basic physical ones, then we shall have a full reductive explanation of phenomenal consciousness. It is true that providing a reductive explanation of representational content is a big problem in its own right – and one which we cannot investigate here. However, a number of reductive theories of content have been developed and many philosophers feel that reducing the problem of consciousness to one of representation would constitute significant progress towards solving the hard problem. So let us look at some representational theories and see how they measure up. We shall begin with a first-order theory.

First-order representationalism

First-order representational theories of consciousness became popular during the 1990s, with a number of philosophers independently developing theories along broadly similar lines. We shall focus on the version set out by Michael Tye in his *Ten Problems of Consciousness* (1995).

Transparency

According to first-order representational theories, the phenomenal character of an experience is identical with its representational content: how the experience *feels* is a matter of what it *represents* – the information it carries. Tye marshals a number of considerations in favour of this view, the most compelling being that experience is *transparent*. Tye explains:

> Focus your attention on a square that has been painted blue. Intuitively, you are directly aware of blueness and squareness as out there in the world away from you, as features of an external surface. Now shift your gaze inward and try to become aware of your experience itself, inside you, apart from its objects. Try to focus your attention on some intrinsic feature of the experience that distinguishes it from other experiences, something other than what it is an experience *of*. The task seems impossible: one's awareness seems always to slip through the experience to blueness and squareness, as instantiated together in an external object. In turning one's mind inward to attend to the experience, one seems to end up concentrating on what is outside again, on external features or properties. And this remains so, even if there really is no blue square in front of one – if, for example, one is subject to an illusion. Again, one experiences blue and square *as* features of an external surface, but introspection does not seem to reveal any further distinctive features of the experience over and above *what* one experiences in undergoing the illusion.

> Visual experience, then is transparent or diaphanous, as is phenomenal consciousness generally. Take, for example, the case of pain. Focus your attention on some particular pain you are feeling, a pain in a leg, say. What do you end up focusing on? In my own case, I find myself attending to what I am experiencing in having the pain, namely, a painful disturbance in the leg. I experience the disturbance *as* located in the relevant part of my leg. But I cannot make myself aware of any features of my experience over and above, or apart from, what I am experiencing. My experience, after all, is not itself in my leg. This is shown by the fact that I could have an experience exactly like my actual

one even if I had no legs, so long as my brain were stimulated electrically in the right way. But if I have a pain in my leg, *all* I end up focusing on, when I introspect my experience, is how things seem to be *in my leg*.

(Tye 1995, 30–1)

ACTIVITY

1 What does Tye mean by saying that experience is *transparent*?

2 How can an experience be transparent even if it is illusory?

3 Tye claims that in focusing on a pain in his leg, he focuses solely on his leg. Why does this imply that he is not aware of any intrinsic features of his pain experience?

DISCUSSION

1 He means that we are not aware of any intrinsic features of our experiences themselves, only of the features they represent as being present in the external world or in some part of our bodies. We see through our experiences, as it were, as we see through a perfectly clear pane of glass. (Note that this use of the term 'transparent' is quite different from Papineau's use in Reading 13, discussed in the previous chapter.)

2 Because it can still represent the presence of something external. If we have the illusion of seeing a blue square, then our attention is still focused on how things seem to be in the external world. Similarly, if a person without legs has an experience as of pain in their leg, then their attention is still directed outward to the region where the pain seems to be. (This does not mean that the subject of the illusion must *believe* that things really are as the experience represents them to be – that there is a blue square in front of them or that they have a leg in which there is a pain. They may know that their experience is misrepresenting the world to them.)

3 Because the pain experience is not in his leg, but in his brain. Thus if he is focusing solely on his leg, he cannot be focusing on features of the experience itself.

To test whether you agree with Tye about visual illusions, you might try the following experiment. Find a brightly coloured object and place it in a good light. Hold your gaze steadily on the object for 60 seconds, then look at a white surface. You will experience an *afterimage* – you will seem to see a shape of the opposite colour to that of the object. Is Tye right that the experience presents this coloured shape to you as located in the external world?

If Tye is right about the transparency of experience, then there is a powerful argument for a first-order representational theory of consciousness.

In the following passage Tye outlines the argument just mentioned. Read the passage and then set out the argument in the form of premises and a conclusion.

> Generalizing, introspection of your perceptual experiences seems to reveal only aspects of *what* you experience, further aspects of the scenes, as represented. Why? The answer, I suggest, is that your perceptual experiences have no *introspectible* features over and above those implicated in their intentional contents. So the phenomenal character of such experiences – itself something that is introspectibly accessible, assuming the appropriate concepts are possessed and there is no cognitive malfunction – is identical with, or contained within, their intentional contents.
>
> The same is true for bodily sensations. Suppose you have a pain in your toe. Then your toe is where you feel the painful disturbance to be. Now try to turn your attention away from what you are experiencing in your toe to your experience itself apart from that. Again, inevitably what you end up focusing on is simply what is going on *in your toe*, or rather what your experience represents is going on there. The phenomenal character of your experience – certainly something you are introspectively aware of on such an occasion – must itself be representational.
>
> (Tye 1995, 136)

The argument goes like this:

> *Premise 1*   The phenomenal character of an experience is an introspectible feature of it.
>
> *Premise 2*   Experiences have no introspectible features over and above their representational content
>
> *Conclusion*   The phenomenal character of an experience is identical with, or an aspect of ('contained within'), its representational content.

Premise 2 of this argument is the controversial one. Not everyone agrees that representational content is all we are aware of when we introspect our experiences. Indeed, it is common to claim that many experiences – bodily sensations and feelings, for example – have no representational content at all. So Tye is going to have to say more in order to convince us that all experiences are transparent. We shall examine his arguments in a moment. First, however,

I want to look at what he has to say about the *type* of representational content possessed by perceptions and other experiences. We shall then be in a better position to understand his account of the content of specific experiences.

PANIC theory

We have seen that Tye holds that phenomenal character is a kind of representational content – he calls it *phenomenal content*. But what kind of content is phenomenal content? Not all states with representational content have phenomenal character. The magnetic patterns on the hard disk of my computer represent things but do not, I am pretty sure, have a phenomenal character. And it is widely accepted that we undergo many non-conscious mental processes, which involve representations but have no feel to them. So what distinguishes those representational states that have phenomenal character from those that do not? Tye's answer takes the form of what calls *PANIC theory*.

In order to understand PANIC theory, it is necessary to know something about Tye's view of the nature of sense experience. On the view Tye endorses, sense experiences are the product of specialized, self-contained subsystems, or *modules*, which operate independently of the rest of the mind and provide the input to higher-level cognitive process such as belief-formation and reasoning. The view that sensory systems are modular is widely held among contemporary psychologists and helps to explain various features of sense experience – in particular the persistence of sensory illusions. Take the well-known Muller–Lyer illusion (Figure 10). The two lines are the same length, but the inverted arrowheads make the one on the top look longer. Moreover, this illusion persists even if we know that the lines are the same length: our belief about the true length of the lines has no effect on way the lines *look*. This strongly suggests that visual experience is the product of a self-contained

Figure 10 The Muller–Lyer diagram.

system whose outputs are not affected by information held in other parts of the mind.

Tye holds that sensory modules operate on computational principles, processing signals from the sense organs in order to build up complex representations of the environment. Here is his sketch of how the vision module works. (A transducer is a device which converts one form of energy into another. For example, a microphone is a transducer because it converts soundwaves into electronic signals. Distal features are features of objects themselves, as opposed to the effects objects have on our sense organs ('proximal features').)

> On the standard computational approach, the receptor cells on the retina are taken to be transducers. They have, as input, physical energy in the form of light, and they convert it immediately into symbolic representations of light intensity and wavelength. These representations are themselves made up of active nerve cells. Hence, they are physical. And they are symbolic, since they are the objects of computational procedures. Moreover, they represent light intensity and wavelength, since that is what they reliably track, assuming the system is functioning properly. The computational procedures operating on these representations generate further symbolic representations first of intensity and wavelength changes in the light, then of lines of such changes, then of edges, ridges, and surfaces, together with representations of local surface features, for example, color, orientation, and distance away...
>
> So representations are built up of distal features of the surfaces of external objects in mechanical fashion by computational processes. The initial, or input, representations for the visual module track light intensity and wavelength, assuming nothing is malfunctioning. The output representations track features of distal stimuli under optimal or ideal perceptual conditions. Thereby, it seems plausible to suppose, they represent those features, they become sensations *of* edges, ridges, colors, shapes, and so on. Likewise for the other senses.
>
> (Tye 1995, 102–3)

Tye suggests that the representations generated by sensory modules are essentially *maplike*. In the case of vision, the output is a map of the visual field on which various features – edges, textures, colours and so on – are marked (Tye 1995, 120–3).

Note that Tye says that mental representations represent features of the external world because they *track* them. To say that one thing tracks another is to say that the two are causally correlated, so that, under ideal conditions, changes in the former mirror changes in the latter. Thus, the number of rings in the trunk of a tree tracks the tree's age; the position of the needle of a car's speedometer tracks the car's speed; the height of the mercury in a thermometer tracks the ambient temperature; and so on. And according to one popular theory, which Tye endorses, tracking is the key to mental representation. A cluster of nerve cells represents some environmental feature because, under ideal conditions, it is activated only when the feature is present and thus tracks its presence.

With this background in place, we can now move on to look at Tye's account of phenomenal content.

Turn to Reading 16 and answer the following questions. (Note that by the 'cognitive system' Tye means the system responsible for conceptualized thought. Note, too, that 'red$_{19}$' and 'red$_{21}$' are made-up names for shades of red for which we have no everyday names.)

ACTIVITY

1   What does Tye mean by saying that phenomenal content is 'poised'?

2   What does Tye mean by saying that phenomenal content is 'abstract'?

3   What does Tye mean by saying that phenomenal content is 'non-conceptual'?

4   What does Tye mean by an 'observational' feature? Why is the property of being a tiger not an observational one? What observational properties does a tiger possess?

DISCUSSION

1   He means that it is ready to be used by the mechanisms which form beliefs and desires. So for example, the content of the perception of a blue square ahead is ready to be used by the belief-forming system to generate the belief that there is a blue square ahead. (This does not mean that the system will in fact make use of it. It may form no belief at all on the matter, or even, if it has evidence that the perception is illusory, form a different one.)

2   He means that individual objects do not enter into it. That is, phenomenal content does not represent the presence of *particular* objects, but only of *general* features that can be shared by different objects. Thus, perceptions of two identical objects seen under identical conditions will have the same phenomenal content, as will an hallucination of an identical object.

3 He means that the features represented in phenomenal content need not be ones for which we have concepts. Sense experience has a richness and detail which far outstrips our ability to conceptualize it. And although we can apply concepts *to* our sense experiences, the concepts applied do not enter into the character of the experiences themselves.

4 An observational feature is one that is represented in sense experience – one which is tracked by our sensory systems. The property of being a tiger is not an observational one since it is not directly tracked by our sensory systems. We cannot literally *see* that something is a tiger – as opposed to some other creature disguised to look exactly like one. The observational properties of a tiger are basic sensory ones – colour, shape, smell and so on.

This, then, is Tye's account of phenomenal content/character. We are concerned here with its broad implications for consciousness, but I shall raise two points of detail before moving on. First, is it true to say that sense experience is wholly non-conceptual? Take the well-known duck–rabbit figure, which can be seen as either a duck or a rabbit. Tye holds that the concepts *duck* and *rabbit* do not enter into the content of the sense experience itself, but only into its classification at a higher level: we see the figure neutrally and then classify it as either a duck or a rabbit. Yet does this reflect the phenomenology of the case? Isn't it the case that the figure actually *looks* different depending on which concept we apply – that its phenomenal character changes?

The second point concerns beliefs and desires. Since the content of these is neither poised nor non-conceptual, Tye denies that they have any phenomenal character. Again, it may be objected that this does not reflect the phenomenology. Don't our beliefs and desires sometimes have a distinctive feel to them? (Certainly Chalmers thinks so – see Reading 1, paragraphs 13–14.) Tye must say that such feels really belong to associated experiences, not to the beliefs and desires themselves.

I shall leave you to assess these objections for yourself. We return now to the question of the transparency of experience.

The content of sensations and feelings

The claim that experience is transparent is central to a first-order representational theory of consciousness such as Tye's. If the theory is correct, then all we are aware of when we introspect our experiences is representational content – information about things. But is that true? Many philosophers hold that it is not. The feel of a perception, they maintain, is something over and above its representational content. Indeed, it is often claimed that some experiences are pure feel, with no representational content at all. Here are three typical comments (all quoted in Tye 1995, 93):

> By sensations, we shall mean bodily feelings... as well as perceptual experiences. These differ in an important respect, which calls for a subdivision within the class of what we are calling sensations: bodily sensations do not have an intentional object in the way that perceptual experiences do. We distinguish between a visual experience and what it is an experience of; but we do not make this distinction in respect of pains. Or again, visual experiences represent the world as being a certain way, but pains have no such representational content.
>
> (McGinn 1982, 8)

> Many conscious states are not Intentional, e.g., a sudden sense of elation.
>
> (Searle 1983, 2)

> Note... that phenomenal content need not be representational at all (my favorite example is the phenomenal content of orgasm).
>
> (Block 1995, 234)

Tye maintains, however, that these views are mistaken and that *all* experiences – bodily sensations and feelings included – have representational content. We are now going to look at a reading in which he argues the case for this view, discussing in detail various types of experience which may seem problematic for a representational theory.

Turn to Reading 17. Begin by reading paragraphs 1–11, which deal with pain. **ACTIVITY**

1   What do pains represent, according to Tye?

2   What reason is there to think that pain is transparent? (Paragraph 3)

3   What is the objection raised in paragraph 6 and what is Tye's response? (He makes two points, one in paragraph 7, the other in paragraph 8.)

4   In what sense are pains painful, according to Tye, and in what sense are they not? (Paragraphs 9–10)

5   In paragraph 11, Tye says that it is possible have a pain in one's left arm even though there is nothing painful there. What are the relevant senses of 'pain' and 'painful'?

6   An amputee will often experience what is known as a 'phantom limb' – the illusion that the missing body part still exists. Phantom limbs are often felt as being extremely painful. What do you think Tye would say about such pains?

DISCUSSION

1   They represent bodily disturbance – in particular, damage. Differences between types of pain correspond to differences in the type of disturbance represented – its volume, location, extent, duration and so on.

2   As before, the key point is that pains are typically experienced as being located in various parts of the body, not directly in the brain. Assuming pains are in fact brain states, this strongly suggests that we are not aware of any intrinsic features of our pains.

3   The objection is that pain can be affected by higher-level ('top-down') activity within the cognitive system – by one's beliefs or emotions, for example. (Processes that can be affected in this way are said to be 'cognitively penetrable'.) This is a problem for Tye since he holds that pains are the product of modular systems that operate independently of the rest of the mind (paragraph 4). Tye's first suggestion is that higher-level processes may affect how *much* of the information from the pain module gets through to the higher brain centres. His second suggestion is that higher-level activity may not affect our pain experiences at all, but merely our *awareness* of them – our readiness to introspect and conceptualize them.

4   Pains are not painful in the way that cuts or bruises are. To say that a cut or bruise is painful is to say that it causes a feeling which in turn causes certain further reactions, such as dislike and anxiety. Pains themselves are not painful in this sense. (They are not causes of the feelings in question, but the feelings themselves.) However, they are painful in the weaker sense that they cause the further reactions mentioned.

5   The relevant senses are 'sensory representation of bodily damage' and 'causing pain' (i.e. causing a sensory representation of bodily damage). So, in the case described, the man has a sensory representation of damage to his arm, even though there is nothing in his arm that is causing such a

representation (the real cause is the damage to his heart). The pain thus misrepresents things.

5   He would say that they represent damage to the body part in question, just as pain in a real limb does. Since the body part does not in fact exist, these pains misrepresent things.

Before continuing with the reading, I want to say a little more about the distinction Tye makes in paragraphs 9–10 between the representational content of a pain and the further reactions it causes. In a later passage Tye illustrates the distinction with an example drawn from neurology:

> Some unfortunate people have a condition known as intractable neuralgia. They suffer very frequent, excruciating pains. When the pains strike, they report the sensation of knives ripping their flesh. During these attacks, they are completely unable to function. Not surprisingly, they become obsessed with their pains. Neurosurgical intervention can help. In particular, prefrontal leukotomies (that is, surgical severing of the neural connections in the deep white matter of both frontal lobes of the brain) can make a dramatic difference. Patients who undergo such a procedure are typically relaxed and cheerful afterward (in sharp contrast to their state before). They report that they still feel pains, but they no longer mind them. Their *suffering* is either gone or greatly diminished.
>
> The way to understand what is going on here is to draw a distinction between what one senses or feels in having a pain and how one reacts to it. The above patients feel or sense much of what they felt before, but they no longer dislike the sensation. Their pains are no longer painful to them.
>
> Perhaps it will be objected that, after the operation, what it is like for these patients to feel pain is not the same as what it was like for them to feel pain before. This, I am prepared to concede, may well be the case. But it is no threat to my position. Disliking something intensely has all sorts of effects, both physical and psychological. The disappearance of the reaction of dislike in the patients after the operation may well feed back down and affect the sensory experience of pain in the way I described in [Reading 17]. So the phenomenal character of the patients' pains may change somewhat. It is also worth noting that the patients no longer feel anxious or concerned, and further they pay much less attention to their pains (so their *awareness* of how the pains feel diminishes).
>
> (Tye 1995, 135)

This distinction between pain and the reactions it provokes also gives Tye a response to a potentially damaging objection. The objection is that the same representation of bodily damage may feel differently to different people. A masochist may enjoy the sensation of the bodily damage caused by whipping, while I find it most unpleasant. Surely, then, what the experience is *like* will differ for each of us, even though its representational content is the same?

ACTIVITY   Can you see how Tye might respond to this objection, drawing on the distinction just mentioned?

DISCUSSION   He might reply that the masochist and I undergo pain experiences with the same phenomenal character, but that these experiences in turn generate quite different reactions – excitement and enjoyment in the one case, distress and aversion in the other.

This is indeed the line Tye takes. Here is what he says

> My reply is that the felt quality of the *pain* is the same for both of us. I find the felt quality horrible and I react accordingly. He [i.e. the masochist] has a different reaction. Our reactions involve further feelings, however. I feel anxiety and concern, he does not. Here there is a phenomenal difference.

(Ibid., 134–5)

The last point is important. The reactions generated by the pain may include further feelings and emotions which themselves have a phenomenal character (itself, of course, on Tye's view identical with a certain sort of representational content). Thus, since the pain generates different feelings and emotions in me and the masochist, Tye can allow that there is a real difference in phenomenology between us.

Let us return now to Reading 17.

ACTIVITY   Read paragraphs 12–19, which deal with bodily sensations and background feelings.

1   Do we always know what our experiences represent, according to Tye? Is this a problem for him? (Paragraph 14)

2   According to Tye, seeing that someone is having an orgasm and feeling an orgasm are both representational states. Both are representations of certain bodily changes. What, then, is the difference between them?

3   What do background feelings represent? Why are they important?

1   No. Tye accepts that we are sometimes ignorant of exactly what our experiences represent – for example, that hunger pangs represent contractions of the stomach walls. This is not a problem, Tye argues, since sensory experiences are not conceptual states. If we do not know what an experience represents, then we cannot conceptualize it correctly, but conceptualization is not necessary for sensory representation.

2   Tye mentions two differences. First, seeing that someone is having an orgasm is a conceptual state, feeling an orgasm is not. Secondly, the state of seeing that someone is having an orgasm represents changes in the other person's body, that of feeling one represents changes in one's own.

3   They represent facts about the overall position and condition of one's body. They are important for our sense of identity, anchoring us to our bodies.

Now complete your study of Reading 17 by reading paragraphs 20–32. You should now be getting to grips with Tye's approach, so I shall leave you to explore these on your own.

I think Tye makes a strong case for the view that all experiences have representational content. But even if he is right, it does not follow that a first-order representational theory of consciousness is defensible. Tye needs to show, not just that all experiences have representational content, but that they have no introspectible features *other than* their representational content – that their phenomenal properties can be identified with their representational ones. We shall pursue this question in the next section.

Assessing first-order representationalism

This section assesses the adequacy of Tye's theory of phenomenal consciousness. We shall look at some proposed counter-examples to the claim that phenomenal character is representational content and then go on to assess the explanatory power of the theory as an account of phenomenal consciousness. Although we shall be concerned specifically with Tye's theory, many of the points made would apply equally to other first-order representational accounts.

Counter-examples?

Over the years, critics have proposed a range of counter-examples to the claim that phenomenal character is identical with representational content – cases where an experience has features that seem to outrun its representational content. I shall mention two examples, one from Ned Block, the other from Christopher Peacocke, together with Tye's responses.

Block's example concerns a case where one simultaneously hears and sees something overhead. The two experiences, Block claims, have the same representational content – that there is something overhead – but are phenomenally quite different. Block explains that he is imagining a case where one just has an impression of the object's location without noticing any other features, so that the difference cannot be attributed to further representational differences (Block 1995, 235). Tye responds that even in such a case the two experiences would differ in their representational content:

> [E]ven if one has no visual experience as of a specific color or shape, there will inevitably be other features one does experience, in addition to relative spatial position, that are not represented in the auditory experience. For example, one is bound to have some visual impression of the thing's size (tiny as a speck, large as a nearby bird, etc.). Likewise, in the case of the auditory experience, one is bound to have some impression of how loud the sound is. And that will not be represented in the visual experience.
>
> (Tye 1995, 157)

Peacocke's case concerns distorted visual experiences 'such as those experienced when your eyes, closed, are directed toward the sun, and swirling shapes are experienced'. In these and similar cases, Peacocke claims, it does not really look as if there are shapes in one's environment and so the character of the experiences cannot be accounted for in representational terms (Peacocke 1993, 675). Tye replies that in these cases it *does* look as if there are shapes in one's environment – it is just that the representations involved are in certain respects indeterminate:

> I have visual sensations of various shapes occupying certain moving, two-dimensional locations relative to my point of view. I experience a square shape,

say, *as* being on my left, next to an oval shape a little to its right and moving away from it. My experience represents these shapes and spatial relations. What it does not do is represent the locations of the shapes in the third dimension either relative to one another or relative to anything in the environment. Nor does it represent the shapes in two dimensions relative to items in the environment. My experience does not comment on these matters. It leaves them open, or at least it does so as long as it is agreed that I do not undergo any sensory representation of the spatial relations just mentioned.

(Tye 1995, 158–9)

You might like to pause here and try to think up further counter-examples for yourself. In each case, ask yourself how Tye might respond.   **ACTIVITY**

I am now going to move on to what many consider the most serious problem for a first-order representational theory – the possibility of spectrum inversion. We have already encountered this idea. The thought is that another person's visual experiences might be inverted relative to yours, so that to them red things look green, blue things look yellow and so on. If this is possible, then phenomenal character cannot be the same thing as representational content. For it is plausible to think that the inverted person's experiences would still have the same representational content as yours. The experience they get from seeing a ripe banana represents the presence of yellowness, even though it has a different phenomenal character from the one that represents yellowness in you. We can also imagine inversions in other senses, such as taste or smell, and the same moral follows.

Now if the claim is merely that spectrum inversion is *conceivable*, then it may not be too serious a threat. For Tye could respond that conceivability does not always correspond to a genuine possibility, drawing on arguments of the sort considered in the previous chapter (see, in particular, Reading 14 from Carruthers). However, there are reasons for thinking that inverted experiences are not just conceivable but genuinely possible – indeed *naturally possible*. That is, there are reasons for thinking that spectrum inversion could occur in our universe, consistently with the laws of nature as they stand. There several ways of arguing for this, but perhaps the neatest involves the example of 'Inverted Earth', devised by Ned Block (1990). Tye summarizes the example for us:

Inverted Earth is an imaginary planet, on which things have complementary colors to the colors of their counterparts on Earth. The sky is yellow, grass is red, ripe tomatoes are green, and so on. The inhabitants of Inverted Earth undergo psychological attitudes and experiences with inverted intentional contents relative to those of people on Earth. They think that the sky is yellow, see that grass is red, and so forth. However, they call the sky 'blue', grass 'green', ripe tomatoes 'red', just as we do. Indeed, in all respects consistent with the alterations just described, Inverted Earth is as much like Earth as possible.

In Block's original version of the tale, one night while you are asleep, a team of alien scientists insert color-inverting lenses in your eyes and take you to Inverted Earth, where you are substituted for your Inverted Earth twin or *doppelgänger*. Upon awakening, you are aware of no difference, since the inverting lenses neutralize the inverted colors. You think that you are still where you were before. What it is like for you when you see the sky or anything else is just what it was like on Earth. But after enough time has passed, after you have become sufficiently embedded in the language and physical environment of Inverted Earth, your intentional contents will come to match those of the other inhabitants. You will come to believe that the sky is yellow, for example, just as they do. Similarly, you will come to have a visual experience that represents the sky as yellow because the experiential state you now undergo, as you view the sky, is the one that, in you, now normally tracks yellow things. So, the later you will come to be subject to inner states that are intentionally inverted relative to the inner states of the earlier you, while the phenomenal aspects of your experiences will remain unchanged.

(Tye 2000, 117–18)

The idea is that, after you have spent some time on Inverted Earth, your colour words and the concepts they express would adjust their meaning to represent the features with which they are now associated, rather than those they used to represent back on Earth. So when you describe the sky as 'blue', you would *mean* that it is yellow, as the native inhabitants do. (This is not to say that you would make a conscious decision to change the meaning. The change is supposed to occur simply because of the changes in your physical and linguistic environment. You might still think you were on Earth and be quite unaware that any changes had occurred.) And, the argument goes, your experiences, too, would change their representational content. The experience you get when you look at the sky would now track, and so represent, yellowness – even though, thanks to the inverting lenses, it would still have the phenomenal character that the experience of blue used to have back on Earth. This story has some implausible and futuristic elements, of course, but nothing – it seems – that violates the laws of nature (though see below). And if so, it creates a problem for Tye's theory.

How does the Inverted Earth example create a problem for Tye?

Compare the experience you get from looking at the sky on Earth with the one you get from looking at it on Inverted Earth. They have the same phenomenal character but different representational content. Representational content can thus vary independently of phenomenal character and the two cannot be one and the same thing, as Tye claims. Hence Tye is wrong.

Tye makes two points in reply to the Inverted Earth objection. The first is that it is not clear that it really would be possible for the aliens to invert your colour experiences in the way described – even allowing them the use of futuristic technology. It is true that colours line up in binary opposites – yellow opposite blue, green opposite red and so on. This reflects the structure of the human visual system. But, as Tye points out, there are asymmetries in this pattern (Tye 1995 203–6; for more detail, see Hardin 1988). For example, yellow things appear brighter than comparable blue things, red things seem warmer and more 'advancing' than green ones, blue can be mixed with black to form a blue-black, but yellow cannot (there is no such colour as yellowy-black). So as well as inserting the inverting lenses, the aliens would also have to adjust your perceptions of brightness, warmth and distance, and restrict the colour combinations you could perceive. And these charges might in turn have knock-on effects on other aspects of your colour experience and even on experiences involving your other senses. All in all, it might well turn out to be impossible to invert your experiences in such a way that you did not notice any change on moving to Inverted Earth.

Tye's second point is that even if we grant the possibility of the Inverted Earth scenario, it still does not follow that phenomenal character and representational content can diverge. For, he argues, your experiences on Inverted Earth would *not* change their representational content: your *thoughts* might alter their meaning to match those of the Inverted Earthlings, but your *experiences* would not. Experiences with the phenomenal feel of blue would still represent blueness, even though they now *tracked* yellowness. There would thus be no mismatch between representational content and phenomenal character and no problem for PANIC theory. Now this might seem to conflict with Tye's claim that representational content is determined by tracking. Tye has a reply to this, however. It is that the content of an experience is determined by what it would track *under optimal conditions* – and such conditions do not hold after the aliens have tampered with you. Tye explains:

> The Inverted Earth story essentially involves an artificial intervention in the operation of certain transducers. Inverting lenses are placed in the eyes of the traveler. These lenses reverse the way in which the light input is processed. Intuitively, the lenses *deceive* the traveler (in Block's original version of the story) so that when he first arrives, he has false beliefs on the basis of the phenomenal character of his visual experiences. He believes that the clear sky is blue, when really it is yellow. Of course, through time the traveler's beliefs adjust. But no matter how long he stays, it remains the case that the scientists from Inverted Earth have tampered with his visual transducers. Their operation is altered by the insertion of the lenses and, at no later time, is the system restored to its initial, natural state. The insertion of the lenses *interferes* with the operation of the sensory transducers. Accordingly, the transduction process is not in itself normal or optimal...
>
> Intuitively, then, it is true of the traveler's sensory state, as he looks at the clear sky on Inverted Earth (after however many years), that *had* there been no interference, that phenomenal state *would have been* causally correlated (in him) with blue things. Accordingly, by the causal covariation proposal, the traveler's sensory state continues to represent the clear sky as *blue*.
>
> (Tye 2000, 137)

ACTIVITY

1 Why, according to Tye, does the experience the traveller gets from looking at yellow things continue to represent blueness?

2 On this view, are the traveller's visual experiences reliable?

DISCUSSION

1 Because it remains the case that, under optimal conditions, it would track blueness. If the implants were removed, thereby restoring optimal conditions, experiences of this type would track blueness, not yellowness.

2 No. They systematically misrepresent things. They represent yellow things as blue, red things as green and so on. (Remember that on Inverted Earth everything has the opposite colour to the one it has on Earth.)

This response rebuts the immediate challenge, but it is debatable whether it is ultimately satisfactory. I shall mention just one objection here. Suppose you are the traveller to Inverted Earth. Tye concedes that after some time there the content of your *beliefs* will adapt to match your new physical and linguistic environment. So you will believe that that the sky is yellow, even though you call it 'blue'. Moreover, you won't know that your visual experiences are misrepresenting colours – you may still be completely unaware that anything has happened to you. So you will, presumably, believe that your experiences represent the sky accurately, as being yellow (though, again, you will express this by saying that they represent it as 'blue'). And you will conceptualize your experiences as representations of yellowness (expressed as 'blueness'), even though they are in fact representations of blueness. In short, your beliefs about colours will get seriously out of step with your experiences of them and you will be massively mistaken about the nature of your own visual experiences. This is, at the very least, counter-intuitive.

It is difficult to judge how serious this objection is – indeed, it is very hard to maintain any clear intuitions about Inverted Earth. But in any case it is unlikely that objections of this kind are going to be decisive in the overall evaluation of first-order representational theories of consciousness. For, whether the objection is successful depends on the particular theory of sensory representation one adopts. So even if Tye's version of first-order representationalism did succumb to it, another version might be immune. That is, we might agree with Tye that phenomenal character is a kind of representational content, but adopt a different account of the nature of representational content itself.

We are going to move on now to a wider question. Suppose there are no genuine counter-examples to the claim that phenomenal character and representational content never vary independently of each other. Still, it does not follow that they are one and the same thing. They might *coincide* but none the less be distinct. So if Tye is to persuade us, he needs to show that his theory has further virtues – and, ideally, that it solves the hard problem.

Explanatory power

What sort of explanatory power does PANIC theory have? Does the hypothesis that phenomenal character is poised abstract non-conceptual intentional content really explain the distinctive features of phenomenally conscious experience?

It can certainly make some progress. To begin with, the theory helps to explain why consciousness seems elusive. If experience is completely transparent, as Tye maintains, then it is not surprising that we find it hard to get a grip on it. Whenever we try to focus on our experiences themselves, we shall look through them to the features of the world which they represent to us. Tye's theory also provides an elegant account of the language we use to describe our experiences – 'phenomenal vocabulary', as Tye calls it. We often apply terms for physical objects to our experiences. We talk of *blue* afterimages, *burning* smells, *stinging* pains and so on. Yet these expressions cannot be taken literally – our experiences are not really blue, burning or stinging. So what do these terms mean when applied in this way? Tye has a neat answer. They mean what they normally do; it is just that they are used in a shorthand way. By a 'blue afterimage', we mean an afterimage that *represents* blue; by a 'burning smell', a smell that *represents* burning, and so on (Tye 1995, 118–19). (Thus on Tye's view, the phenomenal concepts we apply to our experiences (see page 84 above) are the very same concepts we apply to the objects of those experiences. The phenomenal concept *red*, used of an experience, is the same as the colour concept *red*, used of an external object.)

Tye can also explain why the phenomenal character of our experiences seems ineffable – why it is hard to describe it in a way that really captures what it is like. For on Tye's view phenomenal content is *non-conceptual* – it represents fine-grained distinctions for which we have no words and concepts. Any descriptions we give will thus fail to capture the full content of our experiences – the precise shade of a colour, for example. It is true that we might still describe our experiences indirectly by referring to their objects. For example, I might describe my current visual experience by saying that it is an experience of the colour of *that wallpaper over there*. But this would not provide a *general* way of characterizing experiences, which could convey their character to someone who had not experienced the objects in question for themselves.

PANIC theory also vindicates the commonsense view that consciousness has an important function – something which, as we saw in Chapter 2, property dualist accounts struggle to do. On a first-order representationalist view, to say that a mental state has phenomenal character is to say that it carries information about the outside world or about the state of one's body –

information which is poised to be used by higher cognitive processes such as belief-formation and decision-making.

Tye's theory has some attractions, then. But does it really solve the big problem – the problem of explaining phenomenal character itself (the 'what-it-is-likeness' of experience)? There are reasons to doubt it.

For one thing, it is not clear why the particular conditions Tye outlines – the possession of poised abstract non-conceptual intentional content – should be sufficient for a state to be phenomenally conscious. Why those conditions, rather than others? To help see the force of the objection, consider the contrast between conscious and non-conscious perception. As we saw in Chapter 1 (pages 3–5 above), there is reason to think that various kinds of non-conscious perception occur. Neuro-psychological evidence strongly supports this view. In particular, there is evidence that we have two semi-independent visual systems: one (the 'dorsal system') which is devoted to the production of fast behavioural responses and whose contents are non-conscious, and another (the 'ventral system') which feeds into conceptualized thought and reasoning and whose states are usually conscious (Milner and Goodale 1995; for a good summary of the evidence, see Carruthers 2000, Chapter 6). Now at first sight this evidence seems to harmonize well with Tye's theory. For it is only information in the ventral system that is poised to have an impact on the belief system, and so Tye's theory predicts, correctly, that only this will be conscious. But this immediately raises a question. If the representations in the dorsal system have abstract non-conceptual intentional content, why are they not conscious too? Why should being poised to have an impact on the belief system make a difference? (Carruthers forthcoming, Chapter 6). Indeed, why should merely being *poised* to do anything make a difference? Why should the *availability* of information to another system confer what-it-is-likeness upon it?

There is another, more general, objection to Tye's approach. Peter Carruthers has argued that, by their very nature, first-order representational (FOR) theories lack the resources to explain phenomenal consciousness. Carruthers himself advocates a higher-order representational (HOR) theory, according to which consciousness involves awareness of one's own mental states, and his objection goes to the heart of the dispute between first-order and higher-order theories.

ACTIVITY Turn to Reading 18 and make notes on the following questions.

1 What is the distinction that, according to Carruthers, FOR theories cannot make?

2 What is involved in understanding what the *world* is like for an organism ?

3 What is required, according to Carruthers, for an organism's *experiences* to be like something for it (that is, for the organism to exhibit mental-state subjectivity)?

4 What are higher-order representations? Why are they required for mental-state subjectivity, according to Carruthers?

5 Why does a theory of phenomenal consciousness need to explain mental-state subjectivity and not just worldly-subjectivity?

DISCUSSION 1 It is the distinction between what the *world* (or the organism's body) is like for an organism and what its own *experiences* are like for it. Carruthers refers to these as 'worldly subjectivity' and 'mental-state subjectivity' respectively.

2 It involves understanding the organism's *point of view* on the world. This can be characterized by reference to the kinds of perceptual information available to the organism and the kinds of perceptual discrimination it can make. Organisms with different discriminatory powers have different points of view on the world.

3 The organism must have a point of view on its own experiences – that is, must possess information about its experiences and be able to make discriminations among them.

4 They are representations of representations – in this case, of experiences. (First-order representations, by contrast, are representations of states of the world or of one's body.) Mental-state subjectivity requires higher-order representations, according to Carruthers, since it involves possessing information about, and making discriminations among, one's own experiences – which in turn involves representing them to oneself. First-order representations are sufficient only for worldly subjectivity.

5 Because the hard problem is specifically a problem about mental-state subjectivity – about the feel of our experiences themselves.

To sum up: Tye identifies phenomenal consciousness with worldly subjectivity, whereas, if Carruthers is right, it requires mental-state subjectivity, too. And while first-order representations may be sufficient for the former, higher-order representations are required for the latter.

It is important to stress that Tye does not deny that we can form higher-order representations of our experiences. He agrees that we can introspect our experiences, conceptualize them and form beliefs about them. And he concedes that unless we do this, there is a sense in which we are unaware of our experiences:

> We are like the distracted driver who is lost in thought for several miles as he drives along. During this time he keeps his car on the road and perhaps changes gears. So he certainly sees the road and other cars. But he is not aware of his visual sensations. He is not paying attention to them.
>
> (Tye 1995, 115)

Tye insists however that higher-order representations are not necessary for phenomenal consciousness itself. The driver may be unaware of his visual sensations, but they are still phenomenally conscious – still *like something*. Non-human animals too, Tye claims, have phenomenally conscious experiences, even though they seldom or never think about their own experiences:

> Do animals other than humans undergo phenomenally conscious states? It certainly seems that way. Dogs often growl or whimper during REM (rapid eye movement) sleep. Surely, they are undergoing experiences when they do so, just as we are during our dreams. What seems much less plausible is the idea that in every such case, there is consciousness of [the] higher-order type, and hence thought directed on other mental states. After all, one important difference between humans and other animals is that the former are much more reflective than the latter. So with nonhuman animals there is generally much less higher-order consciousness. It is very hard to deny that there is phenomenal consciousness, however. It would be absurd to suppose that there is nothing it is like for a dog that chews a favorite bone or a cat that prefers chopped liver for its dinner over anything else it is offered.
>
> (Ibid., 5)

Carruthers responds that the idea that an experience of which the subject is unaware can none the less be *like something* for it to have is not only counter-intuitive, but verges on incoherence:

For the idea of the *what-it-is-likeness* of *experience* is intended to characterise those aspects of experience which are subjective. But there surely could not be properties of experience which were subjective without being *available to* the subject, and of which the subject was unaware. An experience of which the subject is unaware cannot be one which it *is like something* for the *subject* to have. On the contrary, an experience which it is *like something* to have, must be one which is available to the subject of that experience – and that means being a target (actual or potential) of a suitable HOR.

(Carruthers 1998, 211)

If Carruthers is right, then first-order theories such as Tye's are doomed to failure. But can higher-order theories really do any better? Let us see.

Higher-order representationalism

According to higher-order representational (HOR) theories, phenomenal consciousness involves a kind of inner awareness. Experiences are not phenomenally conscious in their own right, but become so only when we are aware of them in a suitable way. That is, in order to be phenomenally conscious, an experience must be the object of another mental state – a *higher-order* representation.

Several different versions of HOR theory have been proposed. The main point of disagreement between them concerns the nature of the inner awareness involved in consciousness. According to some theories, this awareness is *perceptual* in character – we have an 'inner sense' which generates perceptions of our own experiences. Theories of this kind are known as *higher-order perception* or HOP theories. According to other theories, the awareness involved is *cognitive* and involves having thoughts about our experiences. These are known as *higher-order thought* or HOT theories.

To get an idea of the strengths and weaknesses of the HOR approach, we are going to look at a version of HOT theory developed by the American philosopher David Rosenthal. This will also enable us to compare HOT theory with the rival HOP approach.

Rosenthal's HOT theory

Rosenthal has developed and elaborated his theory in a series of articles published from the mid-1980s onwards. We are going to look at an extract from a 2002 article in which he sets out the case for the theory and argues for its explanatory power.

Turn to Reading 19. Begin by reading the first three paragraphs.

ACTIVITY

1   What is Rosenthal's strategy for developing a theory of consciousness?

2   Give an example of a case where one is aware of possessing a certain mental state without the state itself being a conscious one.

3   What is the difference between state consciousness and transitive consciousness? (If necessary, look back to Chapter 1, page 7.) How are the two related, according to Rosenthal?

DISCUSSION

1   In order for a mental state to be conscious, Rosenthal argues, it is necessary, but not sufficient, for its possessor to be aware of it in some way. His strategy will be to identify the particular type of awareness that is sufficient for consciousness and thereby to establish necessary and sufficient conditions for it.

2   Here is my example. Noticing the way I place my feet as I walk down the street, I infer that I must have a non-conscious desire to avoid treading on the cracks in the pavement. Yet I do not have a conscious desire to avoid doing so. Indeed, I think the idea is silly.

3   State consciousness is a property of mental states. Some mental states are conscious, some are not. Transitive consciousness is a property of individuals. To be transitively conscious of something is to be aware of it – to have some mental state which represents it. According to Rosenthal, state consciousness can be explained in terms of transitive consciousness – for a mental state to be state conscious is for its possessor to be transitively conscious of it. This is not circular since transitive consciousness can be understood independently of state consciousness.

Rosenthal next considers what kind of awareness is involved in consciousness, arguing that it is not perceptual in character.

ACTIVITY Read paragraphs 4–11. Note that by 'intentional states' (paragraph 11) Rosenthal means propositional attitudes – beliefs, desires and so on – as opposed to sense experiences. Rosenthal assumes that conscious intentional states have no phenomenal properties.

1   What does Rosenthal mean by saying that our awareness of our conscious mental states seems *immediate*?

2   What are the two broad ways of being transitively conscious of a mental state?

3   What are the attractions of the perceptual model?

4   What reason does Rosenthal give for rejecting the perceptual model?

DISCUSSION 1   He means that it does not involve any conscious inference; when a mental state is conscious, its possessor knows straight off that they have it, without having to work it out. Contrast the case where I infer from my behaviour that I have a desire to avoid treading on the cracks in the pavement, or the case described by Rosenthal in paragraph 6.

2   Perceiving it or having a thought about it. (Perception here would not, of course, involve our familiar five senses, but some organ of 'inner sense', directed upon our mental states.)

3   Rosenthal lists two. First, since perception is a direct process, which involves no conscious inference, it can explain the immediacy of conscious awareness. Secondly, the perceptual model may be able to explain the qualitative aspect of consciousness (that is, its phenomenal character). The idea is that experiences acquire a phenomenal character as a result of being scanned by the inner sense system.

4   The problem is that our inner sense experiences ought to have distinctive phenomenal properties themselves. Thus, when we have a conscious visual experience of something – a tomato, say – we should expect to be aware of three distinct kinds of properties: (i) the properties of the tomato, (ii) the phenomenal properties of our first-order experience of the tomato and (iii) the phenomenal properties of our higher-order experience of our first-order experience of the tomato. But we are not any aware of any properties of the third kind.

In another paper, Rosenthal expands on his objection to the higher-order perception view. Again, he notes that the view appears initially attractive:

conscious experiences seem to 'light up' subjectively and we might attribute this to their being the object of higher-order perceptions which themselves have a qualitative aspect. But this view, he argues, is fatally flawed:

> Higher-order qualities can't help explain the lighting up unless they are themselves conscious. But, if a state's being conscious consists in its being sensed, the higher-order qualities would be conscious only if there were, in turn, third-order sensations that sensed those second-order sensations. The threat of regress looms. Moreover, the only mental qualities we're ever conscious of are those of first-order conscious states. We're never conscious of distinct, higher-order qualities, even when we become aware of being conscious of the first-order states, as we do when we focus introspectively on those states.
>
> (Rosenthal 2004, 19)

You might like to think about how a HOP theorist could respond to this objection. For example, could they maintain that higher-order perceptions are non-conscious and thus lack any phenomenal character of their own?

ACTIVITY

Return now to Reading 19 and read paragraphs 12–16, in which Rosenthal sets out his own version of HOR theory. Note that an *occurrent* thought is one that is actually being entertained, as opposed to being stored in memory, and that an *assertoric* mental state is one which represents something as being true – a belief as opposed to, for example, a desire, doubt or speculation.

1   What, according to Rosenthal, are the necessary and sufficient conditions for a mental state to be conscious?

2   What is the objection raised in paragraph 14 and what is Rosenthal's reply?

3   What, on Rosenthal's account, is the difference between a mental state that is conscious in the ordinary way and one of which we are introspectively conscious?

4   Summarize the supporting argument outlined in paragraph 16.

DISCUSSION

1   The conditions are that the thinker should currently be having a thought to the effect that they are in the mental state in question and that this thought should not have been arrived at by way of conscious inference.

2   The objection is that we are typically unaware of having higher-order thoughts (HOTs) of the sort described. Rosenthal replies that the thoughts in question are usually not themselves conscious.

3   It is a matter of whether the accompanying HOT is itself non-conscious or conscious. In the latter case, the HOT will be accompanied by a thought of

a yet higher order, to the effect that one is having a thought about the original mental state.

4   If a mental state is conscious, then one can report straight off (non-inferentially) that one is in it. Such a report expresses a thought to the effect that one is in the mental state in question – a HOT. So conscious mental states must be accompanied by HOTs of this kind. Conversely, the fact that we cannot report our non-conscious mental states in this way suggests that they are not accompanied by such HOTs. So it is reasonable to conclude that it is the presence or absence of suitable HOTs that makes the difference between conscious and non-conscious mental states.

So far Rosenthal has stated his account in general terms; it is intended to hold for all conscious mental states – thoughts, as well as experiences. In the next part of the reading he goes on to talk specifically about experiences, or 'sensory states' as he calls them.

ACTIVITY

Now study paragraphs 17–20 of Reading 19, making notes of the answers to the following questions.

1   Under what conditions, according to Rosenthal, is a sensory state conscious?

2   What does Rosenthal mean by 'sensory qualities' and how does sensory quality in his sense differ from *phenomenal character*, in the sense we have been using the term? (Rosenthal does not explicitly address the latter question, so you will need to work out the answer from he does say.)

3   How is phenomenal character related to sensory quality, on Rosenthal's account? (Again, you will need to work out the answer.)

4   Why, according to Rosenthal, do we tend to think that sensory quality cannot exist non-consciously?

DISCUSSION

1   When it possesses the property of state consciousness – which, as Rosenthal has already argued, involves being the object of an appropriate HOT.

2   Sensory qualities are the distinctive properties of sensory states ('whatever properties sensory states have on the basis of which we distinguish among them and sort them into types'). The crucial difference between sensory quality and phenomenal character is that the former can

occur non-consciously. A non-conscious experience has sensory quality, even though it is not like anything to possess it. Phenomenal character, on the other hand, cannot occur non-consciously. The phenomenal character of an experience is *what it is like* to have it, and there is nothing it is like to have a non-conscious experience.

3   An experience acquires a phenomenal character when we are conscious of its sensory qualities – that is, when we have a non-inferential HOT about it.

4   Because, from the first-person point of view, we are never aware of it – it is outside consciousness.

You may be wondering exactly what sensory qualities are supposed to be. Rosenthal says little about them in this paper; elsewhere, however, he makes clear that he regards them as neurological properties, whose existence is not in itself specially problematic (Rosenthal 1999). The key claim is that the really puzzling thing – phenomenal consciousness – occurs when we have HOTs *about* sensory qualities.

But why should that be the case? Why should having a thought about a non-conscious mental state suddenly make it *like something* to have it? Why should the experience 'light up' when it is the object of a HOT? Rosenthal addresses this question in the final part of Reading 19.

Read paragraphs 21–32 of Reading 19.

ACTIVITY

1   Why is first-person evidence unlikely to establish a link between HOTs and what experiences are like?

2   What is Rosenthal's key piece of evidence for such a link?

3   What is the first possible explanation of the evidence and why does Rosenthal dismiss it?

4   What is the second explanation and how does it support HOT theory?

DISCUSSION

1   Because, if Rosenthal is right, the HOTs which render our experiences conscious are usually not themselves conscious. We shall therefore not be subjectively aware of any systematic correlation between our HOTs and what our experiences are like.

2   It is that acquiring new concepts for experiences can alter the phenomenal character of our experiences. Learning to make finer-grained classifications among our experiences can lead to our experiences themselves having a more finely differentiated phenomenal character.

3   The first explanation is that the new concepts somehow cause our experiences to have new sensory qualities which they previously did not have. Rosenthal dismisses this view on the grounds that concepts are abilities to frame thoughts and there is no reason to think they will affect the properties of our sensory states.

4   The second explanation is that the new concepts enable us to become *aware of* sensory qualities that were there, non-consciously, all along. This supports HOT theory since it suggests that it is the ability to frame thoughts about sensory qualities which renders them conscious – and so makes it like something to have the relevant experiences. If we lacked *any* appropriate concepts, Rosenthal suggests, we would be conscious of none of the sensory qualities of our experiences and it would not be like anything to have them.

Assessing HOT theory

Let us try to assess Rosenthal's HOT theory and the HOR approach more generally. On the positive side, Rosenthal's theory avoids some of the problems Tye's theory faced. As we saw, Tye had difficulty accounting for the difference between conscious and non-conscious sensory states; it was not clear why merely being available to the belief system should make the crucial difference. Rosenthal provides a more intuitive answer – a sensory state becomes conscious when we are aware of it, by entertaining an appropriate thought about it. Another problem for Tye was that he seemed unable to account for mental-state subjectivity. Again, Rosenthal's account avoids the problem. According to Rosenthal, we are aware of properties of our experiences – their sensory qualities – as well as of properties of external objects and our own bodies. We thus have a *point of view* on our experiences – something which, if Carruthers is right, is essential for phenomenal consciousness.

There is a cost to these positive features, however, and Rosenthal's account lacks some of the economy of Tye's. Thus, in claiming that we are aware of sensory qualities, Rosenthal is committed to denying that experience is completely *transparent* – that when we attend to our experiences, the only features we are aware of are those represented as being present in the external world or in our own bodies. This is perhaps the key disagreement between Tye and Rosenthal, and you should think carefully about where you stand on it. Rosenthal's account of our phenomenal vocabulary is also more complex than Tye's. Since he holds that we are aware of sensory qualities as well as of properties of external objects, Rosenthal holds that property terms have a different meaning when applied to experiences. When we talk of an afterimage being 'blue', we do not mean simply 'representing blue', as on Tye's account. Rather, we are using the term to refer to the intrinsic sensory quality of the experience – a property which is quite different from that possessed by blue objects. (Rosenthal dubs the former property 'mental blue' and the latter 'physical blue' (Rosenthal 1999).) Similarly with burning smells, stinging pains and so on. When used of experiences, Rosenthal maintains, these terms have a different meaning from the one they have when used of external objects.

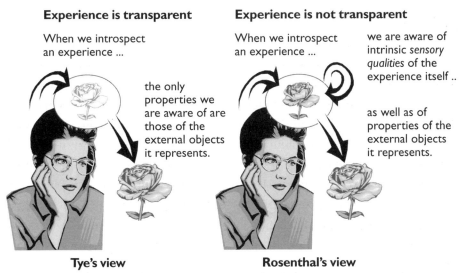

Experience is transparent

When we introspect an experience ...

the only properties we are aware of are those of the external objects it represents.

Tye's view

Experience is not transparent

When we introspect an experience ...

we are aware of intrinsic *sensory qualities* of the experience itself ..

as well as of properties of the external objects it represents.

Rosenthal's view

Figure 11 Is experience transparent?

There are other problems for Rosenthal, too – highlighted both by opponents of a higher-order approach and also by rival HOR theorists. I shall mention three here.

The first concerns the ineffability of conscious experience. We saw that Tye can offer some explanation of this: if phenomenal character is fine-grained, non-conceptual content, then it will have a richness that outstrips our ability to describe it (except indirectly). Rosenthal, by contrast, has a difficulty here. For on his view, sensory qualities become conscious only when we have thoughts about them, and what our experiences are like is directly related to our ability to conceptualize them. If this is right, then, assuming we can verbalize our thoughts, we ought to be able to characterize our experiences adequately simply by expressing the relevant HOTs and should not feel that they possess an inexpressible richness. In this respect, HOP theories may be more attractive than HOT ones. If our awareness of our experiences depends on non-conceptual, perception-like states, then this might explain why we find it so hard to say what our experiences are like (Lycan 2004).

A second problem concerns infants and animals. According to HOT theory, consciousness involves having thoughts about one's mental states. And this requires possession of mental-state concepts, such as that of *experience*. And it is unlikely that infants and (non-human) animals meet this condition. There is evidence that children do not develop mental-state concepts until around the age of three (Perner 1991; Wellman 1990). And, with the possible exception of some primates, animals do not appear to possess them either. But if so, then infants and most animals will be unable to form HOTs and will, consequently, lack conscious experiences. As Fred Dretske points out, this is a counter-intuitive consequence:

> If [infants] are unable to hold higher-order beliefs about lower order thoughts and experiences, are we to conclude, therefore, that none of their thoughts and experience are conscious? They may not, to be sure, be conscious that they have experiences, but that isn't the question. The question is not whether a two-year-old knows what a six-year-old knows (about its own experiences), but whether the experiences of a two-year-old and a six-year-old are, as a result of this fact, fundamentally different – the one being conscious, the other not. If that is a consequence of a HOT theory, it strikes me as very close to a *reductio...*

> The same should be said about animals. I see no reasons to think that because animals have no concept of experience – do not, therefore, know or believe that they have experience – that, therefore, their experience is somehow different from ours. It may be (and probably is) different, of course, but the fact that they have no concept of experience is surely not the reason it is different. When a dog scratches, are we to believe that the itch is not conscious, or that the dog's experience is totally different from ours, because the dog has no conceptual

resources for thinking that it is an itch, that it is irritating, or whatever (on a HOT theory) one has to think about an experience to make it conscious?

(Dretske 1995, 110–11)

Again, HOP theories may be better placed. Perhaps infants and animals can *sense* their own mental states, even though they lack the conceptual resources needed to *think* about them. (Compare the way a cat can see a telephone, even though it cannot think about telephones as such.) This suggestion may have its own problems, however. For why would animals have developed an organ of inner sense if they lacked the conceptual resources needed to think about the information it delivers?

A third problem concerns the function of consciousness. Here all versions of HOR theory face a difficulty. It is natural to think that whether or not a mental state is conscious makes an important difference to its effects. So, for example, we assume that a conscious pain will provoke reactions that a non-conscious one would not. Yet HOR theories seem to be committed to denying this. Again Dretske sums up the objection:

> HO theories of state-consciousness make questions about the function of consciousness hard to answer. Or, worse, they make the answer obvious: it has no function. If what makes E (some experience) conscious is the fact that S (the person in whom the experience occurs) is, somehow, aware of E, then it is clear that E's causal powers (as opposed to S's causal powers) are unaffected by the fact that it is conscious. The causal powers of a rock (as opposed to *my* causal powers) are not changed or enhanced by my observing the rock or having thoughts about it. Why should the causal powers of a thought or an experience be any different? If the consciousness of mental states and processes comes down to higher-order experiences of them, or higher-order thoughts about them, then consciousness is epiphenomenal. Mental states and processes would be no less effective in doing their job – whatever, exactly, we take that job to be – if they were unconscious. According to HO theories of consciousness, asking about the function of conscious states in mental affairs would be like asking what the function of conscious diseases – those we knew about – was in medicine.

(Ibid., 117)

1 In what sense would consciousness be epiphenomenal, according to Dretske, if some version of HOR theory were true?

ACTIVITY

2 Why does Dretske think that HOR theories make consciousness epiphenomenal?

3   Do HOR theories imply that consciousness has no effects at all, according to Dretske?

1   In the sense that it would make no difference to the causal roles of our mental states. A pain, for example, would have exactly the same effects regardless of whether or not it was conscious.

2   Because they identify consciousness with awareness and the fact that someone is aware of an object does not, in itself, alter the causal powers of the object.

3   No. Dretske accepts that consciousness may have effects on the person in whom the conscious experience occurs. Thus, if I am aware that I am having a certain experience, then I may go on to entertain further thoughts about it – speculating about its causes and effects, for example, or even engaging in philosophical reflection on the nature of experience itself.

You might like to think about how HOT theorists could respond to these objections. Take the second. One possible response would be to bite the bullet and deny that infants and animals do have phenomenally conscious experiences. At least one HOT theorist – Peter Carruthers – takes just this line. He accepts that infants and animals have experiences – pains, pleasures, perceptions and so on – and that these have all the usual effects on their behaviour. But he denies that their experiences are conscious – that it is *like anything* to have them (Carruthers 2000, Chapter 7). This view is highly counter-intuitive, of course, but that can be explained. For as Carruthers points out, when we think about the experiences of animals, we try to imagine what they are like. And, of course, when we do this we inevitably imagine *conscious* experiences like our own. It is impossible to imagine what it is like to have a non-conscious experience!

This view could be bolstered by biting the bullet on the third objection and accepting that consciousness is epiphenomenal in the sense described by Dretske. One reason for thinking that infants and animals *do* have conscious experiences is that we think that consciousness is necessary for the sort of behaviour they display. But if consciousness makes little difference to behaviour, then this inference will be unsound. Thus, the view that infants and animals do not have phenomenally conscious experiences may not be as unacceptable as Dreskte supposes.

As a closing thought, it is worth considering whether, if we were to accept that animals and infants lack phenomenal consciousness, important moral consequences would follow. If the pains of infants and animals are not conscious – not *like anything* – would there be any reason for us to care about them? This is one way in which philosophy of mind can link up with wider issues.

Conclusion

In this chapter we have looked at two representational theories of consciousness. Both have weaknesses, of course, and it may be that neither is correct. But this is an area of on-going research and many philosophers believe that a representational approach offers the best hope for constructing a naturalistic theory of phenomenal consciousness. Whether any such theory will ever provide a really convincing solution to the hard problem is another matter. Certainly those, such as Chalmers, who think that physicalism is false will not be persuaded – not, at least, if the proposed theory is coupled with a physicalist theory of representational content. But many physicalists hope that by combining some of the defensive moves discussed in the previous chapter with constructive theorizing of the sort considered in the present one, it will eventually be possible to crack the hard problem.

Further reading

For more detail on Tye's PANIC theory and responses to objections, see:

TYE, M. (1995) *Ten Problems of Consciousness: A Representational Theory of the Phenomenal Mind*, Cambridge, Mass., MIT Press.

TYE, M. (2000) *Consciousness, Color, and Content*, Cambridge, Mass., MIT Press. (A collection of essays elaborating and defending the theory.)

For two other versions of FOR theory, see:

DRETSKE, F. (1995) *Naturalizing the Mind*, Cambridge, Mass., MIT Press, Chapters 3 and 4.

KIRK, R. (1994) *Raw Feeling*, Oxford, Oxford University Press.

Rosenthal has developed his version of HOT theory in a series of papers. See in particular:

ROSENTHAL, D.M. (1991) 'The independence of consciousness and sensory quality', *Philosophical Issues*, 1, 15–36.

ROSENTHAL, D.M. (2002) 'Explaining consciousness', in D.J. Chalmers (ed.), *Philosophy of Mind: Classical and Contemporary Readings*, New York, Oxford University Press, pp.406–21. (The full version of the paper from which Reading 19 is taken.)

At the time of writing (2004) Rosenthal is preparing a collection of papers on consciousness to be published by Oxford University Press under the title *Consciousness and Mind*.

For other versions of HOR theory see:

CARRUTHERS, P. (2000) *Phenomenal Consciousness: A Naturalistic Theory*, Cambridge, Cambridge University Press. (Sets out a sophisticated version of HOR theory which combines elements of HOT and HOP approaches. Also includes an extended critique of FOR theories and rival HOR theories.)

CARRUTHERS, P. (forthcoming). *Consciousness: Essays from a Higher-Order Perspective*, Oxford, Oxford University Press. (A collection of essays exploring different aspects of the theory set out in his 2000.)

GENNARO, R.J. (ed.) (2004) *Higher-Order Theories of Consciousness: An Anthology*, Amsterdam, John Benjamins. (A very useful collection, containing essays by both defenders and critics of the HOR approach. Includes essays by Carruthers, Lycan and Rosenthal, among others.)

LYCAN, W.G. (1996) *Consciousness and Experience*, Cambridge, Mass., MIT Press, Chapter 2. (Defends a version of HOP theory.)

See also Section X of Block et al. 1997, which is devoted to HOR theories and includes papers by Dretske, Lycan and Rosenthal, among others.

If you are interested in the moral consequences of claims about consciousness, you may like to look at some of Carruthers's work on the topic. In his earlier writings he argued that if animal experiences are not phenomenally conscious, then they are not appropriate objects of sympathy and moral concern. See:

CARRUTHERS, P. (1989) 'Brute experience', *The Journal of Philosophy*, 86, 258–69.

CARRUTHERS, P. (1992) *The Animals Issue*, Cambridge, Cambridge University Press, Chapter 8.

In more recent work, however, he rejects this conclusion and argues that the mere fact that animals *desire* their pains to cease is reason enough to sympathize with them – even if their pains and desires are not conscious. See Carruthers 2000, Chapter 7 and also:

CARRUTHERS, P. (1999) 'Sympathy and subjectivity.' *Australasian Journal of Philosophy*, 77, 465–82. (Also included in his forthcoming collection, listed above.)

Rethinking consciousness

I anticipate a day when philosophers and scientists and laypeople will chuckle over the fossil traces of our earlier bafflement about consciousness: 'It still *seems* as if these mechanistic theories of consciousness leave something out, but of course that's an illusion. They do, in fact, explain everything about consciousness that needs explanation.'

(Dennett 2001, 43)

Think back to Chapter 1 and how I introduced the notion of phenomenal consciousness. I drew on your first-person experience – I asked you to imagine the various experiences you would have on coming round from an anaesthetic. It is common to begin discussions of consciousness with an imaginative appeal of this kind. Indeed, it is often said that consciousness is an essentially subjective phenomenon, which can only be grasped from the first-person perspective. (Writers on consciousness like to quote Louis Armstrong's reply when asked what jazz is: 'If you got to ask, you ain't never gonna get to know'.) But some philosophers think that appeals like this can be misleading. They think that introspection fosters misconceptions about consciousness, which make it seem more mysterious than it really is and which bedevil philosophical thinking on the topic. These philosophers maintain that we need to *rethink* consciousness – to strip away the misconceptions and get a clearer view of what it is that we are trying to explain. A vigorous advocate of this view is the American philosopher Daniel Dennett, and I want to use this final chapter to introduce some of his ideas, as set out in his 1991 book *Consciousness Explained*.

The 'Cartesian Theatre'

How could we be wrong about our own experience? Surely, that is the one thing we *cannot* be wrong about? Indeed, it is often claimed that our knowledge of our own experience is *infallible*: we can be mistaken about what the world is like, but not about what our experience of it is like – how the world seems to us. There may be a sense in which this is right, but it is wise to be cautious about the claim. If you are normally sighted, doesn't it seem that your visual field is rich and detailed, right out the edges? Most people are inclined to say yes. But try the following experiment (described in Dennett 1991, 53–4). Take a playing card and, without looking to see what it is, hold it out at arm's length, so that it is positioned at the edge of your visual field (keep your gaze fixed straight ahead). Can you see what the card is – or even what colour it is? Now bring the card closer to the centre of your visual field – again keeping your gaze fixed straight ahead. How close to the centre do you have to bring the card before you can identify it? You may be surprised by the answer.

This suggests that our commonsense views about the nature of our experience can be mistaken and can be corrected by argument and experiment. And, according to Dennett, over-reliance on common sense has lead to some damaging *theoretical* assumptions. The most serious of these, he claims, is the assumption that there is a 'headquarters' in the brain where sensory information is assembled and conscious experience occurs. From a commonsense perspective, this view is very plausible. Take visual experience. It is now known that different aspects of visual experience – colour, shape, movement and so on – are processed in different parts of the brain and at slightly different times. Yet, subjectively, we seem to have a stream of unified visual experience in which all the various elements are bound together and presented in an orderly sequence. So, it seems, there must be some place where visual information is assembled, integrated and displayed for conscious awareness.

Dennett concedes that this view is tempting, but argues that it is both ill-conceived (who is supposed to be watching the inner show?) and contradicted by empirical evidence (neuroanatomy reveals no structure to which all sensory information is routed). In fact, Dennett suggests, the view is a relic of the discredited model of the mind associated with Descartes. Descartes thought that sensory information was channelled to the pineal gland in the centre of the brain, which then relayed it to the immaterial soul. Few contemporary philosophers believe in the soul, but Dennett suggests that many still hold on to the idea that there is a neural headquarters of some sort, where sensory information is presented for conscious awareness – a bit like a show on an interior stage. Dennett dubs this supposed headquarters the 'Cartesian Theatre' and refers to belief in it as 'Cartesian materialism'.

In setting out the case against Cartesian materialism and developing his own alternative view, Dennett uses a variety of argumentative techniques,

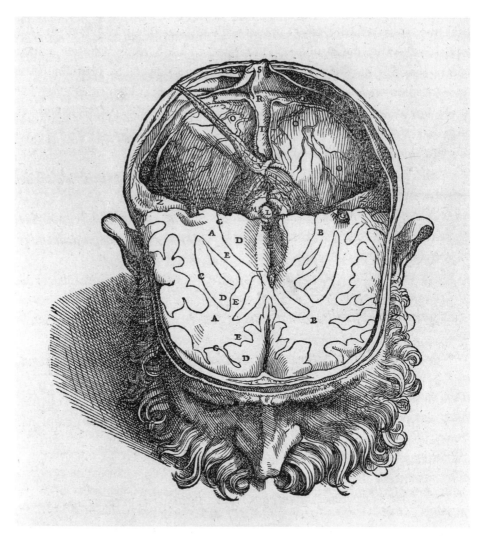

Figure 12 A Cartesian Theatre? Drawing of the brain by Andreas Vesalius ('L' marks the pineal gland). From *De humani corporis fabrica*, Basle, J. Oporinus, 1543. Photo: Wellcome Library, London.

including thought experiments, metaphors and reflection on recent scientific research in psychology and neuroscience. We can get a flavour of his approach from one of his key examples, which concerns a visual illusion known as the 'colour phi phenomenon'.

The illusion works like this. Two spots of light are flashed on and off in front of a spectator: first a red spot and then, to the right, a green one. If the timing is right, the spectator will report seeing, not two spots of different colours, but a single spot moving from left to right and changing from red to green halfway (see Figure 13). The brain mistakenly infers that there was just one spot, which moved and changed colour. (A similar effect can be observed in neon advertising signs which seem to display moving images.) This phenomenon is puzzling, for the spectator seems to see the red spot moving and changing colour *before* the green spot appears. Yet that is impossible! Until the brain had registered the green spot, it could not possibly have known in which direction to represent the red spot as moving or what colour to represent it as changing to.

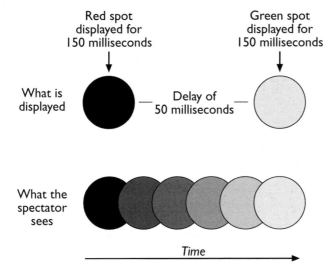

Red spot displayed for 150 milliseconds

Green spot displayed for 150 milliseconds

What is displayed

Delay of 50 milliseconds

What the spectator sees

Time

Figure 13 The colour phi phenomenon.

Now if Cartesian materialism were true, then there would be at least two possible explanations here. One would be that both spots were perceived non-consciously and that conscious awareness of them was delayed until after the brain had finished interpreting the data. Then the final sequence (red spot, red spot moving and turning green, green spot) was displayed in the Cartesian Theatre. Dennett refers to this as the 'Stalinesque' model, since it claims that an 'official' version of events was staged for conscious consumption, like the faked show trials held in the Soviet Union in the 1930s. The second explanation is that the two spots *were* consciously experienced, but that, before the spectator had time to report this, their *memories* were edited to reflect the brain's new interpretation of the situation. That is, conscious experiences of distinct red and green spots were displayed in the Cartesian Theatre, without any illusion of movement, but the memory of this was almost immediately erased and replaced by a false memory of a single spot moving and changing colour. Dennett calls this the 'Orwellian' model, after George

Orwell's novel *Nineteen Eighty-Four*, in which the authorities propagate their version of history by retrospectively revising important documents to make them fit the party line.

If Cartesian materialism were correct, then there would be a fact of the matter as to which of these models was correct. But, Dennett argues, there is no evidence that could settle the issue. Consider the options. First, we might try asking the spectator. This won't help, however, for they will say, quite sincerely, that they saw a single spot moving and changing colour, and this is compatible with both explanations – in one case that they really did have such an experience (albeit an artificially staged one), in the other that they have a false memory of having had one. Secondly, we might investigate the spectator's non-verbal reactions. For example, we might test whether their awareness of the red spot was delayed (as on the Stalinesque model) by asking them to press a button as soon as they see the red spot. But, Dennett argues, this would not be conclusive either. For even if there was no delay in the button-push, it would not follow that there was none in *consciousness*; the button-push might have been generated *non-consciously*. Finally, we might turn to neuroscience for an answer. But again, Dennett argues, any information about the brain would be compatible with both explanations. Defenders of both models can agree about when and where in the brain the presence of each spot was registered and the false belief in movement laid down in memory; they just disagree about whether these events occurred before or after consciousness. Dennett concludes that the difference between the two models is illusory:

> So, in spite of first appearances, there is really only a verbal difference between the two theories... The two theories tell exactly the same story except for where they place a mythical Great Divide, a point in time (and hence a place in space) whose *fine-grained* location is nothing that subjects can help them locate, and whose location is also neutral with regard to all other features of their theories. This is a difference that makes no difference.

> (Dennett 1991, 125)

In short, the two models agree on everything except the exact time and place at which consciousness happened – the moment when the curtain went up in the Cartesian Theatre. And, Dennett argues, since all the data, from both the first-person and third-person perspectives, can be accounted for without reference to this moment of consciousness, there is no need to posit such a time and place at all. Think of it like this. Suppose there are two theories of what is wrong with a car's engine, which agree on all the mechanical details but differ as to the time and place at which an invisible gremlin cast a spell on the machine. The right thing to say in this case would surely be, not that we could never tell which theory was right, but that both were misguided in talking about the gremlin at all. This is exactly Dennett's attitude to the Stalinesque and Orwellian models. Both, he thinks, are fundamentally flawed by their underlying Cartesian materialist assumptions.

Multiple drafts and the 'Joycean machine'

Dennett's alternative to Cartesian materialism has two components – the 'Multiple Drafts' model of conscious experience and an account of what he calls the 'Joycean machine'. Again Dennett's presentation is complex, but I shall briefly introduce the ideas, beginning with the Multiple Drafts model.

According to this model, information gathered by localized neural subsystems does not have to be routed to a headquarters for conscious appreciation:

> Feature detections or discriminations *only have to be made once*. That is, once a particular 'observation' of some feature has been made, by a specialized, localized portion of the brain, the information content thus fixed does not have to be sent somewhere else to be rediscriminated by some 'master' discriminator.
>
> (Ibid., 113)

Moreover, there is no single canonical version of conscious experience. Rather, there are multiple versions in existence at any one time, like different drafts of an academic essay, each subject to continual editing and revision. I shall let Dennett explain further in an extract from *Consciousness Explained*. (In this passage Dennett focuses on visual experience, but he makes it clear that he thinks similar considerations apply to other forms of sense experience.)

Study Reading 20 and summarize Dennett's answers to the following questions. Note that by a 'probe', Dennett means a *question*. Probing someone involves asking them to report on their experience in some way.

ACTIVITY

1 In what ways does the 'skein of contents' generated by our perceptual processes resemble a narrative and in what ways does it differ from one? (Paragraph 2)

2 What is the effect of a probe? (Paragraph 3)

3   Is the content of the stream of consciousness precisely defined? (Paragraphs 5 and 8)

4   How does the Multiple Drafts model account for the colour phi phenomenon? (Paragraphs 5–6)

5   What distinguishes conscious experiences from non-conscious ones? (See in particular paragraphs 7 and 8)

DISCUSSION

1   It resembles a narrative in that it incorporates an account of what is happening which gradually unfolds over time. It is unlike a narrative in that at any one time it contains multiple strands.

2   Probing interrupts the stream and precipitates a narrative corresponding to one of the versions available. Which version emerges depends on exactly when the probe is made.

3   Not apart from probes. A probe elicits a determinate content, but before a probe is made there is no canonical version of experience awaiting expression.

4   The explanation relies on Dennett's claim that there are no fixed facts about the stream of consciousness independent of particular probes. Since the spectator reports having seen a red spot moving and turning green before seeing a stationary green spot, that is the subjective order of events. This subjective time-line can then be compared with the objective order in which these contents were generated in the brain – which was the other way round. There are no further facts about the sequence in which the events appeared in consciousness, since no definitive conscious presentation took place.

5   Conscious experiences are ones that are *available* to report in response to a probe – whether or not a probe is actually made. Thus, the absent-minded driver counts as having consciously experienced the cars around them, since if they had been probed at the time, they would have reported seeing them.

It may be objected that Dennett misses out the heart of the matter – namely how things *seem* to us. Consider the colour phi phenomenon again. Surely, the objector may say, it is not just that the spectator *reports* the events as having occurred in the revised order; the events actually *seemed* to them to occur in that order. They report seeing the red spot moving and turning green before they saw the green spot precisely because they had a prior conscious experience of it happening that way. And surely there would be a fact of the matter about how it seemed to them, even if they immediately forgot all about it and were unable to report it a moment later?

Dennett simply denies this. He argues that there is no need to postulate a prior episode of 'seeming', in addition to the judgement expressed in the subject's report, since all the effects can be accounted for without it:

> Postulating a 'real seeming' *in addition to* the judging or 'taking' expressed in the subject's report is multiplying entities beyond necessity. Worse, it is multiplying entities beyond possibility; the sort of inner presentation in which real seemings happen is a hopeless metaphysical dodge... When you discard Cartesian dualism, you really must discard the show that would have gone on in the Cartesian Theatre...
>
> (Ibid., 134)

Dennett reiterates the point in a later passage, replying to an imaginary opponent:

> You seem to think there's a difference between thinking (judging, deciding, being of the heartfelt opinion that) something seems pink to you and something *really seeming* pink to you. But there is no difference. There is no such phenomenon as really seeming – over and above the phenomenon of judging in one way or another that something is the case.
>
> (Ibid., 364)

Think back to the playing-card experiment. Our visual field *seems* to be rich and detailed right out the edges, but perhaps that it is just to say that we *think* it is and do not notice that it isn't. Here is another of Dennett's examples (ibid., 354–5). Imagine entering a room that is papered with hundreds of identical portraits of Marilyn Monroe. In the first few seconds you would not have time to scan more than one or two of the portraits in any detail. Yet (assuming you have normal vision) you would 'see' hundreds of detailed portraits of Marilyn – not a couple of detailed ones and a lot of blurry Marilyn-shaped blobs. What happens? Does your brain 'copy and paste' the scanned portraits to fill in the gaps, creating a detailed internal image of the room? No, says Dennett: there is no need to do so, since there is no Cartesian Theatre in which to display the image. Rather your brain simply represents *that* the room is papered with hundreds of detailed Marilyns. The room *seems* like that because you *judge* it to be like that.

On this view, then, our memories and reports of our experience are partially *constitutive* of the experience itself: to say that it seemed to the colour phi spectator that the movement and colour change preceded the green spot is to say that that is what they remember and are disposed to report:

> The Multiple Drafts model makes 'writing it down' in memory criterial for consciousness... There is no reality of conscious experience independently of the effects of various vehicles of content on subsequent action (and hence, of course, on memory).

(Ibid., 132)

Dennett does not deny that this view is counter-intuitive, but does not regard that as a problem. For he maintains that our intuitions in this area are seriously misleading. We think there are seemings, but there aren't any really!

It may be helpful at this point to compare Dennett's view of consciousness with those of Tye and Rosenthal.

ACTIVITY

1   Are there any general similarities between Dennett's views and those of Tye and Rosenthal?

2   What differences are there between their views?

3   What would Tye and Rosenthal say about the Orwellian and Stalinesque models of the colour phi phenomenon?

4   Are Tye and Rosenthal committed to the existence of a Cartesian Theatre?

DISCUSSION

1   Yes: like Tye and Rosenthal, Dennett explains consciousness in terms of representational states and their access relations – in terms of perceptual discriminations and their effects on memory and speech. His account, like theirs, thus opens the way to a reductive explanation of consciousness.

2   The key difference is that, unlike Dennett, Tye and Rosenthal think there are fixed facts about consciousness independent of particular probes. Both think that conscious experience may have a determinate content – say, of seeing a blue square for a split second – even if the subject is subsequently unable to remember or report it. On Tye's view, this would be the case if the subject had a momentary sensory state with a PANIC to the effect that a blue square was present; on Rosenthal's view, if they had a similar sensory state that was the target of a HOT. Tye and Rosenthal thus think that there can be 'real seemings', independent of our reports.

CHAPTER 5 RETHINKING CONSCIOUSNESS

3   They would say that the models do correspond to genuine alternatives and that we might obtain evidence that would support one over the other. For example, Tye would say that the Orwellian model would be supported if there were evidence that the spectator had had short-lived sensory states with PANICs *stationary red spot* and *stationary green spot* which left no trace in memory. Rosenthal would say the same if there were evidence that the spectator had had similar sensory states that were the target of appropriate HOTs.

4   This is a tricky question. Dennett would say yes, but Tye and Rosenthal might reply that their position is more subtle. They need not hold that there is a single *place* in the brain to which all sensory information is routed, just that there are *processes* – perhaps distributed over large areas of the brain – by which sensory information is integrated and made available to other mental faculties such as belief formation and higher-order thinking.

Let us turn now, briefly, to the second part of Dennett's theory of consciousness. One obvious problem for the Multiple Drafts model is that it seems unable to account for the unity and coherence of consciousness. Surely our stream of consciousness is not as multi-stranded as the model suggests? Dennett accepts this but argues that it does not undermine the model. The Multiple Drafts model is concerned mainly with the activities of specialized neural subsystems whose development is to a large extent genetically determined. But consciousness of the human kind, Dennett argues, goes beyond this. It involves an extra layer of mental activity, which is the product of human culture rather than genetics.

The idea is that we have learned certain tricks and habits of mind which help to coordinate the activities of our neural subsystems and create the sense of a unified, single-track consciousness. The chief of these tricks, according to Dennett, is the habit of *inner speech* – talking to ourselves in silent soliloquy. This activity, Dennett suggests, is a kind of *self-stimulation*. If you ask yourself a question (*probe* yourself) you may prompt yourself to articulate an answer (a bit of *narrative*) containing information possessed by some neural subsystem. This answer will then be 'heard' by the auditory system and the information it carries broadcast to other neural subsystems, thereby giving the information wider currency and enhanced influence. Similar self-stimulatory effects, Dennett claims, come from reminding yourself of something or exhorting yourself to do something. In this way, inner speech comes to play the role of a central control system – helping to focus attention and promote consistent patterns of behaviour. In tribute to James Joyce, whose 1922 novel *Ulysses* contains vivid depictions of the human stream of consciousness, Dennett dubs this system the *Joycean machine*.

Although the Joycean machine performs the functions of a control system, it is not a headquarters in the brain (not a Cartesian control room), but more like a computer program running on the hardware of the brain (Dennett calls it a 'virtual machine'). The difference is a bit like that between a government department and a newspaper. Whereas a government department makes official decisions and executes them directly, using the resources of the state, the newspaper influences events simply by what its journalists report, without actually being in charge and without presenting a definitive version of events. Again, then, Dennett is inviting us to rethink the way the conscious mind works.

Qualia and what it is like

But what about the what-it-is-likeness of experience – the phenomenal properties, the *qualia*? It depends what we mean by these terms. If we mean properties of the 'real seemings' on show in Cartesian Theatre – the ineffable, intrinsic properties of experience that Chalmers talked about in his catalogue (see Reading 1) – then Dennett flatly denies that they exist. Phenomenal properties in this sense are, he maintains, a figment of philosophers' imaginations. He does not deny, however, that we can meaningfully talk about what an experience is like – provided such talk is stripped of its traditional Cartesian assumptions.

To illustrate Dennett's views I want to introduce an example from an earlier paper of his. Here he describes two coffee tasters, Chase and Sanborn, whose job is to ensure the consistency of taste of a certain brand of coffee. They both agree that, although the coffee has not changed, they no longer enjoy their job. They have different explanations for this, however. Chase says:

> the coffee tastes just the same today as it tasted when I arrived. But, you know, I no longer like it! My tastes have changed. I've become a more sophisticated coffee drinker. I no longer like *that taste* at all.

> (Dennett 1988, 52)

Sanborn, however, gives a different explanation:

> I, like you, really don't care for the coffee we're making. But *my* tastes haven't changed; my... *tasters* have changed. That is, I think something has gone wrong with my taste buds or some other part of my taste-analyzing perceptual machinery. [The coffee] doesn't taste to me the way it used to taste; if only it did, I'd still love it, for I still think *that taste* is the best taste in coffee.
>
> (Ibid.)

ACTIVITY

1   How would you summarize the two explanations?

2   In what way are the two explanations similar to the two models of the colour phi phenomenon discussed earlier?

3   What do you think Dennett would say about the two explanations?

DISCUSSION

1   According to Chase, the coffee produces the same taste experience it always did, but he no longer likes that experience; according to Sanborn, the coffee no longer produces the same taste experience. (Putting it in terms of phenomenal properties, Chase thinks the experience has the same phenomenal properties it used to have, but he no longer reacts positively to them; Chase thinks the experience has different phenomenal properties.)

2   Chase's explanation is similar to the Orwellian model in that it postulates a change *after* the moment of experience. Sanborn's explanation is similar to the Stalinesque model in that it postulates a change *prior* to the moment of experience.

3   He would say that they are misguided. Since there is no precise time or place at which experience occurs – no Cartesian Theatre – it makes no sense to ask whether the changes occurred before or after this point.

The view suggested is indeed the one Dennett takes. He does not deny, of course, that different kinds of changes might have occurred in Chase and Sanborn. A complex sequence of events occurs between the first impact of coffee on the taste buds and the subsequent behavioural reactions and reports, and changes could occur at many different points in this sequence. What he *does* deny is that there is any privileged point in this sequence at which 'the experience' of the coffee occurs and its phenomenal properties are appreciated. In Dennett's view, it is a mistake to think of 'the taste' of the coffee as an introspectible mental property, which we appreciate and react to.

Rather, the taste is *constituted* by the reactions the coffee triggers in us – its effects on speech, memory, perceptual set (see Reading 20), emotional state and other behavioral dispositions. Dennett sums up his view in a later paper:

> Supposing that there is something in addition to these complex families of reactive dispositions is falling for an illusion, plain and simple... [It involves] the natural but treacherous assumption that reactive dispositions must involve the person reacting *to* a quale, presented somehow to the reactor, and causing, by its presentation, the reaction... For instance, here's how pain works: the pain networks produce (somewhere central?) the awfulness quale, which is then the very property to which 'one' reacts with abhorrence. My view is that this confuses cause and effect; it is the reactions that *compose* the 'introspectable property' and it is *through reacting* that one 'identifies' or 'recognizes' the property.

> (Dennett 1993, 927)

On Dennett's view, then, what we are really referring to, when we talk about what an experience is like, is a complex set of reactions and associations. And it is these reactions and associations, Dennett claims, that are the source of our intuitions about qualia:

> What *anchors* our naive sense that there are such properties as qualia are the multiple, asymmetrical, interdependent set of reactive dispositions by which we acquaint ourselves with the sensible world. Our sense that the color red has, as it were, an identity, a 'personality' all its own is *due to* the host of *different* associations that go with each color... [If there were creatures] lacking all such reactive landmarks in their dispositional make-up, [they] would not think they had qualia at all – what it was like to have one sort of experience would not differ at all from what it was like to have a different one!

> (Ibid.)

Thus Chase is mistaken to think that the coffee tastes the same even though his reactions to it have changed. Dennett points the moral in a coda to the story:

> When [Chase] told his wife his original tale, she said 'Don't be silly! Once you add the dislike you change the experience!' – and the more he thought about it, the more he decided she was right.

> (Dennett 1988, 60)

This is a very different view of conscious experience from the one we have been preoccupied with in previous chapters, and I want to round off this chapter by highlighting some of its implications.

1 What would Dennett say about the possibility of undetectable spectrum inversion (the idea that two people might experience colours differently even though their reactions to them are just the same)?

2 What would Dennett say about zombies and the Mary case?

3 What do you think Dennett's attitude to the hard problem would be?

1 He would deny that it is possible or even, strictly speaking, conceivable. If what it is like to see a given colour is a matter of the reactive dispositions things of that colour trigger in us, then any two people who have exactly the same reactive dispositions necessarily have the same colour experiences. Since a person's reactive dispositions are in principle detectable, through questioning or other forms of testing, undetectable differences in colour experience can be ruled out a priori.

2 He would deny that zombies are conceivable – for the same reason given in (1). (Remember, zombies are supposed to be behaviourally identical to us.) He would also deny that Mary would learn anything on leaving her room, since she would already have learned all about the reactive dispositions associated with different colours. (You might find it useful at this point to look again at Readings 9 and 12.)

3 He would say that there isn't one. The hard problem is that of explaining the phenomenal properties of experience, understood as something over and above the associated reactions (explaining the latter is among Chalmers's 'easy' problems). Dennett denies that such properties exist, so he thinks there is no hard problem. Thus, on Dennett's view, consciousness presents no special obstacle to reductive explanation: once we have a clear view of exactly what needs explaining, we can see that physicalist theories (functionalist ones, for example) are adequate to the task. (See the quote at the head of this chapter.)

Conclusion

I am going to leave you to assess Dennett's position for yourself. Its main attraction is that it cuts through the mystery of consciousness. On Dennett's view, when we talk about what our experiences are like, we are not gesturing at some mysterious mental ingredient, presented to us in a private inner realm and standing in a puzzling relation to the rest of the world; rather, we are referring to nothing more than a complex set of reactive dispositions. For many people, however, Dennett's medicine is worse than the illness. They hold that in denying the existence of 'real seemings', independent of our reactions and reports, Dennett is simply ignoring the phenomenon that needs to be explained. (It is often said that he should have called his book *Consciousness Explained Away*.) Dennett would not deny that his account is counter-intuitive – and he has a lot more to say about why we succumb to the illusion of the Cartesian Theatre – but he would insist that the problems associated with other views of consciousness make them even more unpalatable.

Further reading

If you want explore Dennett's views in more detail, the best place to start is with *Consciousness Explained* (Little, Brown, 1991; reprinted in paperback by Penguin Books, 1993). This is a lively and engaging book, full of arguments, thought experiments and fascinating scientific information. Much of it is very controversial, however, and you should maintain a healthy critical stance.

You might also look at:

DENNETT, D.C. (1988) 'Quining qualia', in A. Marcel and E. Bisiach (eds), *Consciousness in Contemporary Science*, Oxford, Oxford University Press, pp.43–77. Reprinted in Block et al. 1997. (Contains a series of *intuition pumps*, including the Chase and Sanborn story, designed to undermine belief in qualia, as traditionally conceived ['to quine' means 'to deny the existence of']).

DENNETT, D.C. & KINSBOURNE, M. (1992) 'Time and the observer: the where and when of consciousness in the brain', *Behavioural and Brain Sciences*, 15, 183–247. Reprinted in Block et al. 1997. (A summary of Dennett's case against the Cartesian Theatre and for the Multiple Drafts model. With a set of replies from philosophers, psychologists and neuroscientists. Technical in places.)

Some of Dennett's later essays on consciousness are included in his 1998 collection, *Brainchildren* (Penguin). These include the paper on zombies from which Reading 12 is taken, a discussion of robot consciousness and a short paper called 'Real Consciousness', which introduces and updates Dennett's accounts of the Cartesian Theatre and the Multiple Drafts model.

At the time of writing, Dennett is preparing a new book, *Sweet Dreams: Philosophical Obstacles to a Science of Consciousness*, which promises a 'revision and renewal' of his theory of consciousness. This will be published by MIT Press in 2005.

Finally, for some critical discussion of Dennett's views, you might look at two symposia on *Consciousness Explained* published in the early 1990s:

VARIOUS AUTHORS (1993) 'Dennett symposium', *Philosophy and Phenomenological Research*, 53, 889–931. (Includes short papers by Jackson, Rosenthal, Tye and Sydney Shoemaker, together with a paper by Dennett replying to them and expanding on some of the themes of *Consciousness Explained*. The papers by Rosenthal and Tye are particularly useful in highlighting points of agreement and disagreement between them and Dennett.)

VARIOUS AUTHORS (1993) 'Symposium on Daniel C. Dennett *Consciousness Explained*', *Inquiry*, 36, 3–159. (Another collection of critical papers, together with Dennett's reply.)

Conclusion

> When it comes to consciousness, it can seem that *all* the alternatives are bad.
>
> (Chalmers 1996, 160)

We are now coming to the end of our study of the problem of consciousness and it is time to pull the threads together. Think back to the discussion of the elusiveness of consciousness in Chapter 1. When we attend to our experiences, they seem to have an intrinsic feel, or *phenomenal character*, which is hard to characterize (*ineffable*) and can be appreciated only from the first-person point of view (*subjective*). Moreover these feels seem to be distinct from brain processes: it seems possible to imagine exactly the same brain processes occurring with a different feel or without any feel at all (the *spectrum inversion* and *zombie intuitions*), and it seems that we could know all the facts about a creature's brain processes without knowing what its experiences were like (the *Mary intuition*). These impressions and intuitions collectively constitute what we may call the *introspective picture* of consciousness, and we can classify different views of consciousness by their attitude towards it.

Property dualists take the introspective picture very seriously. They accept our intuitions about the distinctness of consciousness and hold that introspection really does acquaint us with essentially subjective, non-physical properties. On their view, the phenomenal properties of experience cannot be explained in more basic terms, and our catalogue of the fundamental components of the universe will have to be expanded to include them. The main problem for this position is that it is hard to reconcile with the commonsense view that how our experiences feel affects how we act. In respecting our intuitions about the specialness of consciousness, property dualists threaten to make consciousness *too* special to have any effects within the physical world (the threat of *epiphenomenalism*).

Physicalists are more cautious in their attitude to the introspective picture. They do not trust our intuitions about the distinctness of consciousness and deny that introspection reveals essentially subjective, non-physical properties. Some, such as Dennett, reject the intuitions of distinctness outright, arguing that we cannot clearly imagine zombies and that we are mistaken to suppose that Mary would learn something about vision on leaving her room. Others accept the intuitions but argue that they do not have the metaphysical consequences property dualists think they have. Thus, they agree that zombies and spectrum inversion are conceivable but deny that they are metaphysically possible. Similarly, they concede that Mary would learn something on leaving her room but argue that this does not show that phenomenal properties are essentially subjective, non-physical ones. One popular option here is to argue that in having an experience for ourselves we acquire a new *phenomenal concept* for it, which allows us to think about it in a new way (the *perspectivalist view*).

Many physicalists do none the less accept the key feature of the introspective picture – the claim that experiences have phenomenal properties, of which we are introspectively aware. However, they aim to explain these properties in physical terms – to show how a physical system could have internal states with an ineffable feel to them. *Representationalist* theories, of both the *first-order* and *higher-order* kind, are examples of this general strategy. Each of these theories has its own strengths and weaknesses. For example, it was not clear that Tye's first-order representational theory could explain how we can have a point of view on our own experiences – something which seems necessary for phenomenal consciousness. Rosenthal's higher-order thought theory did better in this respect but had problems explaining the function of consciousness and seemed to entail that non-human animals lack conscious experiences. Moreover, there is a general question as to whether any physicalist theory can really do justice to the introspective data. Whatever theory is proposed, we may still find ourselves asking, 'Why should *that* feel like *this*?'. An *explanatory gap* may always remain.

Rethinkers challenge the introspective picture, with its in-built Cartesian assumptions. Introspection leads us to think of consciousness as resembling a show in an interior theatre, where experiences are presented to us, decked out with phenomenal properties (*qualia*). According to rethinkers – of whom Dennett is the most prominent – this view is seriously misconceived. There is no interior show and when we talk about what it is *like* to experience a certain stimulus, we are referring, not to some introspectible property, but to the complex set of reactive dispositions it triggers in us. Thus, on this view, there is no *hard problem* of explaining how phenomenal properties arise, since there are no such properties. This approach does much to remove the mystery of consciousness and opens the way for a reductive explanation of it. (This is an important motive for Dennett, who is a physicalist, but one does not have to share it in order to endorse his views about consciousness. One might think that the subject needs rethinking, even if one is, for independent reasons, hostile to, or agnostic about, physicalism.) The chief charge against the rethinkers is that they are simply ignoring the phenomenon that needs explaining. They give us an account of something called 'consciousness', but it is not the thing we started out trying to explain: the ineffable subjective feels of which we are introspectively aware.

Who is right? As Chalmers notes in the line quoted above, it can seem that all the options are bad. All involve some implausibilities. (This is, of course, what makes the subject a contentious one; if there were an obviously attractive solution, then there would be little dispute!) One thing perhaps all sides can agree on is that it will be helpful to know more about the psychology and neurology of consciousness – about the associated reactions and the neural mechanisms involved. These data will not settle the fundamental metaphysical issues, but they may help to fill out the various positions and highlight their strengths and weaknesses (even property dualists need to develop an account of how phenomenal properties are *correlated* with neurological ones). And neuroscience may provide direct evidence for or against certain views. (If phenomenal–physical *interaction* occurs, then we should be able to detect its effects in the brain. If consciousness involves higher-order representations, then these states must have some detectable neural basis.) And it is possible that as we understand more about the complex reactions involved in sense experience we shall find ourselves gradually rethinking consciousness. So although there is unlikely to be a decisive discovery that solves or removes the hard problem, scientific research may in time make some positions appear less attractive and others more. We shall probably not reach a consensus for some time, but you may like to place your bets now.

Further reading

If you are interested in exploring the science of consciousness, two recommended books are:

BLACKMORE, S. (2003) *Consciousness: An Introduction*, London, Hodder & Stoughton. (An excellent and comprehensive interdisciplinary textbook on the neurology, psychology and philosophy of consciousness.)

CARTER, R. (2002) *Consciousness*, London, Weidenfeld & Nicholson. (A popular introduction to the neurology of consciousness. More elementary than Blackmore but still useful.)

Glossary

access-conscious (as applied to a mental state) such that its content is available for use in reasoning, the control of action and speech. Aka A-conscious.

basic physical properties the properties invoked by physicists and properties that can be defined in terms of those properties. For example, mass, electrical charge, being composed of atoms of a certain kind.

blindsight a condition which seems to involve non-conscious visual perception.

Cartesian Theatre a location in the brain where sensory information is pooled and conscious awareness occurs.

closure of the physical the view that only physical phenomena have effects within the physical world.

CP thesis (as used in this book) the view that if something is clearly conceivable, then it is **metaphysically possible**. ('CP' stands for 'Conceivability–Possibility'.)

creature consciousness the state of being awake, as opposed to asleep or comatose.

efficacy of consciousness the view that **phenomenal consciousness** has effects within the physical world.

epiphenomenalism the view that **phenomenal consciousness** has no effects within the physical world.

explanatory gap view the view that the **physical facts** about a person cannot explain the **phenomenal facts** about them.

first-order representation a representation of a state of the world or of one's own body.

first-order representationalism see under **representationalism**.

high-level properties properties invoked in sciences other than physics and in non-scientific discourse.

higher-order representation a representation of a representation. In the present context, either a thought about a mental state (a higher-order thought) or a perception of a mental state (a higher-order perception).

higher-order representationalism see under **representationalism**.

interactionism (short for 'interactionist dualism') the view that **phenomenal properties** are not physical but none the less have effects within the physical world. Involves denying the **closure of the physical**.

introspection the activity of attending to one's own mental states. Mental states that are the object of this attention are sometimes said to be introspectively conscious.

metaphysically possible capable of occurring, at least if the laws of nature were different.

naturalism the view that everything that happens in the world around us can be scientifically explained.

naturally possible capable of occurring consistently with the actual laws of nature.

PANIC theory the view that **phenomenal character** is Poised Abstract Non-conceptual Intentional Content. A form of first-order **representationalism**.

panprotopsychism the view that basic physical particles possess **phenomenal properties**, or rudimentary versions of them.

phenomenal character the way an experience feels; the sum of the experience's **phenomenal properties**. Aka feel, felt quality, qualitative feel, phenomenal feel, phenomenal content, phenomenology (in some contexts), **qualia**, subjective character, raw feel, what-it-is-likeness.

phenomenal concepts concepts which are employed in classifying experiences introspectively and which can be acquired only by someone who has undergone the experiences in question.

phenomenal consciousness the possession of mental states with **phenomenal character**. Aka P-consciousness.

phenomenal facts facts about **phenomenal properties**.

phenomenal properties the properties that go to make up the **phenomenal character** of an experience.

physical facts (as used in this book) facts about **physical properties**.

physical properties (as used in this book) properties that either **reduce** to, or are **realized** in, **basic physical properties**.

physicalism see **weak property physicalism**.

property dualism (in discussions of consciousness) the view that **phenomenal properties** are fundamentally distinct from **basic physical** ones.

property physicalism the view that **high-level properties** are not fundamentally distinct from **basic physical** ones.

qualia phenomenal properties (often used with the implication that they are non-physical).

realization roughly, constitution. To say that a **high-level property** is realized in a **basic physical** one is to say that it is constituted by it – that the former exists in virtue of the latter. Many high-level properties can be realized in more than one way ('multiply realized').

recognitional concepts concepts which are linked to simple recognitional capacities.

reduction roughly, identity. To say that a **high-level property** reduces to a **basic physical** one is to say that it can be identified with it in all its instances.

reductive explanation the process of explaining a high-level phenomenon by showing how it arises from lower-level ones.

representational content the information, or misinformation, carried by an experience or a belief. Aka intentional content.

representationalism the view that **phenomenal consciousness** consists in the possession of mental states with certain types of **representational content**. According to first-order versions, **first-order representations** are sufficient; according to higher-order versions (higher-order thought theory, higher-order perception theory), **higher-order representations** are also required.

self-consciousness awareness of oneself as an individual.

spectrum inversion the idea that another person's colour experiences might be systematically inverted relative to yours, so that red things look green to them, blue things look yellow and so on.

strong naturalism (as used in this book) **naturalism** coupled with the view that all **high-level properties** can be **reductively explained**.

strong property physicalism the view that all **high-level properties reduce** to **basic physical** ones.

subjective (as applied to the phenomenal character of an experience) such that it can be appreciated only from the first-person point of view, by the subject of the experience.

substance dualism the view that the universe contains other entities and forces in addition to those described by physics – souls, for example, or psychic energy.

substance physicalism the view that everything in the universe is composed wholly of the basic entities and forces described by physics.

transitive consciousness awareness of something.

transparent (as applied to an experience) not possessing any introspectible properties other than its **representational content**.

weak property physicalism the view that all **high-level properties** either **reduce** to, or are **realized** in, **basic physical** ones. Usually referred to in this book simply as 'physicalism'.

zombie an imagined creature which is physically and behaviourally identical to a normal human being but whose mental states are not **phenomenally conscious**.

Bibliography

ADAMS, B., BREAZEAL, C., BROOKS, R. & SCASSELLATI, B. (2000) 'Humanoid robots: a new kind of tool', *IEEE Intelligent Systems*, 15, 25–31.

ALTER, T. & WALTER, S. (eds) (2005) *Phenomenal Concepts and Phenomenal Knowledge: New Essays on Consciousness and Physicalism*, Oxford, Oxford University Press.

ARMSTRONG, D.M. (1981) *The Nature of Mind*, Brighton, Harvester.

BLOCK, N. (1990) 'Inverted earth', in J. Tomberlin (ed.), *Philosophical Perspectives, 4: Action Theory and Philosophy of Mind*, Atascadero, Ridgeview, pp.53–79.

BLOCK, N. (1995) 'On a confusion about a function of consciousness', *Behavioral and Brain Sciences*, 18, 227–47.

BLOCK, N., FLANAGAN, O. & GÜZELDERE, G. (eds) (1997) *The Nature of Consciousness: Philosophical Debates*, Cambridge, Mass., MIT Press.

BROOKS, R., BREAZEAL, C., MARJANOVIC, M., SCASSELLATI, B. & WILLIAMSON, M. (1998) 'The Cog project: building a humanoid robot', in C. Nehaniv (ed.), *Computation for Metaphors, Analogy and Agents* (vol. 1562 of Springer Lecture Notes in Artificial Intelligence), Heidelberg, Springer-Verlag.

CARRUTHERS, P. (1998) 'Natural theories of consciousness', *European Journal of Philosophy*, 6, 203–22.

CARRUTHERS, P. (2000) *Phenomenal Consciousness: A Naturalistic Theory*, Cambridge, Cambridge University Press.

CARRUTHERS, P. (2004) 'Reductive explanation and the "explanatory gap"', *Canadian Journal of Philosophy*, 34, 153–74.

CARRUTHERS, P. (forthcoming) *Consciousness: Essays from a Higher-Order Perspective*, Oxford, Oxford University Press.

CHALMERS, D.J. (1995) 'Facing up to the problem of consciousness', *Journal of Consciousness Studies*, 2, 200–19.

CHALMERS, D.J. (1996) *The Conscious Mind: In Search of a Fundamental Theory*, New York, Oxford University Press.

CHALMERS, D.J. (1999) 'Materialism and the metaphysics of modality', *Philosophy and Phenomenological Research*, 59, 473–96.

CHALMERS, D.J. (2002a) 'Consciousness and its place in nature', in D.J. Chalmers (ed.), *Philosophy of Mind: Classical and Contemporary Readings*, New York, Oxford University Press, pp.247–72.

CHALMERS, D.J. (2002b) 'Does conceivability entail possibility?', in T.S. Gendler & J. Hawthorne (eds), *Conceivability and Possibility*, Oxford, Oxford University Press, pp.145–200.

CHALMERS, D.J. (ed.) (2002c) *Philosophy of Mind: Classical and Contemporary Readings*, Oxford, Oxford University Press.

CHALMERS, D.J. (2004) 'Phenomenal concepts and the knowledge argument', in P. Ludlow, Y. Nagasawa & D. Stoljar (eds), *There's Something About Mary: Essays on Phenomenal Consciousness and Frank Jackson's Knowledge Argument*, Cambridge, Mass., MIT Press.

CRANE, T. & MELLOR, D.H. (1990) 'There is no question of physicalism', *Mind*, 99, 185–206.

DAVIES, M. & HUMPHREYS, G.W. (eds) (1993) *Consciousness: Psychological and Philosophical Essays*, Oxford, Blackwell.

DENNETT, D.C. (1984) *Elbow Room*, Oxford, Oxford University Press.

DENNETT, D.C. (1991) *Consciousness Explained*, Boston, Little Brown and Co.

DENNETT, D.C. (1993) 'The message is: there is no *medium*', *Philosophy and Phenomenological Research*, 53, 919–31.

DENNETT, D.C. (1995) 'The unimagined preposterousness of zombies', *Journal of Consciousness Studies*, 2, 322–26.

DENNETT, D.C. (2001) 'The zombic hunch: extinction of an intuition?', in A. O'Hear (ed.), *Philosophy at the New Millennium*, Cambridge, Cambridge University Press, pp.27–43.

DIXON, N.F. (1971) *Subliminal Perception: The Nature of a Controversy*. New York: McGraw-Hill.

DRETSKE, F. (1995) *Naturalizing the Mind*, Cambridge, Mass., MIT Press.

FEIGL, H. (1958) 'The "mental" and the "physical"', *Minnesota Studies in the Philosophy of Science*, 2, 370–497.

FLANAGAN, O. & POLGER, T. (1995) 'Zombies and the function of consciousness', *Journal of Consciousness Studies*, 2, 313–21.

HARDIN, C.L. (1988) *Color for Philosophers*, Indianapolis, Hackett.

HAUGELAND, J. (1982) 'Weak supervenience', *American Philosophical Quarterly*, 19, 93–103.

HUMANOID ROBOTICS GROUP, http://www.ai.mit.edu/projects/humanoid-robotics-group/ (accessed 15 December 2004)

JACKSON, F. (1982) 'Epiphenomenal qualia', *Philosophical Quarterly*, 32, 127–36.

JACKSON, F. (1986) 'What Mary didn't know', *The Journal of Philosophy*, 83, 291–5.

JACKSON, F. (1998) *Mind, Method and Conditionals*, London, Routledge.

JACKSON, F. (2003) 'Mind and illusion', in A. O'Hear (ed.), *Minds and Persons* Cambridge, Cambridge University Press, pp.251–71.

JACQUETTE, D. (1995) 'The blue banana trick: Dennett on Jackson's colour scientist', *Theoria*, 61, 217–30.

JAYNES, J. (1976) *The Origins of Consciousness in the Breakdown of the Bicameral Mind*, Boston, Houghton Mifflin.

KRIPKE, S. (1980) *Naming and Necessity*, Oxford, Blackwell.

LEIBNIZ, G.W. (1973) *Philosophical Writings*, London, Dent.

LEVINE, J. (1983) 'Materialism and qualia: the explanatory gap', *Pacific Philosophical Quarterly*, 64, 354–61.

LEVINE, J. (1993) 'On leaving out what it's like', in M. Davies & G.W. Humphreys (eds), *Consciousness: Psychological and Philosophical Essays* Oxford, Blackwell, pp.121–36.

LEVINE, J. (2001) *Purple Haze: The Puzzle of Consciousness*, New York, Oxford University Press.

LEWIS, D. (1983) 'Postscript to "Mad pain and Martian pain"', *Philosophical Papers*, vol. 1, New York, Oxford University Press, pp.130–2.

LEWIS, D. (1990) 'What experience teaches', in W. Lycan (ed.), *Mind and Cognition*, Oxford, Blackwell, pp.499–518.

LOAR, B. (1997) 'Phenomenal states', in N. Block, O. Flanagan & G. Güzeldere (eds), *The Nature of Consciousness: Philosophical Debates*, Cambridge, Mass., MIT Press, pp.597–616.

LOAR, B. (1999) 'David Chalmers's *The Conscious Mind*', *Philosophy and Phenomenological Research*, 59, 465–72.

LOCKE, J. (1961) *An Essay Concerning Human Understanding*, 5th edn, J.W. Yolton (ed.), London, Dent (first published 1706).

LOCKWOOD, M. (1989) *Mind, Brain and the Quantum*, Oxford, Blackwell.

LYCAN, W.G. (1996) *Consciousness and Experience*, Cambridge, Mass., MIT Press.

LYCAN, W.G. (2003) 'Perspectival representation and the knowledge argument', in Q. Smith & A. Jokic (eds), *Consciousness: New Philosophical Perspectives*, Oxford, Oxford University Press, pp.384–95.

LYCAN, W.G. (2004) 'The superiority of HOP to HOT', in R.J. Gennaro (ed.), *Higher-Order Theories of Consciousness: An Anthology*, Amsterdam, John Benjamins, pp.93–113.

MCGINN, C. (1982) *The Character of Mind*, Oxford, Oxford University Press.

MCGINN, C. (1989) 'Can we solve the mind–body problem?', *Mind*, 98, 349–66.

MCGINN, C. (1999) *The Mysterious Flame: Conscious Minds in a Material World*, New York, Basic Books.

MILNER, D. & GOODALE, M. (1995) *The Visual Brain in Action*, Oxford, Oxford University Press.

NAGEL, T. (1974) 'What is it like to be a bat?', *Philosophical Review*, 83, 435–50.

NEMIROW, L. (1980) 'Review of *Mortal Questions*, by Thomas Nagel', *Philosophical Review*, 89, 473–7.

NEMIROW, L. (1990) 'Physicalism and the cognitive role of acquaintance', in W. Lycan (ed.), *Mind and Cognition*, Oxford, Blackwell, pp.490–9.

NORDBY, K. (1990) 'Vision in a complete achromat: a personal account', in R.F. Hess, L.T. Sharpe & K. Nordby (eds), *Night Vision: Basic, Clinical and Applied Aspects*, Cambridge, Cambridge University Press, pp.290–315.

PAPINEAU, D. (1993) *Philosophical Naturalism*, Oxford, Blackwell.

PAPINEAU, D. (1995) 'The antipathetic fallacy and the boundaries of consciousness', in T. Metzinger (ed.), *Conscious Experience*, Thorverton, Imprint Academic, pp.259–70.

PAPINEAU, D. (2002) *Thinking about Consciousness*, Oxford, Oxford University Press.

PEACOCKE, C. (1993) 'Review of M. Tye, *The Imagery Debate*', *Philosophy of Science*, 60, 675–7.

PERNER, J. (1993) *Understanding the Representational Mind*, Cambridge, Mass., MIT Press.

ROBINSON, H. (1993) 'Dennett on the knowledge argument', *Analysis*, 53, 174–7.

ROSENTHAL, D.M. (1993) 'State consciousness and transitive consciousness', *Consciousness and Cognition*, 2, 355–63.

ROSENTHAL, D.M. (1999) 'The colors and shapes of visual experiences', in D. Fisette (ed.), *Consciousness and Intentionality: Models and Modalities of Attribution*, Dordrecht, Kluwer, pp.95–118.

ROSENTHAL, D.M. (2002) 'Explaining consciousness', in D.J. Chalmers (ed.), *Philosophy of Mind: Classical and Contemporary Readings*, New York, Oxford University Press, pp.406–21).

ROSENTHAL, D.M. (2004) 'Varieties of higher-order theory', in R.J. Gennaro (ed.), *Higher-Order Theories of Consciousness: An Anthology*, Amsterdam, John Benjamins, pp.17–44.

ROWLANDS, M. (2002) 'Two dogmas of consciousness', *Journal of Consciousness Studies*, 9, 158–80.

SACKS, O. (1995) *An Anthropologist on Mars*, London, Picador.

SEARLE, J. (1983) *Intentionality*, Cambridge, Cambridge University Press.

SMART, J.J.C. (1959) 'Sensations and brain processes', *Philosophical Review*, 68, 141–56.

SMITH, A. (1985) *The Mind*, Harmondsworth, Penguin Books.

SUTHERLAND, S. (ed.) (1995) *The Macmillan Dictionary of Psychology*, London, Palgrave Macmillan.

TYE, M. (1995) *Ten Problems of Consciousness: A Representational Theory of the Phenomenal Mind*, Cambridge, Mass., MIT Press.

TYE, M. (2000) *Consciousness, Color, and Content*, Cambridge, Mass., MIT Press.

TYE, M. (2002) 'Visual qualia and visual content revisited', in D.J. Chalmers (ed.), *Philosophy of Mind: Classical and Contemporary Readings*, New York, Oxford University Press, pp.447–56.

WEISKRANTZ, L. (1986) *Blindsight*, Oxford, Oxford University Press.

WEISKRANTZ, L. (1997) *Consciousness Lost and Found*, Oxford, Oxford University Press.

WELLMAN, H.M. (1990) *The Child's Theory of the Mind*, Cambridge, Mass., MIT Press.

READINGS

A catalog of conscious experiences

David J. Chalmers

Source: Chalmers, David J. (1996) *The Conscious Mind*, Oxford, Oxford University Press, pp.6–11. Used by permission of Oxford University Press Inc.

1   Conscious experience can be fascinating to attend to. Experience comes in an enormous number of varieties, each with its own character. A far-from-complete catalog of the aspects of conscious experience is given in the following pretheoretical, impressionistic list. Nothing here should be taken too seriously as philosophy, but it should help focus attention on the subject matter at hand.

2   *Visual experiences.* Among the many varieties of visual experience, color sensations stand out as the paradigm examples of conscious experience, due to their pure, seemingly ineffable qualitative nature. Some color experiences can seem particularly striking, and so can be particularly good at focusing our attention on the mystery of consciousness. In my environment now, there is a particularly rich shade of deep purple from a book on my shelf; an almost surreal shade of green in a photograph of ferns on my wall; and a sparkling array of bright red, green, orange, and blue lights on a Christmas tree that I can see through my window. But any color can be awe-provoking if we attend to it, and reflect upon its nature. Why should it feel like *that*? Why should it feel like anything at all? How could I possibly convey the nature of this color experience to someone who has not had such an experience?

3   Other aspects of visual experience include the experience of shape, of size, of brightness, and of darkness. A particularly subtle aspect is the experience of depth. As a child, one of my eyes had excellent vision, but the other was very poor. Because of my one good eye, the world looked crisp and sharp, and it certainly seemed three-dimensional. One day, I was fitted with glasses, and the change was remarkable. The world was not much sharper than before, but it suddenly looked *more* three-dimensional: things that had depth

before somehow got deeper, and the world seemed a richer place. If you cover one eye and then uncover it, you can get an idea of the change. In my previous state, I would have said that there was no way for the depth of my vision to improve; the world already seemed as three-dimensional as it could be. The change was subtle, almost ineffable, but extremely striking. Certainly there is an intellectual story one can tell about how binocular vision allows information from each eye to be consolidated into information about distances, thus enabling more sophisticated control of action, but somehow this causal story does not reveal the way the experience *felt*. Why that change in processing should be accompanied by such a remaking of my experience was mysterious to me as a ten-year-old, and is still a source of wonder today.

4   *Auditory experiences*. In some ways, sounds are even stranger than visual images. The structure of images usually corresponds to the structure of the world in a straightforward way, but sounds can seem quite independent. My telephone receives an incoming call, an internal device vibrates, a complex wave is set up in the air and eventually reaches my eardrum, and somehow, almost magically, I hear a *ring*. Nothing about the quality of the ring seems to correspond directly to any structure in the world, although I certainly know that it originated with the speaker, and that it is determined by a waveform. But why should that waveform, or even these neural firings, have given rise to a sound quality like *that*?

5   Musical experience is perhaps the richest aspect of auditory experience, although the experience of speech must be close. Music is capable of washing over and completely absorbing us, surrounding us in a way that a visual field can surround us but in which auditory experiences usually do not. One can analyze aspects of musical experience by breaking the sounds we perceive into notes and tones with complex interrelationships, but the experience of music somehow goes beyond this. A unified qualitative experience arises from a chord, but not from randomly selected notes. An old piano and a far-off oboe can combine to produce an unexpectedly haunting experience. As always, when we reflect, we ask the question: why should *that* feel like *this*?

6   *Tactile experiences*. Textures provide another of the richest quality spaces that we experience: think of the feel of velvet, and contrast it to the texture of cold metal, or a clammy hand, or a stubbly chin. All of these have their own unique quality. The tactile experiences of water, of cotton candy, or of another person's lips are different again.

7   *Olfactory experiences.* Think of the musty smell of an old wardrobe, the stench of rotting garbage, the whiff of newly mown grass, the warm aroma of freshly baked bread. Smell is in some ways the most mysterious of all the senses, due to the rich, intangible, indescribable nature of smell sensations. Ackermann (1990) calls it 'the mute sense; the one without words'. While there is something ineffable about any sensation, the other senses have properties that facilitate some description. Visual and auditory experiences have a complex combinatorial structure that can be described. Tactile and taste experiences generally arise from direct contact with some object, and a rich descriptive vocabulary has been built up by reference to these objects. Smell has little in the way of apparent structure, and often floats free of any apparent object, remaining a primitive presence in our sensory manifold. (Perhaps animals might do better [Figure 1].) The primitiveness is perhaps partly due to the slot-and-key process by which our olfactory receptors are sensitive to various kinds of molecules. It seems arbitrary that a given sort of molecule should give rise to *this* sort of sensation, but give rise it does.

Calvin and Hobbes   by Bill Watterson

Figure 1 Effability and ineffability in olfactory experience. (Calvin and Hobbes © Watterson. Distributed by Universal Press Syndicate. Reprinted with permission. All rights reserved.)

8   *Taste experiences.* Psychophysical investigations tell us that there are only four independent dimensions of taste perception: sweet, sour, bitter, and salt. But this four-dimensional space combines with our sense of smell to produce a great variety of possible experiences: the taste of Turkish Delight, of curried black-eyed pea salad, of a peppermint Lifesaver, of a ripe peach.

9   *Experiences of hot and cold.* An oppressively hot, humid day and a frosty winter's day produce strikingly different qualitative experiences. Think also of the heat sensations on one's skin from being close to a fire, and the hot-cold sensation that one gets from touching ultracold ice.

10   *Pain.* Pain is a paradigm example of conscious experience, beloved by philosophers. Perhaps this is because pains form a very distinctive class of qualitative experiences, and are difficult to map directly onto any structure in the world or in the body, although they are usually associated with some part of the body. Because of this, pains can seem even more subjective than most sensory experiences. There are a great variety of pain experiences, from shooting pains and fierce burns through sharp pricks to dull aches.

11   *Other bodily sensations.* Pains are only the most salient kind of sensations associated with particular parts of the body. Others include headaches (which are perhaps a class of pain), hunger pangs, itches, tickles, and the experience associated with the need to urinate. Many bodily sensations have an entirely unique quality, different in kind from anything else in our experience: think of orgasms, or the feeling of hitting one's funny bone. There are also experiences associated with proprioception, the sense of where one's body is in space.

12   *Mental imagery.* Moving ever inward, toward experiences that are not associated with particular objects in the environment or the body but that are in some sense generated internally, we come to mental images. There is often a rich phenomenology associated with visual images conjured up in one's imagination, though not nearly as detailed as those derived from direct visual perception. There are also the interesting colored patterns that one gets when one closes one's eyes and squints, and the strong after-images that one gets after looking at something bright. One can have similar kinds of auditory 'images' conjured up by one's imagination, and even tactile, olfactory, and gustatory images, although these are harder to pin down and their associated qualitative feel is usually fainter.

13   *Conscious thought.* Some of the things we think and believe do not have any particular qualitative feel associated with them, but many do. This applies particularly to explicit, occurrent thoughts that one thinks to oneself, and to various thoughts that affect one's stream of consciousness. It is often hard to pin down just what the qualitative feel of an occurrent thought is, but it is certainly there. There is *something* it is like to be having such thoughts.

14   When I think of a lion, for instance, there seems to be a whiff of leonine quality to my phenomenology: what it is like to think of a lion is subtly different from what it is like to think of the Eiffel tower. More obviously, cognitive attitudes such as desire often have a strong phenomenal flavor. Desire seems to exert a phenomenological 'tug', and memory often has a qualitative component, as with the experience of nostalgia or regret.

15   *Emotions*. Emotions often have distinctive experiences associated with them. The sparkle of a happy mood, the weariness of a deep depression, the red-hot glow of a rush of anger, the melancholy of regret: all of these can affect conscious experience profoundly, although in a much less specific way than localized experiences such as sensations. These emotions pervade and color all of our conscious experiences while they last.

16   Other more transient feelings lie partway between emotions and the more obviously cognitive aspects of mind. Think of the rush of pleasure one feels when one gets a joke. Another example is the feeling of tension one gets when watching a suspense movie, or when waiting for an important event. The butterflies in one's stomach that can accompany nervousness also fall into this class.

17   *The sense of self*. One sometimes feels that there is something to conscious experience that transcends all these specific elements: a kind of background hum, for instance, that is somehow fundamental to consciousness and that is there even when the other components are not. This phenomenology of self is so deep and intangible that it sometimes seems illusory, consisting in nothing over and above specific elements such as those listed above. Still, there seems to be *something* to the phenomenology of self, even if it is very hard to pin down.

18   This catalog covers a number of bases, but leaves out as much as it puts in. I have said nothing, for instance, about dreams, arousal and fatigue, intoxication, or the novel character of other drug-induced experiences. There are also rich experiences that derive their character from the combination of two or many of the components described above. I have mentioned the combined effects of smell and taste, but an equally salient example is the combined experience of music and emotion, which interact in a subtle, difficult-to-separate way. I have also left aside the unity of conscious experience – the way that all of these experiences seem to be tied together as the experience of a single experiencer. Like the sense of self, this unity

sometimes seems illusory – it is certainly harder to pin down than any specific experiences – but there is a strong intuition that unity is there.

References

ACKERMAN, D. (1990) *A Natural History of the Senses*, New York, Random House.

The easy problems and the hard problem

David J. Chalmers

Source: Chalmers, David J. (1995) 'Facing up to the problem of consciousness', *Journal of Consciousness Studies*, 2, no.3, 200–19.

1   There is not just one problem of consciousness. 'Consciousness' is an ambiguous term, referring to many different phenomena. Each of these phenomena needs to be explained, but some are easier to explain than others. At the start, it is useful to divide the associated problems of consciousness into 'hard' and 'easy' problems. The easy problems of consciousness are those that seem directly susceptible to the standard methods of cognitive science, whereby a phenomenon is explained in terms of computational or neural mechanisms. The hard problems are those that seem to resist those methods.

2   The easy problems of consciousness include those of explaining the following phenomena:

- the ability to discriminate, categorize, and react to environmental stimuli;
- the integration of information by a cognitive system;
- the reportability of mental states;
- the ability of a system to access its own internal states;
- the focus of attention;
- the deliberate control of behaviour;
- the difference between wakefulness and sleep.

All of these phenomena are associated with the notion of consciousness. For example, one sometimes says that a mental state is conscious when it is verbally reportable, or when it is internally accessible. Sometimes a system is said to be conscious of some information when it has the ability to react on the basis of that information, or, more strongly, when it attends to that information, or when it can integrate that information and exploit it in the sophisticated control of behaviour. We sometimes say that an action is conscious precisely when it is deliberate. Often, we say that an organism is conscious as another way of saying that it is awake.

3   There is no real issue about whether *these* phenomena can be explained scientifically. All of them are straightforwardly vulnerable to explanation in terms of computational or neural mechanisms. To explain access and reportability, for example, we need only specify the mechanism by which information about internal states is retrieved and made available for verbal report. To explain the integration of information, we need only exhibit mechanisms by which information is brought together and exploited by later processes. For an account of sleep and wakefulness, an appropriate neurophysiological account of the processes responsible for organisms' contrasting behaviour in those states will suffice. In each case, an appropriate cognitive or neurophysiological model can clearly do the explanatory work.

4   If these phenomena were all there was to consciousness, then consciousness would not be much of a problem. Although we do not yet have anything close to a complete explanation of these phenomena, we have a clear idea of how we might go about explaining them. This is why I call these problems the easy problems. Of course, 'easy' is a relative term. Getting the details right will probably take a century or two of difficult empirical work. Still, there is every reason to believe that the methods of cognitive science and neuroscience will succeed.

5   The really hard problem of consciousness is the problem of *experience*. When we think and perceive, there is a whir of information-processing, but there is also a subjective aspect. As Nagel (1974) has put it, there is *something it is like* to be a conscious organism. This subjective aspect is experience. [...]

6   It is undeniable that some organisms are subjects of experience. But the question of how it is that these systems are subjects of experience is perplexing. Why is it that when our cognitive systems engage in visual and auditory information-processing, we have visual or auditory experience: the quality of deep blue, the sensation of middle C? How can we explain why there is something it is like to entertain a mental image, or to experience an emotion? It is widely agreed that experience arises from a physical basis, but we have no good explanation of why and how it so arises. Why should physical processing give rise to a rich inner life at all? It seems objectively unreasonable that it should, and yet it does. If any problem qualifies as *the* problem of consciousness, it is this one. [...]

7   Why are the easy problems easy, and why is the hard problem hard? The easy problems are easy precisely because they concern the explanation of cognitive *abilities* and *functions*. To explain a cognitive function, we need only specify a mechanism that can perform the function. The methods of cognitive science are well-suited for this sort of explanation, and so are well-suited to the easy problems of consciousness. By contrast, the hard problem is hard precisely because it is not a problem about the performance of functions. The problem persists even when the performance of all the relevant functions is explained.[1]

8   To explain reportability, for instance, is just to explain how a system could perform the function of producing reports on internal states. To explain internal access, we need to explain how a system could be appropriately affected by its internal states and use information about those states in directing later processes. To explain integration and control, we need to explain how a system's central processes can bring information contents together and use them in the facilitation of various behaviours. These are all problems about the explanation of functions.

9   How do we explain the performance of a function? By specifying a *mechanism* that performs the function. Here, neurophysiological and cognitive modelling are perfect for the task. If we want a detailed low-level explanation, we can specify the neural mechanism that is responsible for the function. If we want a more abstract explanation, we can specify a mechanism in computational terms. Either way, a full and satisfying explanation will result. Once we have specified the neural or computational mechanism that performs the function of verbal report, for example, the bulk of our work in explaining reportability is over.

10   In a way, the point is trivial. It is a *conceptual* fact about these phenomena that their explanation only involves the explanation of various functions, as the phenomena are *functionally definable*. All it *means* for reportability to be instantiated in a system is that the system has the capacity for verbal reports of internal information. All it means for a system to be awake is for it to be appropriately receptive to information from the environment and for it to be able to use this information in directing behaviour in an appropriate way. To see that this sort of thing is a conceptual fact, note that someone who says 'you have explained the performance of the verbal report function, but you have not explained reportability' is making a trivial conceptual mistake about reportability. All it could *possibly* take to explain reportability is an explanation

of how the relevant function is performed; the same goes for the other phenomena in question.

11   Throughout the higher-level sciences, reductive explanation works in just this way. To explain the gene, for instance, we needed to specify the mechanism that stores and transmits hereditary information from one generation to the next. It turns out that DNA performs this function; once we explain how the function is performed, we have explained the gene. To explain life, we ultimately need to explain how a system can reproduce, adapt to its environment, metabolize, and so on. All of these are questions about the performance of functions, and so are well-suited to reductive explanation. The same holds for most problems in cognitive science. To explain learning, we need to explain the way in which a system's behavioural capacities are modified in light of environmental information, and the way in which new information can be brought to bear in adapting a system's actions to its environment. If we show how a neural or computational mechanism does the job, we have explained learning. We can say the same for other cognitive phenomena, such as perception, memory, and language. Sometimes the relevant functions need to be characterized quite subtly, but it is clear that insofar as cognitive science explains these phenomena at all, it does so by explaining the performance of functions.

12   When it comes to conscious experience, this sort of explanation fails. What makes the hard problem hard and almost unique is that it goes *beyond* problems about the performance of functions. To see this, note that even when we have explained the performance of all the cognitive and behavioural functions in the vicinity of experience – perceptual discrimination, categorization, internal access, verbal report – there may still remain a further unanswered question: *Why is the performance of these functions accompanied by experience?* A simple explanation of the functions leaves this question open.

13   There is no analogous further question in the explanation of genes, or of life, or of learning. If someone says 'I can see that you have explained how DNA stores and transmits hereditary information from one generation to the next, but you have not explained how it is a *gene*', then they are making a conceptual mistake. All it means to be a gene is to be an entity that performs the relevant storage and transmission function. But if someone says 'I can see that you have explained how information is discriminated, integrated, and

reported, but you have not explained how it is *experienced*', they are not making a conceptual mistake. This is a nontrivial further question.

14   This further question is the key question in the problem of consciousness. Why doesn't all this information-processing go on 'in the dark', free of any inner feel? Why is it that when electromagnetic waveforms impinge on a retina and are discriminated and categorized by a visual system, this discrimination and categorization is experienced as a sensation of vivid red? We know that conscious experience *does* arise when these functions are performed, but the very fact that it arises is the central mystery. There is an *explanatory gap* (a term due to Levine 1983) between the functions and experience, and we need an explanatory bridge to cross it. A mere account of the functions stays on one side of the gap, so the materials for the bridge must be found elsewhere.

References

LEVINE, J. (1983) 'Materialism and qualia: the explanatory gap', *Pacific Philosophical Quarterly*, 64, 354–61.

NAGEL, T. (1974) 'What is it like to be a bat?', *Philosophical Review*, 4, 435–50.

Note

[1] Here 'function' is not used in the narrow teleological sense of something that a system is designed to do, but in the broader sense of any causal role in the production of behaviour that a system might perform.

The knowledge argument

Frank Jackson

Source: Jackson, Frank (1982) 'Epiphenomenal qualia', *Philosophical Quarterly*, 32, 127, 127–36. Grateful acknowledgement is made to the following source for permission to reproduce material within this book: Blackwell Publishing Ltd.

1   I am what is sometimes known as a 'qualia freak'. I think that there are certain features of the bodily sensations especially, but also of certain perceptual experiences, which no amount of purely physical information includes. Tell me everything physical there is to tell about what is going on in a living brain, the kind of states, their functional role, their relation to what goes on at other times and in other brains, and so on and so forth, and be I as clever as can be in fitting it all together, you won't have told me about the hurtfulness of pains, the itchiness of itches, pangs of jealousy, or about the characteristic experience of tasting a lemon, smelling a rose, hearing a loud noise or seeing the sky.

2   There are many qualia freaks, and some of them say that their rejection of Physicalism is an unargued intuition. I think that they are being unfair to themselves. They have the following argument. Nothing you could tell of a physical sort captures the smell of a rose, for instance. Therefore, Physicalism is false. By our lights this is a perfectly good argument. It is obviously not to the point to question its validity, and the premise is intuitively obviously true both to them and to me.

3   I must, however, admit that it is weak from a polemical point of view. There are, unfortunately for us, many who do not find the premise intuitively obvious. The task then is to present an argument whose premises are obvious to all, or at least to as many as possible. This I try to do in [the following paragraphs] with what I will call 'the Knowledge argument'. [...]

4   People vary considerably in their ability to discriminate colours. Suppose that in an experiment to catalogue this variation Fred is discovered. Fred has better colour vision than anyone else on record; he makes every discrimination that anyone has ever made, and moreover he makes one that we

cannot even begin to make. Show him a batch of ripe tomatoes and he sorts them into two roughly equal groups and does so with complete consistency. That is, if you blindfold him, shuffle the tomatoes up, and then remove the blindfold and ask him to sort them out again, he sorts them into exactly the same two groups.

5   We ask Fred how he does it. He explains that all ripe tomatoes do not look the same colour to him, and in fact that this is true of a great many objects that we classify together as red. He sees two colours where we see one, and he has in consequence developed for his own use two words 'red$_1$' and 'red$_2$' to mark the difference. Perhaps he tells us that he has often tried to teach the difference between red$_1$ and red$_2$ to his friends but has got nowhere and has concluded that the rest of the world is red$_1$-red$_2$ colour-blind – or perhaps he has had partial success with his children, it doesn't matter. In any case he explains to us that it would be quite wrong to think that because 'red' appears in both 'red$_1$' and 'red$_2$' that the two colours are shades of the one colour. He only uses the common term 'red' to fit more easily into our restricted usage. To him red$_1$ and red$_2$ are as different from each other and all the other colours as yellow is from blue. And his discriminatory behaviour bears this out: he sorts red$_1$ from red$_2$ tomatoes with the greatest of ease in a wide variety of viewing circumstances. Moreover, an investigation of the physiological basis of Fred's exceptional ability reveals that Fred's optical system is able to separate out two groups of wavelengths in the red spectrum as sharply as we are able to sort out yellow from blue.

6   I think that we should admit that Fred can see, really see, at least one more colour than we can; red$_1$ is a different colour from red$_2$. We are to Fred as a totally red-green colour-blind person is to us. H.G. Wells' story 'The Country of the Blind' is about a sighted person in a totally blind community. This person never manages to convince them that he can see, that he has an extra sense. They ridicule this sense as quite inconceivable, and treat his capacity to avoid falling into ditches, to win fights and so on as precisely that capacity and nothing more. We would be making their mistake if we refused to allow that Fred can see one more colour than we can.

7   What kind of experience does Fred have when he sees red$_1$ and red$_2$? What is the new colour or colours like? We would dearly like to know but do not; and it seems that no amount of physical information about Fred's brain and optical system tells us. We find out perhaps that Fred's cones respond differentially to certain light waves in the red section of the spectrum that

make no difference to ours (or perhaps he has an extra cone) and that this leads in Fred to a wider range of those brain states responsible for visual discriminatory behaviour. But none of this tells us what we really want to know about his colour experience. There is something about it we don't know. But we know, we may suppose, everything about Fred's body, his behaviour and dispositions to behaviour and about his internal physiology, and everything about his history and relation to others that can be given in physical accounts of persons. We have all the physical information. Therefore, knowing all this is *not* knowing everything about Fred. It follows that Physicalism leaves something out.

8   To reinforce this conclusion, imagine that as a result of our investigations into the internal workings of Fred we find out how to make everyone's physiology like Fred's in the relevant respects; or perhaps Fred donates his body to science and on his death we are able to transplant his optical system into someone else – again the fine detail doesn't matter. The important point is that such a happening would create enormous interest. People would say, 'At last we will know what it is like to see the extra colour, at last we will know how Fred has differed from us in the way he has struggled to tell us about for so long'. Then it cannot be that we knew all along all about Fred. But *ex hypothesi* we did know all along everything about Fred that features in the physicalist scheme; hence the physicalist scheme leaves something out.

9   Put it this way. *After* the operation, we will know *more* about Fred and especially about his colour experiences. But beforehand we had all the physical information we could desire about his body and brain, and indeed everything that has ever featured in physicalist accounts of mind and consciousness. Hence there is more to know than all that. Hence Physicalism is incomplete.

10   Fred and the new colour(s) are of course essentially rhetorical devices. The same point can be made with normal people and familiar colours. Mary is a brilliant scientist who is, for whatever reason, forced to investigate the world from a black and white room *via* a black and white television monitor. She specializes in the neurophysiology of vision and acquires, let us suppose, all the physical information there is to obtain about what goes on when we see ripe tomatoes, or the sky, and use terms like 'red', 'blue', and so on. She discovers, for example, just which wavelength combinations from the sky stimulate the retina, and exactly how this produces *via* the central nervous system the contraction of the vocal chords and expulsion of air from the lungs that results

in the uttering of the sentence 'The sky is blue'. (It can hardly be denied that it is in principle possible to obtain all this physical information from black and white television, otherwise the Open University would *of necessity* need to use colour television.)

11   What will happen when Mary is released from her black and white room or is given a colour television monitor? Will she *learn* anything or not? It seems just obvious that she will learn something about the world and our visual experience of it. But then it is inescapable that her previous knowledge was incomplete. But she had *all* the physical information. *Ergo* there is more to have than that, and Physicalism is false.

12   Clearly the same style of Knowledge argument could be deployed for taste, hearing, the bodily sensations and generally speaking for the various mental states which are said to have (as it is variously put) raw feels, phenomenal features or qualia. The conclusion in each case is that the qualia are left out of the physicalist story. And the polemical strength of the Knowledge argument is that it is so hard to deny the central claim that one can have all the physical information without having all the information there is to have.

The conceivability of zombies

David J. Chalmers

Source: Chalmers, David J. (1996) *The Conscious Mind*, Oxford, Oxford University Press, pp.94–8. Copyright © 1996 by David J. Chalmers. Used by permission of Oxford University Press Inc.

1   [C]onsider my zombie twin. This creature is molecule for molecule identical to me, and identical in all the low-level properties postulated by a completed physics, but he lacks conscious experience entirely. (Some might prefer to call a zombie 'it', but I use the personal pronoun; I have grown quite fond of my zombie twin.) To fix ideas, we can imagine that right now I am gazing out the window, experiencing some nice green sensations from seeing the trees outside, having pleasant taste experiences through munching on a chocolate bar, and feeling a dull aching sensation in my right shoulder.

2   What is going on in my zombie twin? He is physically identical to me, and we may as well suppose that he is embedded in an identical environment. He will certainly be identical to me *functionally*: he will be processing the same sort of information, reacting in a similar way to inputs, with his internal configurations being modified appropriately and with indistinguishable behavior resulting. He will be *psychologically* identical to me [...]. He will be perceiving the trees outside, in the functional sense, and tasting the chocolate, in the psychological sense. All of this follows logically from the fact that he is physically identical to me, by virtue of the functional analyses of psychological notions. He will even be 'conscious' in the functional senses [...] – he will be awake, able to report the contents of his internal states, able to focus attention in various places, and so on. It is just that none of this functioning will be accompanied by any real conscious experience. There will be no phenomenal feel. There is nothing it is like to be a zombie.

3   This sort of zombie is quite unlike the zombies found in Hollywood movies, which tend to have significant functional impairments (Figure 1). The sort of consciousness that Hollywood zombies most obviously lack is a psychological version: typically, they have little capacity for introspection and lack a refined ability to voluntarily control behavior. They may or may not lack

phenomenal consciousness; as Block (1995) points out, it is reasonable to suppose that there is something it tastes like when they eat their victims. We can call these *psychological zombies*; I am concerned with *phenomenal zombies*, which are physically and functionally identical, but which lack experience. (Perhaps it is not surprising that phenomenal zombies have not been popular in Hollywood, as there would be obvious problems with their depiction.)

Calvin and Hobbes   by Bill Watterson

Figure 1 Calvin and Hobbes on zombies. (Calvin and Hobbes © Watterson. Distributed by Universal Press Syndicate. Reprinted with permission. All rights reserved.)

4   The idea of zombies as I have described them is a strange one. For a start, it is unlikely that zombies are naturally possible. In the real world, it is likely that any replica of me would be conscious. For this reason, it is most natural to imagine unconscious creatures as physically different from conscious ones – exhibiting impaired behavior, for example. But the question is not whether it is plausible that zombies could exist in our world, or even whether the idea of a zombie replica is a natural one; the question is whether the notion of a zombie is conceptually coherent. The mere intelligibility of the notion is enough to establish the conclusion.

5   Arguing for a logical possibility is not entirely straightforward. How, for example, would one argue that a mile-high unicycle is logically possible? It just seems obvious. Although no such thing exists in the real world, the description certainly appears to be coherent. If someone objects that it is not logically possible – it merely seems that way – there is little we can say, except to repeat the description and assert its obvious coherence. It seems quite clear that there is no hidden contradiction lurking in the description.

6   I confess that the logical possibility of zombies seems equally obvious to me. A zombie is just something physically identical to me, but which has no conscious experience – all is dark inside. While this is probably empirically impossible, it certainly seems that a coherent situation is described; I can discern no contradiction in the description. In some ways an assertion of this logical possibility comes down to a brute intuition, but no more so than with the unicycle. Almost everybody, it seems to me, is capable of conceiving of this possibility. Some may be led to deny the possibility in order to make some theory come out right, but the justification of such theories should ride on the question of possibility, rather than the other way around.

7   In general, a certain burden of proof lies on those who claim that a given description is logically *impossible*. If someone truly believes that a mile-high unicycle is logically impossible, she must give us some idea of where a contradiction lies, whether explicit or implicit. If she cannot point out something about the intensions of the concepts 'mile-high' and 'unicycle' that might lead to a contradiction, then her case will not be convincing. On the other hand, it is no more convincing to give an obviously false analysis of the notions in question – to assert, for example, that for something to qualify as a unicycle it must be shorter than the Statue of Liberty. If no reasonable analysis of the terms in question points toward a contradiction, or even makes the existence of a contradiction plausible, then there is a natural assumption in favor of logical possibility.

8   That being said, there are some positive things that proponents of logical possibility can do to bolster their case. They can exhibit various indirect arguments, appealing to what we know about the phenomena in question and the way we think about hypothetical cases involving these phenomena, in order to establish that the obvious logical possibility really is a logical possibility, and really is obvious. One might spin a fantasy about an ordinary person riding a unicycle when suddenly the whole system expands a thousandfold. Or one might describe a series of unicycles, each bigger than the last. In a sense, these are all appeals to intuition, and an opponent who wishes to deny the possibility can in each case assert that our intuitions have misled us, but the very obviousness of what we are describing works in our favor, and helps shift the burden of proof further onto the other side.

9   For example, we can indirectly support the claim that zombies are logically possible by considering *nonstandard realizations* of my functional organization. My functional organization – that is, the pattern of causal

organization embodied in the mechanisms responsible for the production of my behaviour – can in principle be realized in all sorts of strange ways. To use a common example (Block 1978), the people of a large nation such as China might organize themselves so that they realize a causal organization isomorphic to that of my brain, with every person simulating the behavior of a single neuron, and with radio links corresponding to synapses. The population might control an empty shell of a robot body, equipped with sensory transducers and motor effectors.

10   Many people find it implausible that a set-up like this would give rise to conscious experience – that somehow a 'group mind' would emerge from the overall system. I am not concerned here with whether or not conscious experience would *in fact* arise; I suspect that in fact it would [...]. All that matters here is that the idea that such a system lacks conscious experience is *coherent*. A meaningful possibility is being expressed, and it is an open question whether consciousness arises or not. We can make a similar point by considering my silicon isomorph, who is organized like me but who has silicon chips where I have neurons. Whether such an isomorph would *in fact* be conscious is controversial, but it seems to most people that those who deny this are expressing a coherent possibility. From these cases it follows that the existence of my conscious experience is not logically entailed by the facts about my functional organization.

11   But given that it is conceptually coherent that the group-mind set-up or my silicon isomorph could lack conscious experience, it follows that my zombie twin is an equally coherent possibility. For it is clear that there is no more of a *conceptual* entailment from biochemistry to consciousness than there is from silicon or from a group of homunculi. If the silicon isomorph without conscious experience is conceivable, we need only substitute neurons for silicon in the conception while leaving functional organization constant, and we have my zombie twin. Nothing in this substitution could force experience into the conception; these implementational differences are simply not the sort of thing that could be conceptually relevant to experience. [...]

12   Some may think that conceivability arguments are unreliable. For example, sometimes it is objected that we cannot really imagine in detail the many billions of neurons in the human brain. Of course this is true; but we do not need to imagine each of the neurons to make the case. Mere complexity among neurons could not conceptually entail consciousness; if all that neural

structure is to be relevant to consciousness, it must be relevant *in virtue* of some higher-level properties that it enables. So it is enough to imagine the system at a coarse level, and to make sure that we conceive it with appropriately sophisticated mechanisms of perception, categorization, high-bandwidth access to information contents, reportability, and the like. No matter how sophisticated we imagine these mechanisms to be, the zombie scenario remains as coherent as ever. Perhaps an opponent might claim that all the unimagined neural detail is conceptually relevant in some way independent of its contribution to sophisticated functioning; but then she owes us an account of what that way might be, and none is available. Those implementational details simply lie at the wrong level to be conceptually relevant to consciousness.

References

BLOCK, N. (1978) 'Troubles with functionalism', in C.W. Savage (ed.), *Perception and Cognition: Issues in the Foundation of Psychology*, Minneapolis, University of Minnesota Press. [Reprinted in N. Block (ed.), (1980) *Readings in the Philosophy of Psychology*, vol. 1. Cambridge, Mass., Harvard University Press.]

BLOCK, N. (1995) 'On a confusion about a function of consciousness', *Behavioral and Brain Sciences*, 18, 227–47.

Naturalistic dualism

David J. Chalmers

Source: Chalmers, David J. (1996) *The Conscious Mind*, Oxford, Oxford University Press, pp.124–8. Copyright © 1996 by David J. Chalmers. Used by permission of Oxford University Press Inc.

1   Th[e] failure of materialism leads to a kind of *dualism*: there are both physical and nonphysical features of the world. [...] But there are many varieties of dualism, and it is important to see just where the argument leads us.

2   The [anti-physicalist] arguments [...] establish that consciousness does not supervene *logically* on the physical, but this is not to say that it does not supervene at all. There appears to be a systematic dependence of conscious experience on physical structure in the cases with which we are familiar, and nothing in the arguments [...] suggests otherwise. It remains as plausible as ever, for example, that if my physical structure were to be replicated by some creature in the actual world, my conscious experience would be replicated, too. So it remains plausible that consciousness supervenes *naturally* on the physical. It is this view – natural supervenience without logical supervenience – that I will develop.

3   The arguments do not lead us to a dualism such as that of Descartes, with a separate realm of mental substance that exerts its own influence on physical processes. The best evidence of contemporary science tells us that the physical world is more or less causally closed: for every physical event, there is a physical sufficient cause. If so, there is no room for a mental 'ghost in the machine' to do any extra causal work. [...]

4   The dualism implied here is instead a kind of *property* dualism: conscious experience involves properties of an individual that are not entailed by the physical properties of that individual, although they may depend lawfully on those properties. Consciousness is a *feature* of the world over and above the physical features of the world. This is not to say it is a separate 'substance'; the issue of what it would take to constitute a dualism of substances seems quite

unclear to me. All we know is that there are properties of individuals in this world – the phenomenal properties – that are ontologically independent of physical properties. [...]

5   It remains plausible, however, that consciousness *arises* from a physical basis, even though it is not *entailed* by that basis. The position we are left with is that consciousness arises from a physical substrate in virtue of certain contingent laws of nature, which are not themselves implied by physical laws. [...]

6   Some people will think that the view should count as a version of materialism rather than dualism, because it posits such a strong lawful dependence of the phenomenal facts on the physical facts, and because the physical domain remains autonomous. Of course there is little point arguing over a name, but it seems to me that the existence of further contingent facts over and above the physical facts is a significant enough modification to the received materialist world view to deserve a different label. Certainly, if all that is required for materialism is that all facts be lawfully connected to the physical facts, then materialism becomes a weak doctrine indeed.

7   Although it is a variety of dualism, there is nothing antiscientific or supernatural about this view. The best way to think about it is as follows. Physics postulates a number of *fundamental* features of the world: space-time, mass-energy, charge, spin, and so on. It also posits a number of fundamental laws in virtue of which these fundamental features are related. Fundamental features cannot be explained in terms of more basic features, and fundamental laws cannot be explained in terms of more basic laws; they must simply be taken as primitive. Once the fundamental laws and the distribution of the fundamental features are set in place, however, almost everything about the world follows. That is why a fundamental theory in physics is sometimes known as a 'theory of everything'. But the fact that consciousness does not supervene on the physical features shows us that this physical theory is not *quite* a theory of everything. To bring consciousness within the scope of a fundamental theory, we need to introduce *new* fundamental properties and laws.

8   In his book *Dreams of a Final Theory* (1992), physicist Steven Weinberg notes that what makes a fundamental theory in physics special is that it leads to an explanatory chain all the way up, ultimately explaining everything. But he is forced to concede that such a theory may not explain consciousness. At best,

he says, we can explain the 'objective correlates' of consciousness. 'That may not be an explanation of consciousness, but it will be pretty close' (p. 45). But it is not close enough, of course. It does not explain everything that is happening in the world. To be consistent, we must acknowledge that a truly final theory needs an additional component.

9   There are two ways this might go. Perhaps we might take experience itself as a fundamental feature of the world, alongside space–time, spin, charge, and the like. That is, certain phenomenal properties will have to be taken as *basic* properties. Alternatively, perhaps there is some *other* class of novel fundamental properties from which phenomenal properties are derived. Previous arguments have shown that these cannot be physical properties, but perhaps they are nonphysical properties of a new variety, on which phenomenal properties are logically supervenient. Such properties would be related to experience in the same way that basic physical properties are related to nonbasic properties such as temperature. We could call these properties *protophenomenal* properties, as they are not themselves phenomenal but together they can yield the phenomenal. Of course it is very hard to imagine what a protophenomenal property could be like, but we cannot rule out the possibility that they exist. [...]

10   Where we have new fundamental properties, we also have new fundamental laws. Here the fundamental laws will be *psychophysical* laws, specifying how phenomenal (or protophenomenal) properties depend on physical properties. These laws will not interfere with physical laws; physical laws already form a closed system. Instead, they will be *supervenience laws*, telling us how experience arises from physical processes. We have seen that the dependence of experience on the physical cannot be derived from physical laws, so any final theory must include laws of this variety.

11   Of course, at this stage we have very little idea what the relevant fundamental theory will look like, or what the fundamental psychophysical laws will be. But we have reason to believe that such a theory exists. There is good reason to believe that there is a lawful relationship between physical processes and conscious experience, and any lawful relationship must be supported by fundamental laws. The case of physics tells us that fundamental laws are typically simple and elegant; we should expect the same of the fundamental laws in a theory of consciousness. Once we have a fundamental theory of consciousness to accompany a fundamental theory in physics, we may truly have a theory of everything. Given the basic physical and

psychophysical laws, and given the distribution of the fundamental properties, we can expect that all the facts about the world will follow. Developing such a theory will not be straightforward, but it ought to be possible in principle.

12   In a way, what is going on here with consciousness is analogous to what happened with electromagnetism in the nineteenth century. There had been an attempt to explain electromagnetic phenomena in terms of physical laws that were already understood, involving mechanical principles and the like, but this was unsuccessful. It turned out that to explain electromagnetic phenomena, features such as electromagnetic charge and electromagnetic forces had to be taken as fundamental, and Maxwell introduced new fundamental electromagnetic laws. Only this way could the phenomena be explained. In the same way, to explain consciousness, the features and laws of physical theory are not enough. For a theory of consciousness, new fundamental features and laws are needed.

13   This view is entirely compatible with a contemporary scientific worldview, and is entirely naturalistic. On this view, the world still consists in a network of fundamental properties related by basic laws, and everything is to be ultimately explained in these terms. All that has happened is that the inventory of properties and laws has been expanded, as happened with Maxwell. Further, nothing about this view contradicts anything in physical theory; rather, it supplements that theory. A physical theory gives a theory of physical processes, and a psychophysical theory tells us how those processes give rise to experience.

14   To capture the spirit of the view I advocate, I call it *naturalistic dualism*. It is naturalistic because it posits that everything is a consequence of a network of basic properties and laws, and because it is compatible with all the results of contemporary science. And as with naturalistic theories in other domains, this view allows that we can *explain* consciousness in terms of basic natural laws. There need be nothing especially transcendental about consciousness; it is just another natural phenomenon. All that has happened is that our picture of nature has expanded. Sometimes 'naturalism' is taken to be synonymous with 'materialism', but it seems to me that a commitment to a naturalistic understanding of the world can survive the failure of materialism. [...] Some might find a certain irony in the name of the view, but what is most important is that it conveys the central message: to embrace dualism is not necessarily to embrace mystery.

References

WEINBERG, S. (1992) *Dreams of a Final Theory*, New York, Pantheon Books.

The bogey of epiphenomenalism

Frank Jackson

Source: Jackson, Frank (1982) 'Epiphenomenal qualia', *Philosophical Quarterly*, 32, 127, 127–36. Grateful acknowledgement is made to the following source for permission to reproduce material within this book: Blackwell Publishing Ltd.

1   The major factor in stopping people from admitting qualia is the belief that they would have to be given a causal role with respect to the physical world and especially the brain; and it is hard to do this without sounding like someone who believes in fairies. I seek [...] to turn this objection by arguing that the view that qualia are epiphenomenal is a perfectly possible one. [...]

2   Three reasons are standardly given for holding that a quale like the hurtfulness of a pain must be causally efficacious in the physical world, and so, for instance, that its instantiation must sometimes make a difference to what happens in the brain. None, I will argue, has any real force. (I am much indebted to Alec Hyslop and John Lucas for convincing me of this.)

3   (i) It is supposed to be just obvious that the hurtfulness of pain is partly responsible for the subject seeking to avoid pain, saying 'It hurts' and so on. But, to reverse Hume, anything can fail to cause anything. No matter how often *B* follows *A*, and no matter how initially obvious the causality of the connection seems, the hypothesis that *A* causes *B* can be overturned by an over-arching theory which shows the two as distinct effects of a common underlying causal process.

4   To the untutored the image on the screen of Lee Marvin's fist moving from left to right immediately followed by the image of John Wayne's head moving in the same general direction looks as causal as anything. And of course throughout countless Westerns images similar to the first are followed by images similar to the second. All this counts for precisely nothing when we know the over-arching theory concerning how the relevant images are both effects of an underlying causal process involving the projector and the film. The epiphenomenalist can say exactly the same about the connection

between, for example, hurtfulness and behaviour. It is simply a consequence of the fact that certain happenings in the brain cause both.

5   (ii) The second objection relates to Darwin's Theory of Evolution. According to natural selection the traits that evolve over time are those conducive to physical survival. We may assume that qualia evolved over time – we have them, the earliest forms of life do not – and so we should expect qualia to be conducive to survival. The objection is that they could hardly help us to survive if they do nothing to the physical world.

6   The appeal of this argument is undeniable, but there is a good reply to it. Polar bears have particularly thick, warm coats. The Theory of Evolution explains this (we suppose) by pointing out that having a thick, warm coat is conducive to survival in the Arctic. But having a thick coat goes along with having a heavy coat, and having a heavy coat is *not* conducive to survival. It slows the animal down.

7   Does this mean that we have refuted Darwin because we have found an evolved trait – having a heavy coat – which is not conducive to survival? Clearly not. Having a heavy coat is an unavoidable concomitant of having a warm coat (in the context, modern insulation was not available), and the advantages for survival of having a warm coat outweighed the disadvantages of having a heavy one. The point is that all we can extract from Darwin's theory is that we should expect any evolved characteristic to be *either* conducive to survival *or* a by-product of one that is so conducive. The epiphenomenalist holds that qualia fall into the latter category. They are a by-product of certain brain processes that are highly conducive to survival.

8   (iii) The third objection is based on a point about how we come to know about other minds. We know about other minds by knowing about other behaviour, at least in part. The nature of the inference is a matter of some controversy, but it is not a matter of controversy that it proceeds from behaviour. That is why we think that stones do not feel and dogs do feel. But, runs the objection, how can a person's behaviour provide any reason for believing he has qualia like mine, or indeed any qualia at all, unless this behaviour can be regarded as the *outcome* of the qualia. Man Friday's footprint was evidence of Man Friday because footprints are causal outcomes of feet attached to people. And an epiphenomenalist cannot regard behaviour, or indeed anything physical, as an outcome of qualia.

9   But consider my reading in *The Times* that Spurs won. This provides excellent evidence that *The Telegraph* has also reported that Spurs won, despite the fact that (I trust) *The Telegraph* does not get the results from *The Times*. They each send their own reporters to the game. *The Telegraph*'s report is in no sense an outcome of *The Times*', but the latter provides good evidence for the former nevertheless.

10   The reasoning involved can be reconstructed thus. I read in *The Times* that Spurs won. This gives me reason to think that Spurs won because I know that Spurs' winning is the most likely candidate to be what caused the report in *The Times*. But I also know that Spurs' winning would have had many effects, including almost certainly a report in *The Telegraph*.

11   I am arguing from one effect back to its cause and out again to another effect. The fact that neither effect causes the other is irrelevant. Now the epiphenomenalist allows that qualia are effects of what goes on in the brain. Qualia cause nothing physical but are caused by something physical. Hence the epiphenomenalist can argue from the behaviour of others to the qualia of others by arguing from the behaviour of others back to its causes in the brains of others and out again to their qualia.

The paradox of phenomenal judgment

David J. Chalmers

1   When I say in conversation, 'Consciousness is the most mysterious thing there is', that is a behavioral act. When I wrote in an earlier chapter 'Consciousness cannot be reductively explained', that was a behavioral act. When I comment on some particularly intense purple qualia that I am experiencing, that is a behavioral act. Like all behavioral acts, these are in principle explainable in terms of the internal causal organization of my cognitive system. There is some story about firing patterns in neurons that will explain why these acts occurred; at a higher level, there is probably a story about cognitive representations and their high-level relations that will do the relevant explanatory work. We certainly do not know the details of the explanation now, but if the physical domain is causally closed, then there will be some reductive explanation in physical or functional terms.

2   In giving this explanation of my claims in physical or functional terms, we will never have to invoke the existence of conscious experience itself. The physical or functional explanation will be given independently, applying equally well to a zombie as to an honest-to-goodness conscious experiencer. It therefore seems that conscious experience is irrelevant to the explanations of phenomenal claims and irrelevant in a similar way to the explanation of phenomenal judgments, even though these claims and judgments are centrally concerned with conscious experience! [...]

3   To see the problem in a particularly vivid way, think of my zombie twin in the universe next door. He talks about conscious experience all the time – in fact, he seems obsessed by it. He spends ridiculous amounts of time hunched over a computer, writing chapter after chapter on the mysteries of

consciousness. He often comments on the pleasure he gets from certain sensory qualia, professing a particular love for deep greens and purples. He frequently gets into arguments with zombie materialists, arguing that their position cannot do justice to the realities of conscious experience.

4   And yet he has no conscious experience at all! In his universe, the materialists are right and he is wrong. Most of his claims about conscious experience are utterly false. But there is certainly a physical or functional explanation of why he makes the claims he makes. After all, his universe is fully law-governed, and no events therein are miraculous, so there must be *some* explanation of his claims. But such an explanation must ultimately be in terms of physical processes and laws, for these are the *only* processes and laws in his universe. [...]

5   Now my zombie twin is only a logical possibility, not an empirical one, and we should not get *too* worried about odd things that happen in logically possible worlds. Still, there is room to be perturbed by what is going on. After all, any explanation of my twin's behavior will equally count as an explanation of *my* behavior, as the processes inside his body are precisely mirrored by those inside mine. The explanation of *his* claims obviously does not depend on the existence of consciousness, as there is no consciousness in his world. It follows that the explanation of my claims is also independent of the existence of consciousness.

6   To strengthen the sense of paradox, note that my zombie twin is himself engaging in reasoning just like this. He has been known to lament the fate of *his* zombie twin, who spends all his time worrying about consciousness despite the fact that he has none. He worries about what that must say about the explanatory irrelevance of consciousness in his own universe. Still, he remains utterly confident that consciousness exists and cannot be reductively explained. But all this, for him, is a monumental delusion. There *is* no consciousness in his universe – in his world, the eliminativists have been right all along. Despite the fact that his cognitive mechanisms function in the same way as mine, *his* judgments about consciousness are quite deluded.

Panprotopsychism

David J. Chalmers

Source: Chalmers, David J. (2002) 'Consciousness and its place in nature', in David J. Chalmers (ed.), *Philosophy of Mind: Classical and Contemporary Readings*, New York, Oxford University Press, pp.247–72. Also in S.P. Stich and T.A. Warfield (eds) (2003) *The Blackwell Guide to Philosophy of Mind*, Oxford, Blackwell, pp.102–42. Grateful acknowledgement is made to the following source for permission to reproduce material within this book: Blackwell Publishing Ltd.

1   [Consider] the view that consciousness is constituted by the intrinsic properties of fundamental physical entities [...]. On this view, phenomenal or protophenomenal properties are located at the fundamental level of physical reality, and in a certain sense, underlie physical reality itself.

2   This view takes its cue from Bertrand Russell's discussion of physics in *The Analysis of Matter*. Russell pointed out that physics characterizes physical entities and properties by their relations to one another and to us. For example, a quark is characterized by its relations to other physical entities, and a property such as mass is characterized by an associated dispositional role, such as the tendency to resist acceleration. At the same time, physics says nothing about the intrinsic nature of these entities and properties. Where we have relations and dispositions, we expect some underlying intrinsic properties that ground the dispositions, characterizing the entities that stand in these relations. But physics is silent about the intrinsic nature of a quark, or about the intrinsic properties that play the role associated with mass. So this is one metaphysical problem: what are the intrinsic properties of fundamental physical systems?

3   At the same time, there is another metaphysical problem: how can phenomenal properties be integrated with the physical world? Phenomenal properties seem to be intrinsic properties that are hard to fit in with the structural/dynamic character of physical theory; and arguably, they are the only intrinsic properties that we have direct knowledge of. Russell's insight was that we might solve both these problems at once. Perhaps the intrinsic properties of the physical world are themselves phenomenal properties. Or

perhaps the intrinsic properties of the physical world are not phenomenal properties, but nevertheless constitute phenomenal properties: that is, perhaps they are protophenomenal properties. If so, then consciousness and physical reality are deeply intertwined.

4   This view holds the promise of integrating phenomenal and physical properties very tightly in the natural world. Here, nature consists of entities with intrinsic (proto)phenomenal qualities standing in causal relations within a spacetime manifold. Physics as we know it emerges from the relations between these entities, whereas consciousness as we know it emerges from their intrinsic nature. As a bonus, this view is perfectly compatible with the causal closure of the microphysical, and indeed with existing physical laws. The view can retain the *structure* of physical theory as it already exists; it simply supplements this structure with an intrinsic nature. And the view acknowledges a clear causal role for consciousness in the physical world: (proto)phenomenal properties serve as the ultimate categorical basis of all physical causation.

5   This view has elements in common with both materialism and dualism. From one perspective, it can be seen as a sort of materialism. If one holds that physical terms refer not to dispositional properties but the underlying intrinsic properties, then the protophenomenal properties can be seen as physical properties, thus preserving a sort of materialism. From another perspective, it can be seen as a sort of dualism. The view acknowledges phenomenal or protophenomenal properties as ontologically fundamental, and it retains an underlying duality between structural–dispositional properties (those directly characterized in physical theory) and intrinsic protophenomenal properties (those responsible for consciousness). One might suggest that while the view arguably fits the letter of materialism, it shares the spirit of antimaterialism. [...]

6   One could also characterize this form of the view as a sort of panpsychism, with phenomenal properties ubiquitous at the fundamental level. One could give the view in its most general form the name *panprotopsychism*, with either protophenomenal or phenomenal properties underlying all of physical reality. [...]

7   [This] view is admittedly speculative, and it can sound strange at first hearing. Many find it extremely counterintuitive to suppose that fundamental physical systems have phenomenal properties: e.g., that there is something it

is like to be an electron. The protophenomenal version of the view rejects this claim, but retains something of its strangeness: it seems that any properties responsible for constituting consciousness must be strange and unusual properties, of a sort that we might not expect to find in microphysical reality. Still, it is not clear that this strangeness yields any strong objections. Like epiphenomenalism, the view appears to be compatible with all our evidence, and there is no direct evidence against it. One can argue that if the view were true, things would appear to us just as they in fact appear. And we have learned from modern physics that the world is a strange place: we cannot expect it to obey all the dictates of common sense.

8   One might also object that we do not have any conception of what protophenomenal properties might be like, or of how they could constitute phenomenal properties. This is true, but one could suggest that this is merely a product of our ignorance. [...] Of course it would be very desirable to form a positive conception of protophenomenal properties. Perhaps we can do this indirectly, by some sort of theoretical inference from the character of phenomenal properties to their underlying constituents; or perhaps knowledge of the nature of protophenomenal properties will remain beyond us. Either way, this is no reason to reject the truth of the view.

9   There is one sort of principled problem in the vicinity. Our phenomenology has a rich and specific structure: it is unified, bounded, differentiated into many different aspects, but with an underlying homogeneity to many of the aspects, and appears to have a single subject of experience. It is not easy to see how a distribution of a large number of individual microphysical systems, each with their own protophenomenal properties, could somehow add up to this rich and specific structure. Should one not expect something more like a disunified, jagged collection of phenomenal spikes? [...]

10   [W]e need a much better understanding of the *compositional* principles of phenomenology: that is, the principles by which phenomenal properties can be composed or constituted from underlying phenomenal properties, or protophenomenal properties. We have a good understanding of the principles of physical composition, but no real understanding of the principles of phenomenal composition. This is an area that deserves much close attention: I think it is easily the most serious problem for [this] view. At this point, it is an open question whether or not the problem can be solved. [...]

11   Overall, [this view] promises a deeply integrated and elegant view of nature. No-one has yet developed any sort of detailed theory in this class, and it is not yet clear whether such a theory can be developed. But at the same time, there appear to be no strong reasons to reject the view. As such [it] is likely to provide fertile grounds for further investigation, and it may ultimately provide the best integration of the physical and the phenomenal within the natural world.

References

RUSSELL, B. (1927) *The Analysis of Matter*, London, Kegan Paul.

Mary and the blue banana

Daniel C. Dennett

Source: Dennett, Daniel C. (1991) *Consciousness Explained*, London, Allen Lane, pp.399–401. Copyright © 1992 Daniel Dennett. Reproduced with permission from Penguin Group, UK and Abner Stein.

1   Mary has had *no* experience of color at all (there are no mirrors to look at her face in, she's obliged to wear black gloves, etc., etc.), and so, at that special moment when her captors finally let her come out into the colored world which she knows only by description (and black-and-white diagrams), 'it seems just obvious', as Jackson says, that she will learn something. Indeed, we can all vividly imagine her, seeing a red rose for the first time and exclaiming, 'So *that's* what red looks like!' And it may also occur to us that if the first colored things she is shown are, say, unlabeled wooden blocks, and she is told only that one of them is red and the other blue, she won't have the faintest idea which is which until she somehow learns which color words go with her newfound experiences.

2   That is how almost everyone imagines this thought experiment – not just the uninitiated, but the shrewdest, most battle-hardened philosophers [...]. Only Paul Churchland (1985, 1990) has offered any serious resistance to the *image*, so vividly conjured up by the thought experiment, of Mary's dramatic discovery. The image is wrong; if that is the way you imagine the case, you are simply not following directions! The reason no one follows directions is because what they ask you to imagine is so preposterously immense, you can't even try. The crucial premise is that 'She has *all* the physical information'. That is not readily imaginable, so no one bothers. They just imagine that she knows lots and lots – perhaps they imagine that she knows everything that anyone knows *today* about the neurophysiology of color vision. But that's just a drop in the bucket, and it's not surprising that Mary would learn something if *that* were all she knew.

3   To bring out the illusion of imagination here, let me continue the story in a surprising – but legitimate – way:

And so, one day, Mary's captors decided it was time for her to see colors. As a trick, they prepared a bright blue banana to present as her first color experience ever. Mary took one look at it and said 'Hey! You tried to trick me! Bananas are yellow, but this one is blue!' Her captors were dumfounded. How did she do it? 'Simple', she replied. 'You have to remember that I know *everything* – absolutely everything – that could ever be known about the physical causes and effects of color vision. So of course before you brought the banana in, I had already written down, in exquisite detail, exactly what physical impression a yellow object or a blue object (or a green object, etc.) would make on my nervous system. So I already knew exactly what *thoughts* I would have (because, after all, the 'mere disposition' to think about this or that is not one of your famous qualia, is it?). I was not in the slightest surprised by my experience of blue (what surprised me was that you would try such a second-rate trick on me). I realize it is *hard for you to imagine* that I could know so much about my reactive dispositions that the way blue affected me came as no surprise. Of course it's hard for you to imagine. It's hard for anyone to imagine the consequences of someone knowing absolutely everything physical about anything!'

4   Surely I've cheated, you think. I must be hiding some impossibility behind the veil of Mary's remarks. Can you prove it? My point is not that my way of telling the rest of the story proves that Mary *doesn't* learn anything, but that the usual way of imagining the story doesn't *prove* that she *does*. It doesn't prove anything; it simply pumps the intuition that she does ('it seems just obvious') by lulling you into imagining something other than what the premises require.

5   It is of course true that in any realistic, readily imaginable version of the story, Mary would come to learn something, but in any realistic, readily imaginable version she might know a lot, but she would not know everything physical. Simply imagining that Mary knows a lot, and leaving it at that, is not a good way to figure out the implications of her having 'all the physical information' – any more than imagining she is filthy rich would be a good way to figure out the implications of the hypothesis that she owned everything. It may help us imagine the extent of the powers her knowledge gives her if we begin by enumerating a few of the things she obviously knows in advance. She knows black and white and shades of gray, and she knows the difference between the color of any object and such surface properties as glossiness versus matte, and she knows all about the difference between luminance boundaries and color boundaries (luminance boundaries are those that show up on black-and-white television, to put it roughly). And she knows precisely

which effects – described in neurophysiological terms – each particular color will have on her nervous system. So the only task that remains is for her to figure out a way of identifying those neurophysiological effects 'from the inside'. You may find you can readily imagine her making a *little* progress on this – for instance, figuring out tricky ways in which she would be able to tell that some color, whatever it is, is *not* yellow, or *not* red. How? By noting some salient and specific reaction that her brain would have only for yellow or only for red. But if you allow her even a little entry into her color space in this way, you should conclude that she can leverage her way to complete advance knowledge, because she doesn't just know the *salient* reactions, she knows them all. [...]

6   I know that this will not satisfy many of Mary's philosophical fans, and that there is a lot more to be said, but – and this is my main point – the actual proving must go on in an arena far removed from Jackson's example, which is a classic provoker of Philosophers' Syndrome: mistaking a failure of imagination for an insight into necessity.

References

CHURCHLAND, P.M. (1985) 'Reduction, qualia and the direct inspection of brain states', *Journal of Philosophy*, 82, 8–28.

CHURCHLAND, P.M. (1990) 'Knowing qualia: a reply to Jackson', in Churchland, P.M., *A Neurocomputational Perspective: The Nature of Mind and the Structure of Science*, Cambridge, MA., MIT Press/A Bradford Book, pp. 67–76.

The ability hypothesis

David Lewis

Source: Lewis, David Lewis (1988) 'What experience teaches', in William G. Lycan (ed.) (1990) *Mind and Cognition: A Reader*, Oxford, Blackwell, pp.499–519. (Originally published in *Proceedings of the Russellian Society*, University of Sydney.)

1   If you have a new experience, you gain abilities to remember and to imagine. After you taste Vegemite, and you learn what it's like, you can afterward remember the experience you had. By remembering how it once was, you can afterward imagine such an experience. Indeed, even if you eventually forget the occasion itself, you will very likely retain your ability to imagine such an experience.

2   Further, you gain an ability to recognize the same experience if it comes again. If you taste Vegemite on another day, you will probably know that you have met the taste once before. And if, while tasting Vegemite, you know that it is Vegemite you are tasting, then you will be able to put the name to the experience if you have it again. Or if you are told nothing at the time, but later you somehow know that it is Vegemite that you are then remembering or imagining tasting, again you can put the name to the experience, or to the memory, or to the experience of imagining, if it comes again. Here, the ability you gain is an ability to gain information if given other information. Nevertheless, the information gained is not phenomenal, and the ability to gain information is not the same thing as information itself. [...]

3   As well as gaining the ability to remember and imagine the experience you had, you also gain the ability to imagine related experiences that you never had. After tasting Vegemite, you might for instance become able to imagine tasting Vegemite ice cream. By performing imaginative experiments, you can predict with some confidence what you would do in circumstances that have never arisen – whether you'd ask for a second helping of Vegemite ice cream, for example.

4   These abilities to remember and imagine and recognize are abilities you cannot gain (unless by super-neurosurgery, or by magic) except by tasting Vegemite and learning what it's like. You can't get them by taking lessons [...]. The Ability Hypothesis says that knowing what an experience is like just *is* the possession of these abilities to remember, imagine, and recognize. It isn't the possession of any kind of information, ordinary or peculiar. It isn't knowing that certain possibilities aren't actualized. It isn't knowing-that. It's knowing-how. Therefore it should be no surprise that lessons won't teach you what an experience is like. Lessons impart information; ability is something else. Knowledge-that does not automatically provide know-how.

5   There are parallel cases. Some know how to wiggle their ears; others don't. If you can't do it, no amount of information will help. Some know how to eat with chopsticks, others don't. Information will help up to a point – for instance, if your trouble is that you hold one chopstick in each hand – but no amount of information, by itself, will bring you to a very high level of know-how. Some know how to recognize a C-38 locomotive by sight, others don't. If you don't, it won't much help if you memorize a detailed geometrical description of its shape, even though that does all the eliminating of possibilities that there is to be done. (Conversely, knowing the shape by sight doesn't enable you to write down the geometrical description.) Information very often contributes to know-how, but often it doesn't contribute enough. That's why music students have to practice.

6   Know-how is ability. But of course some aspects of ability are in no sense knowledge: strength, sufficient funds. Other aspects of ability are, purely and simply, a matter of information. If you want to know how to open the combination lock on the bank vault, information is all you need. It remains that there are aspects of ability that do *not* consist simply of possession of information, and that we *do* call knowledge. The Ability Hypothesis holds that knowing what an experience is like is that sort of knowledge.

7   If the Ability Hypothesis is the correct analysis of knowing what an experience is like, then phenomenal information is an illusion. We ought to explain that illusion. It would be feeble, I think, just to say that we're fooled by the ambiguity of the word 'know': we confuse ability with information because we confuse knowledge in the sense of knowing-how with knowledge in the sense of knowing-that. There may be two senses of the word 'know', but they are well and truly entangled. They mark the two pure endpoints of a range of mixed cases. The usual thing is that we gain information and ability together.

If so, it should be no surprise if we apply to pure cases of gaining ability, or to pure cases of gaining information, the same word 'know' that we apply to all the mixed cases.

Mary's room

Michael Tye

Source: Tye, Michael (1995) *Ten Problems of Consciousness*, Cambridge Mass:, MIT Press, pp.172–4. Grateful acknowledgement is made to the following source for permission to reproduce material within this book: MIT Press.

1 [The knowledge] argument has provoked extensive discussion. Part of the difficulty in evaluating it is that it uses the very slippery term 'fact'. Let us begin, then, with a discussion of how the term 'fact' is to be understood.

2 Facts are sometimes taken to be as fine-grained in their individuation conditions as the contents of the propositional attitudes. Facts, in this sense, are what are expressed by the that-clauses of true beliefs. On this view, the fact that there is water ahead is not the same as the fact that there is H_2O ahead, since the beliefs are different. The one belief can be had without the other. Likewise, the fact that Tom is now asleep is not the same as the fact that Tom is asleep at 2:00 p.m. on Tuesday, even given that it is now 2:00 p.m., Tuesday. What distinguishes these facts are the different conceptual modes of representation they incorporate. The external, objective states of affairs are the same, but the ways in which they are conceptualized are different. The fact that Tom is now asleep, in the given circumstances, consists of the same real, external state of affairs as the fact that Tom is asleep at 2:00 p.m. Tuesday – in each case, there is the same real individual in the real state at the same time – but the one brings in a temporal indexical concept with reference to the individual's being in the state, whereas the other does not. Facts are identical, then, if and only if they consist of the same objective, actual states of affairs under the same concepts.

3 There is another, more coarse-grained view of facts that identifies them outright with states of affairs that obtain in the objective world, regardless of how those states of affairs are conceived. On this view, the fact that there is water ahead is identical with the fact that there is H_2O ahead.

4 On the former conception of facts, the existence of facts that are neither functional nor (lower-level) physical is something that can be accepted by the

functionalist or the physicalist.[1] For, there are such facts if there are concepts that are neither functional nor (lower-level) physical. And the existence of concepts of neither of these sorts can be accepted by everyone. What matters is whether there are real, nonconceptual items that cannot be accommodated within a physicalist framework.

5   This perhaps calls for a little further explanation. Consider the fact that I am tall. This fact is not the same as the fact that Michael Tye is tall, on the fine-grained conception of facts, since the first-person concept expressed by 'I' is not a constituent of the latter fact. Nevertheless, there is here only a single, real, external state of affairs, which consists of the individual, Michael Tye, exemplifying the property of being tall. The existence of the fact that I am tall, as distinct from the fact that Michael Tye is tall, is no objection to physicalism. One and the same thing can be conceived in different ways.

6   Moreover, the first-person concept is not a concept with a functional or (lower-level) physical content. In thinking of Michael Tye as me, I do not think of Michael Tye as the person who plays a certain functional role or as the bearer of certain physiological or chemical or other lower-level, physical properties. So the concept expressed by 'I' is not a physiological or chemical or functional concept. [...]

7   The question, then, is whether the case of Mary reveals any real, nonconceptual items that pose problems for physicalism. If it does, then there will be facts that cannot be accommodated by the physicalist view, even on the broader conception of facts.

8   Mary does not know what it is like to experience red. So, on my view, she does not know the phenomenal content of the state of experiencing red (whatever the determinate shade). She does not know this for two reasons. First, she *lacks* the phenomenal concept *red*; second, she cannot *apply* the phenomenal concept *this* to the color represented in the experience of red. After all, Mary has never had the experience of red, nor is she now having the experience of red. She is thus in no position to conceptualize the phenomenal content properly. There really is, then, something Mary does not know. Still, the state of experiencing red can have a [physical] essence [...]. And Mary will know that essence [...] if she knows all the facts countenanced by physicalism. So there is nothing of a nonconceptual sort not known to Mary. The fact she does not know is a fine-grained one within which there are phenomenal concepts. However, the coarse-grained, nonconceptual fact it contains *is*

(broadly) physical. Once the different notions of fact are sorted out, Mary creates no trouble for physicalism.

Note

[1] Here, I take lower-level physical facts to be facts expressible in the vocabulary of microphysics, chemistry, neurophysiology, or molecular biology.

The unimagined preposterousness of zombies

Daniel C. Dennett

Source: Dennett, Daniel C. (1995) 'The unimagined preposterousness of zombies', *Journal of Consciousness Studies*, 2 (4), 322–6. Also in Daniel C. Dennett (1998) *Brainchildren*, Harmondsworth, Penguin Books, pp.171–7. Grateful acknowledgement is made to the following source for permission to reproduce material within this book: Imprint Academic.

1   [W]hen philosophers claim that zombies are conceivable, they invariably underestimate the task of conception (or imagination), and end up imagining something that violates their own definition. This conceals from them the fact that the philosophical concept of a zombie is sillier than they have noticed. [...] If, *ex hypothesi*, zombies are behaviourally indistinguishable from us normal folk, then they are really behaviourally indistinguishable! They say just what we say, they understand what they say (or, not to beg any questions, they understand^Z what they say), they believe^Z what we believe, right down to having beliefs^Z that perfectly mirror all our beliefs about inverted spectra, 'qualia' *and every other possible topic of human reflection and conversation.* [...]

2   In Dennett (1991), I introduced the category of a *zimbo*, by definition a zombie equipped for higher-order reflective informational states (e.g., beliefs^Z about its other beliefs^Z and its other zombic states). This was a strategic move on my part, I hasten to add. Its point was to make a distinction within the imaginary category of zombies that would have to be granted by believers in zombies, and that could do all the work they imputed to consciousness, thereby showing either that their concept was subtly self-contradictory, since some zombies – zimboes – were conscious after all, or that their concept of consciousness was not tied to anything familiar and hence amounted to an illicit contrast: consciousness as a 'player to be named later' or an undeclared wild-card. As I pointed out when I introduced the term, zombies behaviourally indistinguishable from us are zimboes, capable of all the higher-order reflections we are capable of, because they are competent, *ex*

hypothesi, to execute all the behaviours that, when we perform them, manifestly depend on our higher-order reflections. Only zimboes could pass a demanding Turing Test, for instance, since the judge can ask as many questions as you like about what it was like answering the previous question, what it is like thinking about how to answer this question, and so forth. Zimboes think^Z they are conscious, think^Z they have qualia, think^Z they suffer pains – they are just 'wrong' (according to this lamentable tradition), in ways that neither they nor we could ever discover!

3   According to Flanagan and Polger, there is still a difference between the inner lives of zombies and ours: theirs are merely 'informationally sensitive' while ours are also 'experientially sensitive'. This contrast, drawn from Flanagan (1992) is ill-conceived, so far as I can see. [...] The contrast Flanagan and Polger would draw between zombies and us [...], I draw between simple zombies and fancier zombies – zimboes. [...]

4   Flanagan and Polger compound this mistake when they go on to ask what the adaptive advantage of consciousness (as contrasted with mere 'informational sensitivity') would be. [...] The question of adaptive advantage, however, is ill-posed in the first place. If consciousness is (as I argue) not a single wonderful separable thing ('experiential sensitivity') but a huge complex of many different informational capacities that individually arise for a wide variety of reasons, there is no reason to suppose that 'it' is something that stands in need of its own separable status as fitness-enhancing. It is not a separate organ or a separate medium or a separate talent.

5   To see the fallacy, consider the parallel question about what the adaptive advantage of *health* is. Consider 'health inessentialism': for any bodily activity *b*, performed in any domain *d*, even if *we* need to be healthy to engage in it (e.g., pole vaulting, swimming the English Channel, climbing Mount Everest), it could in principle be engaged in by something that wasn't healthy at all. So what is health *for*? Such a mystery! But the mystery would arise only for someone who made the mistake of supposing that health was some *additional* thing that could be added or subtracted to the proper workings of all the parts. In the case of health we are not apt to make such a simple mistake, but there is a tradition of supposing just this in the case of consciousness. Supposing that by an act of stipulative imagination you can remove consciousness while leaving all cognitive systems intact – a quite standard but entirely bogus feat of imagination – is like supposing that by an act of stipulative imagination, you can remove health while leaving all bodily functions and powers intact. If you

think you can imagine this, it's only because you are confusedly imagining some health-module that might or might not be present in a body. Health isn't that sort of thing, and neither is consciousness.

6   All I can do at this point is to reiterate my plea: consider the suggestion, once again, that when you've given an evolutionary account of the talents of zimboes, you've answered all the real questions about consciousness *because the putative contrast between zombies and conscious beings is illusory*. I know that many philosophers are sure that it is not illusory. I know that they are sure that *they* don't make such mistakes of imagination when they claim to conceive of zombies. Maybe they don't. But [...] I have never seen an argument in support of the zombie distinction that didn't make a mistake of the imagination of this sort. [...] My conviction is that the philosophical tradition of zombies would die overnight if philosophers ceased to mis-imagine them, but of course I cannot prove it *a priori*. We will just have to wait for some philosopher to write an essay in defence of zombies that doesn't commit any such misdirections, and see what happens.

7   To make sure the challenge is clear, let me review the burden and its attendant requirements. One must show that there is a difference between conscious beings and zombies, *and* one must show that one's demonstration of this difference doesn't depend on underestimating in the well-nigh standard way the powers of zombies. Here's a handy way of checking one's exercises of imagination: demonstrate that a parallel difference does *not* exist between zimboes and less fancy zombies. One may in this way ensure that one hasn't simply underestimated the power of zombies by imagining some crude non-zimbo zombie, rather than a zombie with all the 'informational sensitivity' of us human beings.

References

DENNETT, D.C. (1991) *Consciousness Explained*, Boston, MA, Little, Brown and Company.

FLANAGAN, O. (1992) *Consciousness Reconsidered*, Cambridge, MA, MIT Press.

Conceivability and possibility

David Papineau

Source: Papineau, David (2002) *Thinking about Consciousness*, Oxford, Oxford University Press, pp.91–2.

1   Some philosophers hold that [...] conceivability always guarantees a real possibility. They maintain that, to every conceivable non–identity (N ≠ M, say), there corresponds a genuine possibility. In cases where N *is* M, this can't of course be the possibility that N is not itself. Rather, in such cases, it must be that N (or M) refers by association with contingent descriptions, which then generates the possibility that the entity referred to might not satisfy those descriptions.

2   Putting all this together, these philosophers thus hold that, whenever N ≠ M is conceivable, either (a) one of the terms involved refers by description, or (b) N really isn't identical to M. This makes it clear why materialists must deny the initial premiss: they cannot allow that conceivability always points to a real possibility. For, if it did, then the manifest conceivability of zombies would imply either (a) that phenomenal concepts refer by contingent description, or (b) that phenomenal properties aren't material properties. But the former alternative is ruled out by Kripke's argument, and the latter refutes materialism straight off.

3   My response is that conceivability does not always point to a real possibility. I take the Cicero-Tully example [...] to provide strong support for this view. It is conceivable, for Jane, that Cicero ≠ Tully, even though (a) Cicero *is* Tully and (b) she associates neither Cicero nor Tully with any descriptions.

4   Someone who wants to uphold conceivability as a guarantee of possibility will need to argue here that Jane must have some further ideas about Cicero and Tully, if she is to have genuine concepts of them. That is, she must associate certain descriptions a priori with 'Cicero' and 'Tully', if she is really to be capable of thinking with these terms. This will then restore the link

between conceivability and possibility, since it will give us the possibility that Cicero/Tully does not satisfy those descriptions.

5   But why suppose that any such associations are necessary for Jane to be competent with these terms? The theory of names is a large subject, and this is not the place to start pursuing it. But one clear lesson of the last thirty years of work in this area is surely that Jane's conceptual competence with 'Cicero' and 'Tully' need owe nothing to any specific ideas she associates with these terms. Rather, it will be enough if she has picked up the names 'Cicero' and 'Tully' from competent speakers, and intends to use them as they do. And this clearly doesn't require that she associate any further descriptions with these names.

6   More generally, the contention that conceivability is a guide to possibility places implausibly strong constraints on the theory of reference. It requires that, whenever two directly referring terms refer to the same thing, it must be a priori knowable that they do so. For, on the conceivability → possibility assumption, if it is so much as *conceivable* that some *directly* referring 'N' and 'M' do not co-refer, then it must be *true* that N ≠ M, for without any associated descriptions there is no other possibility around to explain the conceivability. On the conceivability → possibility view, then, we can be confident that two entities really are distinct whenever directly referring thoughts about them allow them to *seem* possibly distinct.

7   [...] I shall use the term 'the transparency thesis' for the claim that identities involving two directly referring terms are always a priori knowable. I see no reason whatsoever to accept this thesis. It seems to me to hinge on some atavistic view of reference. For the transparency thesis to be true, the basic referential relations, direct referential relations, would have to involve some kind of unmediated mental grasp of the entities referred to, a grasp which left no room for mistakes about identity. Far from accepting this, I take the basic referential relations to depend on all kinds of facts external to thinkers' heads, facts which create plenty of room for a thinker to be wrong about whether two terms refer directly to the same thing.

On properties and recognitional concepts

Peter Carruthers

Source: Carruthers, Peter (2000) *Phenomenal Consciousness: A Naturalistic Theory*, Cambridge, Cambridge University Press, pp.55–7.

1   Some of our mental-state concepts are *recognitional*, or at least admit of recognitional applications. This seems especially plausible in connection with sensation-concepts, and, more generally, concepts of states which are phenomenally conscious. In these cases our concepts can consist in a capacity to recognise, straight off, the corresponding state.

2   I can recognise the feel of pain purely by its feel, without having to appeal to any of my beliefs about causal roles and functions. And then I can conceive of a world where all of the physical facts and causal roles remain as they are, but where the *feel* is different or absent. But it does not follow from this that *what I recognise* – namely, the feel – *is not* some physical or functionally-identifiable state. The failure of *feel* to supervene logically on *function* shows something about how we conceptualise phenomenally conscious mental states; but it shows nothing about the nature of those states themselves. [...] [I]t is an open question whether the very properties which we recognise on the basis of *feel* may actually be physical and/or functional and/or representational ones.

3   Consider, for comparison, some other domain in which people can come to possess purely-recognitional concepts (or at least concepts which are *nearly* so – see below). It is said, for example, that people can be trained to sex very young chicks entirely intuitively by handling them, without having any idea of what they are doing, or of the basis on which they effect their classifications. So suppose that Mary is someone who has been trained to classify chicks into As and Bs – where the As are in fact male, and the Bs are in fact female – but without Mary knowing that this is what she is doing, and without her having any idea of what it is about the As which underpins recognition.

4   Then we ask Mary: 'Can you conceive of a world which is micro-physically identical with our own, except that the chicks which are As in this world are Bs in that, and vice versa?' If *A* really does express a purely recognitional concept for Mary – if she really has no beliefs at all about the nature of *A-hood* beyond the fact that some chicks have it – then she should answer 'Yes'. For then all she has to imagine is that she is confronted with a chick exactly like this A-chick in all micro-physical respects, but that it is one which evokes a recognitional application of the concept *B*. Plainly Mary should not – if she is sensible – conclude from this thought-experiment that *A-hood* is not a physical or functional property of the chicks. And if she did, she would reason fallaciously. For as we know, the property picked out by her recognitional concept is in fact the property of being male.

5   It is unlikely, of course, that Mary will have no beliefs at all about the nature of *A-hood*. She will probably at least believe that *A-hood* is a perceptible property of the chicks. And if, like us, she believes that perception is a causal process, then she must believe that instances of *A-hood* can have some sort of causal impact upon her sense-organs. These beliefs may well lead her to believe that the property of *A-hood* is somehow or other constituted by physical facts about the chicks, and so to reject the possibility of a world where all micro-physical facts remain the same but *A-hood* and *B-hood* are reversed. But then the only differences here from recognitional concepts of feel are (first) that many of us may have *no* beliefs about the causal nature of introspective recognition. And (second) even if we do believe that introspection is causally mediated, we lack any beliefs about the nature of the introspective process which might imply physicality, in the way that we *do* believe that outer perception of the properties of physical objects requires those properties to have physical effects upon our sense-organs.

6   The morals of this example for phenomenal consciousness should be clear. [...] Possessing purely recognitional concepts of *feel*, we can deploy those concepts in thought experiments in ways which are unconstrained by the physical or functional facts. But nothing follows about the non-physical, non-functional, nature of the properties which those concepts pick out. So although we can *conceive of* worlds in which all the micro-physical facts remain as they are, but in which phenomenal consciousness is different or absent, it may be that there are really no such worlds. For it may be that phenomenal consciousness is constituted by some physical or functional fact, in which case

there are no possible worlds where the facts of consciousness can be different while the constituting facts remain the same.

The explanatory gap

Joseph Levine

Source: Levine, Joseph (1993) 'On leaving out what it's like', in M. Davies and G.W. Humphreys (eds), *Consciousness: Psychological and Philosophical Essays*, Oxford, Blackwell, pp.121–36.

1   For a physicalist theory to be successful, it is not only necessary that it provide a physical description for mental states and properties, but also that it provide an *explanation* of these states and properties. In particular, we want an explanation of why when we occupy certain phsyico-functional states we experience qualitative character of the sort we do. It's not enough for these purposes to explain the contribution of qualitative states to the production of behaviour, or the fixation of perceptual belief; this is a job that a physicalist theory can presumably accomplish. [...] Rather what is at issue is the ability to explain qualitative character itself; why it is like what it is like to see red or feel pain. Conceivability arguments serve to demonstrate the inability of physicalist theories to provide just this sort of explanation of qualitative character. [...]

2   [There is] an important epistemological difference between the purported reductions of water to H_2O and pain to the firing of C-fibres; namely, that the chemical theory of water explains what needs to be explained, whereas a physicalist theory of qualia still 'leaves something out'. It is because the qualitative character itself is left *unexplained* by the physicalist or functionalist theory that it remains conceivable that a creature should occupy the relevant physical or functional state and yet not experience qualitative character.

3   The basic idea is that a reduction should explain what is reduced, and the way we tell whether this has been accomplished is to see whether the phenomenon to be reduced is epistemologically necessitated by the reducing phenomenon, i.e. whether we can see why, given the facts cited in the reduction, things must be the way they seem on the surface. I claim that we have this with the chemical theory of water but not with a physical or

functional theory of qualia. The robustness of the absent and inverted qualia intuitions is testimony to this lack of explanatory import.

4   Let me make the contrast between the reduction of water to H_2O and a physico-functional reduction of qualia more vivid. What is explained by the theory that water is H_2O? Well, as an instance of something that's explained by the reduction of water to H_2O let's take its boiling point at sea level. The story goes something like this. Molecules of H_2O move about at various speeds. Some fast-moving molecules that happen to be near the surface of the liquid have sufficient kinetic energy to escape the intermolecular attractive forces that keep the liquid intact. These molecules enter the atmosphere. That's evaporation. The precise value of the intermolecular attractive forces of H_2O molecules determines the vapour pressure of liquid masses of H_2O, the pressure exerted by molecules attempting to escape into saturated air. As the average kinetic energy of the molecules increases, so does the vapour pressure. When the vapour pressure reaches the point where it is equal to atmospheric pressure, large bubbles form within the liquid and burst forth at the liquid's surface. The water boils.

5   I claim that given a sufficiently rich elaboration of the story above, it is inconceivable that H_2O should not boil at 212°F at sea level (assuming, again, that we keep the rest of the chemical world constant). But now contrast this situation with a physical or functional reduction of some conscious sensory state. No matter how rich the information processing or the neurophysiological story gets, it still seems quite coherent to imagine that all that should be going on without there being anything it's like to undergo the states in question. Yet, if the physical or functional story really explained the qualitative character, it would not be so clearly imaginable that the qualia should be missing. For, we would say to ourselves something like the following:

> Suppose creature X satisfies functional (or physical) description F. I understand – from my functional (or physical) theory of consciousness – what it is about instantiating F that is responsible for its being a conscious experience. So how could X occupy a state with those very features and yet *not* be having a conscious experience?

Phenomenal content: the PANIC theory

Michael Tye

Source: Tye, Michael (1995) *Ten Problems of Consciousness*, Cambridge Mass:, MIT Press, pp.137–42. Grateful acknowledgement is made to the following source for permission to reproduce material within this book: MIT Press.

1   Sensory representations serve as inputs for a number of systems of higher-level cognitive processing. They are themselves outputs of specialized sensory modules (for perceptual experiences, bodily sensations, primary emotions, and moods).[1] Representations occurring within the modules supply information the creature needs to construct or generate sensory representations, but they are not themselves sensory. [...] [E]xperience and feeling arise at the level of the outputs from the sensory modules and the inputs to a cognitive system. It is here that phenomenal content is found.

2   Sensory representations (viewed in the above way) represent either internal or external physical items. Bodily sensations represent internal bodily changes. They are directly tuned to such changes (in optimal conditions). Likewise emotions and moods. In the case of perceptual experiences, the items sensorily represented are external environmental states or features.

3   Phenomenal content, I maintain, is content that is appropriately poised for use by the cognitive system, content that is abstract and nonconceptual. I call this the PANIC theory of phenomenal character: phenomenal character is one and the same as Poised Abstract Nonconceptual Intentional Content. I hope that this will not be taken as a literal indication of the state of mind to which I have been driven by the problems of consciousness! It follows that representations that differ in their PANICs differ in their phenomenal character, and representations that are alike with respect to their PANICs are alike in their phenomenal character.

4   The claim that the contents relevant to phenomenal character must be *poised* is to be understood as requiring that these contents attach to the

(fundamentally) maplike output representations of the relevant sensory modules and stand ready and in position to make a direct impact on the belief/desire system. To say that the contents stand ready in this way is not to say that they always do have such an impact. The idea is rather that they supply the inputs for certain cognitive processes whose job it is to produce beliefs (or desires) directly from the appropriate nonconceptual representations, *if* attention is properly focused and the appropriate concepts are possessed. So, attentional deficits can preclude belief formation as can conceptual deficiencies. [...]

5   The PANIC theory entails that no belief could have phenomenal character. A content is classified as phenomenal only if it is nonconceptual and poised. Beliefs are not nonconceptual, and they are not appropriately poised. They lie within the cognitive system, rather than providing inputs to it. Beliefs are not sensory representations at all.

6   The claim that the contents relevant to phenomenal character must be *abstract* is to be understood as demanding that no particular concrete objects enter into these contents (except for the subjects of experiences in some cases). Since different concrete objects can look or feel exactly alike phenomenally, one can be substituted for the other without any phenomenal change. Which particular object is present, then, does not matter. Nor does it matter if *any* concrete object is present to the subject at all. Whether or not you have a left leg, for example, you can feel a pain in your left leg; in both cases, the phenomenal character of your experience can be exactly the same. So the existence of that particular leg is not required for the given phenomenal character. What is crucial to phenomenal character is the representation of general features or properties. Experiences nonconceptually represent that there is *a* surface or *an* internal region having so-and-so features at such-and-such locations, and thereby they acquire their phenomenal character.

7   The claim that the contents relevant to phenomenal character must be *nonconceptual* is to be understood as saying that the general features entering into these contents need not be ones for which their subjects possess matching concepts. [...]

8   Consider [...] the case of color. The *Dictionary of Color*, by Maerz and Paul (1950), contains 7,056 color samples and 4,000 color names. Most of us have a *much* more limited color vocabulary, but even Maerz and Paul have no names for many of their samples. And humans can discriminate many, many

more colors than those presented in Maerz and Paul, something on the order of ten million, according to some estimates. So we have names for only a few of the colors we can discriminate, and we also have no stored representations in memory for most colors either. There simply is not enough room.

9   Beliefs and thoughts involve the application of concepts. One cannot believe that a given animal is a horse, for example, unless one has the concept *horse*. At a minimum, this demands that one has the stored memory representation *horse*, which one brings to bear in an appropriate manner (by, for example, activating the representation and applying it to the sensory input). However, as noted above [...], phenomenal seemings or experiences are *not* limited in this way. My experience of red_{19}, for example, is phenomenally different from my experience of red_{21}, even though I have no stored memory representations of these specific hues and hence no such concepts as the concepts red_{21} and red_{19}. These points generalize to the other senses. Phenomenal character, and hence phenomenal content, on my view, is nonconceptual.

10   Sensory experiences, then, are *determinate* in a way that our stored memory representations are not. We have general concepts for the determinables but not for their determinate values. I do not deny, of course, that we can represent the determinables via indexical concepts when we focus our cognitive gaze upon them. But experience outstrips such acts of noticing (and can occur without them altogether). Indexical concepts do not enter into phenomenal character any more than general concepts. Phenomenal character, I claim, is wholly nonconceptual.

11   Which features involved in bodily and environmental states are elements of phenomenal contents? There is no a priori answer. Empirical research is necessary. The relevant features will be the ones represented in the output representations of the sensory modules. I call these features, whatever they might be, *observational* features. They are the features our sensory states track in optimal conditions. Since the receptors associated with the various sensory modules and the processing that goes on within them vary, features that are observational for one module need not be observational for another. What gets outputted obviously depends on what gets inputted and how the module operates. I conjecture that for perceptual experience, the observational features will include properties like being an edge, being a corner, being square, being red_{29}.

12   In classifying being square as observational, I am not supposing that it has that status for all possible species of creatures. Observationality, in my view, is relative to creatures with a certain sort of sensory equipment. Thus, some features that are observational for us might not be for other possible creatures (and vice versa).

13   Suppose, for example, it looks to me that there is a tiger present. It seems plausible to suppose that the property of being a tiger is not itself a feature represented by the outputs of the sensory modules associated with vision. Our sensory states do not track *this* feature. There might conceivably be creatures other than tigers that look to us phenomenally just like tigers. Still, perhaps the property of being a tiger *could* have been sensorily represented by some creatures. Perhaps we can imagine that there are alien creatures with microscope eyes whose visual sensory states are tuned to the genetic essence of tigers. If so, what it is like for these creatures, when they view tigers, will be very different from what it is like for us. The phenomenal contents of their states will be very different from ours. What will it be like for them? We cannot say (or think): we lack the right sensory perspective.

References

MAERZ, A. & PAUL, M. (1950) *A Dictionary of Color*, New York, McGraw-Hill.

Note

[1] By a primary emotion or mood, I mean one that is universally experienced from very early on in life.

The intentionality of feelings and experiences

Michael Tye

Source: Tye, Michael (1995) *Ten Problems of Consciousness*, Cambridge Mass:, MIT Press, pp.113–31. Grateful acknowledgement is made to the following source for permission to reproduce material within this book: MIT Press.

1   [I]n optimal conditions, sensory experiences of the pain sort track certain sorts of disturbances in the body, paradigmatically, bodily damage. So pains represent such disturbances.

2   For example, a twinge of pain represents a mild, brief disturbance. A throbbing pain represents a rapidly pulsing disturbance. Aches represent disorders that occur *inside* the body rather than on the surface. These disorders are represented as having volume, as gradually beginning and ending, as increasing in severity and then slowly fading away. The volumes so represented are not represented as precise or sharply bounded. This is why aches are not felt to have precise locations, unlike pricking pains, for example. A stabbing pain is one that represents sudden damage over a particular well-defined bodily region. This region is represented as having volume (rather than being two-dimensional), as being the shape of something sharp-edged and pointed (like that of a dagger). In the case of a pricking pain, the relevant damage is represented as having a sudden beginning and ending on the surface or just below, and as covering a very tiny area. A racking pain is one that represents that the damage involves the stretching of internal body parts (e.g., muscles).

3   In each of the above cases, the subject of the pain undergoes a sensory representation of a certain sort of bodily disturbance. The disturbances vary with the pains. Consider, for example, a pricking pain in the leg. Here, it seems phenomenologically undeniable that pricking is experienced *as* a feature tokened within the leg, and not as an intrinsic feature of the experience itself. What is experienced as being pricked is a part of the surface of the leg. This is

nicely accounted for by the above proposal. It should also be noted that since pricking pains do not represent pins, my account does not have the implausible consequence that creatures who live in worlds without pins cannot have pricking sensations or that in these worlds creatures undergoing such sensations are misrepresenting what is going on in them.

4   My proposal, then, is that pains are sensory representations of bodily damage or disorder. More fully, they are mechanical responses to the relevant bodily changes in the same way that basic visual sensations are mechanical responses to proximate visual stimuli. In the case of pain, the receptors (known as nociceptors) are distributed throughout the body. These receptors function analogously to the receptors on the retina. They are transducers. They are sensitive only to certain changes in the tissue to which they are directly connected (typically, damage), and they convert this input immediately into symbols. Representations are then built up mechanically of internal bodily changes, just as representations are built up of external surfaces in the case of vision. These representations, to repeat, are sensory. They involve no concepts. One does not need to be able to conceptualize a given bodily disturbance in order to feel pain. And even if one can, it is not relevant, because feeling pain demands the sensory experience of that disturbance.

5   It is interesting to note that there are circumstances in which people cannot tell whether they are feeling pressure or pain, for example, during dental drilling under partial anesthetic. This has a simple explanation on the above account. Both sensations involve the representation of a bodily disturbance. Some disturbances – tissue distortions of certain sorts – fall on the border between those paradigmatic of pain and those paradigmatic of pressure. Sensory representations of such disturbances are neither clearly pain experiences nor clearly pressure experiences.

6   Perhaps it will now be said that it is not clear how the above proposal accomodates the well-established fact that pain is susceptible to top-down influences. For example, in one experiment, joggers were found to run faster in a lovely wooded area than on a track. Apparently, they experienced less pain in their arms and legs while viewing the trees and flowers and, as a result, ran at a quicker pace. [...] Anxiety, by contrast, increases the experience of pain, as, for example, when one compares a present injury to some past one.

7   These facts, if indeed they are facts (see below), about pain are no threat to my position. They may be explained by supposing that the pain receptor pathway in the spinal column leading to the somatosensory cortex (the primary center of pain) has a gate in it that is controlled by input from the higher brain centers (the gate control theory). When this gate is partly closed, less information gets through, and the feeling of pain diminishes. As it opens further, more information is enabled to pass. Anxiety, excitement, joy, concentration, and other higher-level activities affect the orientation of the gate. So, the fact that the experience of pain is, *in the above sense*, cognitively penetrable presents no real difficulty for my proposal. What happens is simply that one's cognitive assessment of the situation feeds back down into the sensory module for the experience of pain and affects how much information gets through about bodily damage.

8   I might add that it is also not obvious to what degree the experience of pain itself, considered as a sensory state, really can be changed by the cognitive centers. What seems undeniable is that cognitive reactions can affect one's *awareness* of pain experiences. But awareness of a pain experience is itself a cognitive state. It involves bringing the experience under concepts. These concepts are what allow us to form conceptions through introspection of what it is like for us to undergo the experiences. [...]

9   So far I have said nothing directly about the painfulness of pains. How is this feature of pains to be accounted for within the above proposal? To begin with, it should be noted that we often speak of bodily damage as painful. When it is said that a cut or a burn or a bruise is painful or hurts, what is meant is (roughly) that it is *causing* a feeling, namely, the very feeling the person is undergoing, and that this feeling elicits an immediate dislike for itself together with anxiety about, or concern for, the state of the bodily region where the disturbance feels located.

10   Now pains do not themselves cause feelings that cause dislike: they *are* such feelings, at least in typical cases. So pains are not painful in the above sense. Still, they are painful in a slightly weaker sense: they typically elicit the *cognitive* reactions described above. Moreover, when we introspect our pains, we are aware of their sensory contents as painful. This is why, if I have a pain in my leg, intuitively, I am aware of something in my leg (and not in my head, which is where the experience itself is) as painful. My pain represents damage in my leg, and I then cognitively classify that damage as painful (via the application of the concept *painful* in introspection).

11   In normal circumstances, a person who has a pain in a leg and who reports that something in her leg is painful is not under any sort of illusion. But a man who reports to his doctor that he has a pain in his left arm is in a different situation if it is discovered that the real cause of his pain lies in his heart. Such a man has a pain in his left arm – he undergoes a sensory experience that represents to him damage there – but there really is nothing *in his left arm* that is painful. What is painful is something happening in his heart. [...]

12   The intentionalist approach to pain extends in a natural way to all bodily sensations. To have a tickle in a toe is to undergo a certain sort of experience. What experiences of the tickle sort track (in optimal conditions) is the presence of something lightly touching or brushing against the surface of the body. So that is what they represent. Tickles are sensory representations of bodily disturbances, just as pains are. Tickles also have a standard reactive component (like pains in normal cases): they cause an impulse to break contact with the object brushing lightly against the skin, together with a further desire to rub or scratch the affected bodily region, if contact continues.

13   Itches also represent surface disturbances, though not ones of the same sort as tickles. In addition, itches cause in their owners reactions of dislike (less intense than for pains) plus the impulse to rub or scratch the relevant bodily part.

14   Tingling sensations represent patterns of bodily disturbance that consist of a large number of tiny distinct parts, each of which is quickly varying or pulsating. The feeling of thirst represents dryness in the throat and mouth. Feeling hot is a state that represents an increase in body temperature above the normal one. Hunger pangs represent contractions of the stomach walls when the stomach is empty.[1] In these cases, the representations themselves are sensory experiences, not conceptual states. So the fact that for some bodily sensations – for example, the feeling of hunger – the person in the street may not be able to say just which bodily state is represented has no significance. Whereof you cannot speak (or think), thereof you can still sense.

15   What about Block's example of the sensations involved in orgasm? In this case, one undergoes sensory representations of certain physical changes in the genital region. These changes quickly undulate in their intensity. Furthermore, they are highly pleasing. They elicit an immediate and strong positive reaction.

16   It is important to stress again that the representations of bodily changes involved in orgasms are nonconceptual. This is why if I see that my partner is having an orgasm, it does not follow that I am having one myself. Seeing-that is conceptual. It involves believing-that together with associated visual sensations. Feeling an orgasm requires nonconceptual sensory experience of the pertinent bodily changes, not conceptual representation of the generic state. No belief about myself or my partner is necessary. Furthermore, my orgasms represent physical changes in *my* body, not in my partner. But what I see, if I see that she is having an orgasm, is something about *her*. [...]

17   So far I have said nothing about background feelings. These are what we feel from moment to moment when we are not gripped by any particular emotion or mood. As I write, I am not especially happy or unhappy; I am not angry or sad or fearful. Nothing out of the ordinary is happening, feeling-wise. But it would be a serious mistake to infer from this that there is no feeling going on at all. I am constantly feeling all sorts of things pertaining to my body, for example, where all my limbs are, and how they are connected to one another, even though I rarely attend to these feelings.

18   The importance of background feelings to our mental lives is difficult to overstate. Think about lying motionless in bed in the dark, breathing rhythmically, and yet being unable to fall asleep. Imagine that you are focusing on your breathing. Still, you can feel all your limbs and where they are in the bed. Now imagine losing those feelings of your body, going completely numb all over. Would you still have a clear sense of yourself? Imagine that you even lose any feeling with respect to your own head, your own breathing, the pressure of the pillow on your head. It seems to me that if this situation were to continue your sense of yourself would, at best, be seriously threatened. [...]

19   So background feelings, I maintain, are representations that fit into the general category of bodily sensations, although they are not confined in their contents to single, discrete bodily regions like pains. They are constantly present in normal persons, anchoring them in their bodies. [...]

20   I come finally to the case of emotions and moods. Some felt moods and emotions obviously have intentional content. Feeling elated that an exam has been passed or feeling angry that it is raining yet again are two straightforward examples. These states are plausibly taken to be compound, however, having a belief and a simple mood or emotion as a component. In the one case, there is the belief that an exam has been passed, which elicits the feeling of elation, and,

in the other, the belief that it is raining yet again, which causes the feeling of anger. The beliefs here are certainly intentional, but the simple feelings of elation and of depression do not themselves seem to be intentional at all. Or so it is widely supposed.

21   This view is much too hasty. Simple felt moods and emotions are sensory representations similar in their intentional character to background feelings and bodily sensations like pain. Let me begin with some comments on the emotions.

22   Suppose you suddenly feel extremely angry. Your body will change in all sorts of ways: for example, your blood pressure will rise, your nostrils will flare, your face will flush, your chest will heave as the pattern of your breathing alters, your voice will become louder, you will clench your teeth and hands, the muscles in your cheeks will become more tense, your immune system will alter rapidly. These physical changes are registered in the sensory receptors distributed throughout your body. In response to the activity in your receptors, you will mechanically build up a complex sensory representation of how your body has changed, of the new body state you are in. In this way, you will *feel* the physical changes. The feeling you undergo consists in the complex sensory representation of these changes.

23   In different circumstances, you might still feel very angry without feeling *just* the way you do above. For your body might change in somewhat different ways. The felt difference arises because of the different body state that is sensorily represented. You might even feel anger if you lose your body altogether and you are kept alive as a brain in a vat, stimulated to undergo the very brain states you do when you are angry in normal circumstances, via instructions from a computer. This is because you need not actually undergo changes like those I have described. It suffices that you undergo a sensory *representation* of those changes. Where there is representation, there can be misrepresentation. And misrepresentation, or illusion, is what is going on in the case of the brain in the vat.

24   Here is another example. Suppose you think that you are about to be robbed, and you feel very scared. Again, assuming circumstances are normal, your body will change both internally and externally. For example, your face will go white, your stomach will turn, your heart rate will speed up, your lips will tremble, your legs will go weak.[2] There are sensory states in your head that

track all these changes and others. So you will sense the changes and, sensing them, will feel great fear.

25   Why accept this view? For one thing, it comports very nicely with the views expressed in the earlier sections on bodily sensations and background feelings. For another, consider what it would he like to feel angry if you felt *no changes at all* of the sort specified above in connection with anger. I myself can form no clear conception of what is being asked. Take away the sensations of all such changes, and there seems to me no feeling of anger left. Likewise fear. [...]

26   To claim that emotions are sensory representations need not be to claim that they *only* have sensory aspects. In fact, I reject the latter position. Part of what makes a given state an instance of anger is its effects on what the person wants and/or believes, and relatedly on how he or she behaves. Anger, for example, normally causes the desire or urge to act violently with respect to the perceived cause. Fear normally causes the impulse to flee. Any sensory state that did not play causal roles like these would not be classified as an instance of anger or fear. So cognitive reaction is undoubtedly an important factor in each emotion.

27   Furthermore, emotions are often triggered by cognitive assessments. My thinking that I am about to be robbed causes various physical reactions in my body of the sort described earlier. These reactions activate sensory receptors located throughout my body, and a complex sensory representation is then generated of the physical changes that have occurred in me. This representation tracks those changes (in optimal conditions). In turn, it causes certain cognitive reactions, for example, the desire to run and the belief that the best way out is to my left, which may themselves produce further bodily changes that are also sensorily registered.

28   Emotions are not always produced by cognitive states, however. Some very basic emotions, which are universally felt, are often produced by noncognitive stimuli. In these cases, we are wired to experience the emotions in response to the stimuli. Consider, for example, the sensations of chest pain and pressure involved in a heart attack. These stimuli elicit the feelings of anxiety and fear. Arguably, we are innately built to respond mechanically to activity in the relevant nociceptors first by generating the nonconceptual pain and pressure experiences and then, in reaction to those experiences, by generating the feelings of anxiety and fear. It does seem plausible to suppose

that it is not necessary to *think* to oneself that one is about to die or that danger is present in order to feel fear in these circumstances. Of course, not all felt emotions are like this. Many require a cognitive cause. Think, for example, of the feeling of embarrassment or gratitude or indignation.

29   The view I have taken of emotions and background feelings can be extended to moods. We think of moods as descending on us, as filling us up, as coming over us. As John Haugeland (1985, p. 235) has noted, moods are like 'vapors that seep into and infect everything we are about'. Moreover, this is what our experience of moods tells us. We experience moods *as* descending on us, *as* being located where we are, *as* taking us over.

30   Mood experiences, I maintain, like emotions, are sensory representations. What exactly they represent is not easy to pin down, but the general picture I have is as follows: For each of us, there is at any given time a range of physical states constituting functional equilibrium. Which states these are might vary from time to time. But when functional equilibrium is present, we operate in a balanced, normal way without feeling any particular mood. When moods descend on us, we are responding in a sensory way to a *departure* from the pertinent range of physical states. We are sensing physical changes in our 'body landscapes' (as Damasio [1994] puts it). [...]

31   So moods, like emotions, are intentional states; and like emotions, moods also have certain standard cognitive effects that are partly definitive of their presence. These effects, however, are not as straightforward to specify as they are in the case of emotions. For depression or anxiety, there is no characteristic activity standardly caused by them as in the case of fear or anger. Rather, there is a characteristic style or manner of behavior. Depression is a state that causes people who are subject to it to behave in a depressed manner, whatever they may be doing. Similarly, anxiety causes people to behave anxiously. [...]

31   The overall conclusion I draw is that feelings and experiences generally have intentional content. Philosophical orthodoxy on this topic is just plain wrong.

References

DAMASIO, A. (1994) *Descartes' Error*, New York, G.P. Putnam's Sons.

HAUGELAND, J. (1985) *Artificial Intelligence: The Very Idea*, Cambridge, Mass., MIT Press, Bradford Books.

JAMES, W. (1890) *The Principles of Psychology*, vol. 2, New York, Dover (1950).

Notes

[1] This feeling typically elicits the desire or urge to eat, just as the feeling of pain typically causes the strong desire that it cease.

[2] Cf. William James 1890.

A problem for FOR-theories

Peter Carruthers

Source: Carruthers, Peter (1998) 'Natural theories of consciousness', *European Journal of Philosophy*, 6, 208–9. Grateful acknowledgement is made to the following source for permission to reproduce material within this book: Basil Blackwell Ltd.

1   One major difficulty with FOR-accounts in general, is that they cannot distinguish between what the *world* (or the state of the organism's own body) is like for an organism, and what the organism's *experience of the world* (or of its own body) is like for the organism. This distinction is very frequently overlooked in discussions of consciousness. And Tye, for example, will move (sometimes in the space of a single sentence) from saying that his account explains what *colour* is like for an organism with colour-vision, to saying that it explains what *experiences of colour* are like for that organism. But the first is a property of the world (or of a world-perceiver pair, perhaps), whereas the latter is a property of the organism's experience of the world (or of an experience-experiencer pair). These are plainly distinct.

2   It is commonplace to note that each type of organism will occupy a distinctive point of view on the world, characterised by the kinds of perceptual information which are available to it, and by the kinds of perceptual discriminations which it is capable of making (Nagel 1974). This is part of what it means to say that bats (with echolocation) and cats (without colour vision) occupy a different point of view on the world from ourselves. Put differently but equivalently: the world (including subjects' own bodies) is *subjectively presented* to different species of organism somewhat differently. And to try to characterise this is to try and understand what the world for such subjects *is like*. But it is one thing to say that *the world* takes on a subjective aspect by being presented to subjects with differing conceptual and discriminatory powers, and it is quite another thing to say that the subject's *experience of the world* also has such a subjective aspect, or that there is something which the *experience* is *like*. Indeed, by parity of reasoning, this would seem to require subjects to possess information about, and to make discriminations amongst, their own states of experience. And it is just this

which provides the rationale for HOR-accounts as against FOR-accounts, in fact.

3   According to HOR-theories, first-order perceptual states (if non-conscious [...]) may be adequately accounted for in FOR terms. The result will be an account of the point of view – the subjective perspective – which the organism takes towards its world (and the states of its own body), giving us an account of what the world, for that organism, *is like*. But the HOR-theorist maintains that something else is required in accounting for what an *experience* is like for a subject, or in explaining what it is for an organism's *mental states* to take on a subjective aspect. For this, we maintain, higher-order representations – states which meta-represent the subject's own mental states – are required. And it is hard to see how it could be otherwise, given the distinction between what the world is like for an organism, and what its experience of the world is like.

4   We therefore need to distinguish between two different sorts of subjectivity – between worldly-subjectivity and mental-state-subjectivity. [...] FOR-theory may be adequate to account for the former; but not to explain the latter, where some sort of HOR-theory is surely needed. Which of these two deserves the title 'phenomenal consciousness'? There is nothing (or nothing much) in a name; and I am happy whichever reply is given. But it is the subjectivity of experience which seems to be especially problematic – if there is a 'hard problem' of consciousness (Chalmers 1996), it surely lies here. At any rate, nothing can count as a complete theory of phenomenal consciousness which cannot explain it – as FOR-theory plainly cannot.

References

CHALMERS, D. (1996) *The Conscious Mind: towards a fundamental theory*, Oxford, Oxford University Press.

NAGEL, T. (1974) 'What is it like to be a bat?', *Philosophical Review*, 82, 435–56.

Explaining consciousness

David M. Rosenthal

Source: Rosenthal David M. (2002) 'Explaining consciousness', in David J. Chalmers (ed.), *Philosophy of Mind: Classical and Contemporary Readings*, Oxford, Oxford University Press, pp.406–21. Copyright © 2002 by David J. Chalmers. Used by permission of Oxford University Press Inc.

1   Whatever else we may discover about consciousness, it's clear that, if one is totally unaware of some mental state, that state is not a conscious state. A state may of course be conscious without one's paying conscious attention to it and, indeed, even without one's being conscious of every mental aspect of the state. But if one is not at all aware of a state, that state is not a conscious state. This observation provides a useful start towards a theory of state consciousness. Because it is sufficient for a state not to be conscious that one be completely unaware of it, being aware of a state is perforce a necessary condition for that state to be a conscious state.

2   Being aware of a mental state, however, is not also a sufficient condition for the state to be conscious. There are ways we can be aware of our mental states even when those states are not conscious states. So, if we can rule out those ways, we'll be left with the particular way in which we are aware of our mental states when those states are conscious states. And this would give us a condition that's both necessary and sufficient for a mental state to be conscious.

3   For present purposes, I'll speak interchangeably of being aware of something and being conscious of that thing. So my strategy is to explain a state's being a conscious state in terms of our being conscious of that state in some particular way. No circle is involved here, since we are explaining one phenomenon in terms of another. It is one thing for us to be conscious *of* something – what we may call *transitive consciousness* – and another for a state to be a conscious state –what I'm calling state consciousness. And we understand transitive consciousness – our being conscious *of* things – independently of understanding what it is for mental states to be conscious states. We are transitively conscious of something by virtue of being either in

an intentional or a sensory state whose content is directed upon that thing. And a state's having a certain content is a distinct property from that of a state's being conscious. [...]

4   Let us turn, then, to the question of what it is that is special about the way we are transitively conscious of our mental states when those states are conscious states. Perhaps the most obvious thing is that, when a state is conscious, we are conscious of it in a way that seems immediate. [...]

5   Our being conscious of [our conscious mental states] seems unmediated because we are conscious of them in a way that relies on no conscious inference, no inference, that is, of which we are aware.

6   Consider a case. I am annoyed, but unaware of it. Though my annoyance is not conscious, you observe my annoyed behavior and tell me I am annoyed. There are two ways I might react. I might accept what you tell me, but still feel no conscious annoyance. My belief that I'm annoyed would be the result of a conscious inference based on your remark, and possibly also a conscious inference from my coming to notice my own relevant behavior. But there is another possibility; your remark might cause me to become conscious of my annoyance independently of any such conscious inference. In that case my annoyance would have become a conscious state.

7   A state's being conscious involves one's being noninferentially conscious of that state. Can we pin down any further the way we are transitively conscious of our conscious states? There are two broad ways of being transitively conscious of things. We are conscious of something when we see it or hear it, or perceive it in some other way. And we are conscious of something when we have a thought about it. Which kind of transitive consciousness is relevant here? When our mental states are conscious, do we somehow sense those states or do we have thoughts about them?

8   The perceptual model may seem inviting. When we perceive things, we seem intuitively to be directly conscious of them; nothing seems to mediate between our perceptions and the objects we perceive. So perhaps the perceptual model can explain the apparent immediacy of the way we are conscious of our conscious states. But this advantage of the perceptual model won't help us decide between that model and the alternative view that we are conscious of our conscious states by having thoughts about them. Even though our thoughts do often rely on conscious inferences involving perceptions or other thoughts, they often don't.

9   There is, however, another consideration that seems to favor the perceptual model. A theory of consciousness must explain the qualitative dimension of our conscious sensory states. And sensing always involves some sensory quality. So if we are conscious of our conscious states by sensing them, perhaps we can explain the qualitative dimension of consciousness as due to that higher-order sensing. Such an explanation, however, would at best just put off the problem, since the qualitative aspect of this higher-order perceiving would itself need to be explained in turn.

10   Not only do the considerations favoring the perceptual model fail to hold up; there is also reason to reject the model. Higher-order sensing would have to exhibit characteristic mental qualities; what qualities might those be? One possibility is that the higher-order perception and the state we perceive would both exhibit the same sensory quality. But this is theoretically unmotivated. When we perceive something, the quality of our perceptual state is distinct from any property of the object we perceive. When we see a tomato, for example, the redness of our sensation is not the same property as the redness of the tomato. So we have no reason to think that the higher-order qualities would be the same as those of our lower-order states.

11   If the higher- and lower-order qualities were distinct, however, it's a mystery what those higher-order qualities could be. What mental qualities are there in our mental lives other than those which characterize our first-order sensory states? And if the higher-order qualities are neither the same as nor distinct from our first-order qualities, the higher-order states in virtue of which we are conscious of our conscious states cannot have qualities at all. But if those higher-order states have no qualitative properties, they can only be higher-order intentional states of some sort.

12   We must therefore reject the perceptual model of how we are transitively conscious of our conscious states. The only alternative is that we are conscious of our conscious states by virtue of having thoughts about them. Since these thoughts are about other mental states, I shall refer to them as *higher-order thoughts* (HOTs).

13   This narrows down somewhat the way we are transitively conscious of our mental states when those states are conscious. But we can narrow things down even more. When a mental state is conscious, we are conscious of being in that state; so the content of our HOT must be, roughly, that one is in that very state. And, since merely being disposed to have a thought about

something does not make one conscious of that thing, the HOT must be an occurrent thought, rather than just a disposition to think that one is in the target state. Moreover, when we are conscious of something by being in an intentional state that's about that thing, the intentional state is normally assertoric. Indeed, it's likely that being in an intentional state whose mental attitude is not assertoric does not result in one's being conscious of the thing the intentional state is about. So we should require that the HOT has an assertoric mental attitude. Finally, to capture the intuition about immediacy, we have seen that our HOTs must be independent of any inference of which we are aware. Our hypothesis, therefore, is that a mental state is conscious just in case it is accompanied by a noninferential, nondispositional, assertoric thought to the effect that one is in that very state.

14   One problem that seems to face this hypothesis is that, even when we are in many conscious states, we are typically unaware of having any such HOTs. But this is not a difficulty; we are conscious of our HOTs only when those thoughts are themselves conscious, and it's rare that they are. Moreover, the hypothesis readily explains why this should be so. The HOTs it posits are conscious thoughts only when they are accompanied, in turn, by yet higher-order thoughts about them, and that seldom happens. Not having conscious HOTs, moreover, does nothing at all to show that we do not have HOTs that fail to be conscious.

15   There is another reason it's useful to distinguish cases in which HOTs are conscious from cases in which they are not. The way we are ordinarily conscious of our conscious states differs from the way we are conscious of mental states of which we are introspectively conscious. Being introspectively conscious of a mental state involves, roughly, our deliberately focusing on that state, and very few of our conscious states are the subjects of any such introspective scrutiny. If being conscious of a mental state were the same as being introspectively conscious of it, it would be rare that we are conscious of our conscious states, and we would be unable to explain state consciousness in terms of transitive consciousness. Not distinguishing the two, moreover, would lead one mistakenly to see the HOT hypothesis as providing a theory only of introspective consciousness, and not of state consciousness generally. But the present hypothesis actually allows us to explain what is distinctive about introspective consciousness. A state is introspectively conscious when the accompanying HOT is a conscious thought. Ordinary, nonintrospective

state consciousness, by contrast, occurs instead when the HOT is not itself conscious. [...]

16   There is an especially interesting argument that supports the appeal to HOTs. When a mental state is conscious, one can noninferentially report being in that state, whereas one cannot report one's nonconscious mental states. Every speech act, moreover, expresses an intentional state with the same content as that of the speech act [...]. So a noninferential report that one is in a mental state will express a noninferential thought that one is in that state, that is, a HOT about the state. We can best explain this ability noninferentially to report our conscious states by supposing that the relevant HOT is there to be expressed. Correspondingly, the best explanation of our inability to report nonconscious states is that no HOTs accompany them. [...]

17   On this argument, sensory consciousness is simply a special case of state consciousness – the special case in which the state that's conscious is a sensory state. Sensory states are states with sensory quality. So sensory consciousness occurs when a mental state has two properties: sensory quality and the property of state consciousness.

18   Moreover, these two properties are distinct and can occur independently of one another. State consciousness can of course occur without sensory quality, since nonsensory, intentional states are often conscious. But the converse is possible as well; sensory qualities can occur without state consciousness. Sensory qualities are just whatever properties sensory states have on the basis of which we distinguish among them and sort them into types. Since state consciousness consists in our being conscious of a mental state in some suitable way, these properties are independent of state consciousness. We would need some special reason to think that the properties on the basis of which we distinguish among sensations cannot occur except when we're conscious of the states that have those properties. It's hard to see what special reason there could be.

19   This conclusion conflicts with the familiar contention that sensory quality cannot occur nonconsciously. On that view, state consciousness is intrinsic, or essential, to sensory quality. But it's far from clear that this view is correct. Subliminal perception and peripheral vision both involve perceptual sensations of which we're wholly unaware, and the same is very likely true of such dissociative phenomena as blindsight. Bodily sensations such as pains can also occur without being conscious. For example, we often have a

headache or other pain throughout an extended period even when distractions intermittently make us wholly unaware of the pain. [...]

20   There is, of course, nothing it's like to have a pain or a sensation of red unless the sensation in question is conscious. And some have argued from this to the conclusion that sensory quality simply cannot exist unless there's something it's like to have it. But what it's like for one to have a pain, in the relevant sense of that idiom, is simply what it's like for one to be conscious of having that pain. So there won't be anything it's like to have a pain unless the pain is conscious. Of course, if nonconscious pains were impossible, there would be no difference between a pain's existing and its being conscious, and its sensory quality would then exist only when there is something it's like to have it. But it begs the question simply to assume that pains, or other sensations, cannot exist nonconsciously. Moreover, the intuition that sensory states cannot exist nonconsciously gets whatever force it has from our first-person point of view. And it's unreasonable to rely on consciousness to tell us whether some phenomenon can exist outside of consciousness. [...]

21   Nonetheless, there does seem to be a serious problem about what it is for sensory states to be conscious. When a sensory state is conscious, there is something it's like for us to be in that state. When it's not conscious, we do not consciously experience any of its qualitative properties; so then there is nothing it's like for us to be in that state. How can we explain this difference? A sensory state's being conscious means that we are transitively conscious of that state in some suitable way. So being transitively conscious of a sensory state, in that particular way, must result in there being something it's like to be in that state. But how can being transitively conscious of a sensory state have this result? What way of being transitively conscious of our sensory states could, by itself, give rise to there being something it's like for us to be in those states? [...]

22   The difficulty seems particularly pressing for the HOT hypothesis. An attraction of the perceptual model was that it might help explain the qualitative dimension of our conscious sensory states. Since perceiving involves sensory qualities, if a state's being conscious consisted in our perceiving it, perhaps we could explain the way we are conscious of the qualities of our conscious sensations. As we saw, that explanation fails, since the higher-order qualities it appeals to would themselves need to be explained. But the HOT hypothesis may seem even less well-suited to deal with this problem. How can one's being

in an intentional state, of whatever sort, result in there being something it's like for one to be in a conscious sensory state?

23   There are two ways the HOT theorist might try to show that being in a suitable intentional state can have this result. One would be to show that it's evident, from a first-person point of view, that one has a suitable HOT when, and only when, there is something it's like for one to be in some sensory state. We could then argue that one's having that HOT is responsible for there being something it's like for one to be in that state.

24   But if the HOT hypothesis is correct, we cannot expect to find any such first-person correlations. That's because, on that hypothesis, the HOTs in virtue of which our sensory states are conscious are seldom conscious thoughts. And when a thought is not conscious, it will seem, from a first-person point of view, that one does not have it.

25   So if the HOT hypothesis is correct, it will rarely seem, from a first-person point of view, that HOTs accompany one's conscious sensory states. Our first-person access reveals correlations only with conscious HOTs, not HOTs generally. And HOTs are conscious only in those rare cases in which one has a third-order thought about the HOT. But on the HOT hypothesis, HOTs need not be conscious for there to be something it's like to be in the target sensory states. So we cannot hope to test the hypothesis by correlating in a first-person way the occurrence of HOTs with there being something it's like to be in conscious sensory states.

26   But we need not rely solely on first-person considerations; there are other factors that help establish the correlation between having HOTs and there being something it's like for one to be in conscious sensory states. In particular, there is a striking connection between what HOTs we are able to have and what sensory qualities we are able to be aware of. And the best explanation of this connection is that accompanying HOTs do result in there being something it's like for one to be in states with those sensory qualities.

27   Consider wine tasting. Learning new concepts for our experiences of the gustatory and olfactory properties of wines typically leads to our being conscious of more fine-grained differences among the qualities of our sensory states. Similarly with other sensory modalities; acquiring new concepts for specific musical and artistic experiences, for example, enables us to have conscious experiences with more finely differentiated sensory qualities.

Somehow, the new concepts appear to generate new conscious sensory qualities.

28   There are two ways this might happen. One is that coming to have new concepts results in our sensory states' coming to have distinguishing properties that they did not previously have. This is highly implausible. How could merely having new concepts give rise to our sensory states' having new properties? On a widespread view, concepts are abilities to think certain things; how could having a new ability change the properties of the sensory states that result from the same type of stimulus?

29   But there is another possibility. The new concepts might result in new conscious qualities not by generating those properties, but by making us conscious of properties that were already there. The new concepts would enable us to be conscious of sensory qualities we already had, but had not been conscious of.

30   Possessing a concept allows us to form intentional states that have a certain range of contents. So which contents our intentional states can have must somehow make a difference to which sensory qualities can occur consciously. Moreover, the new concepts, which make possible conscious experiences with qualities that seem new to us, are the concepts of those very qualities.[1] So being able to form intentional states about certain sensory qualities must somehow result in our being able to experience those qualities consciously. It must result, that is, in there being something specific that it's like for us to be in the relevant sensory states.

31   How could this happen? The only plausible explanation is that a sensory quality's being conscious does actually consist in our having a HOT about that quality. This is true not only of the relatively finely differentiated qualities we have just now been considering. We can extrapolate to any sensory quality, however crudely individuated, and extrapolate even to whether or not we are conscious of any quality at all.

32   Take the conscious experience of hearing the sound of an oboe. If one's HOTs couldn't classify one's sensations in terms of the sound of an oboe but only that of some undifferentiated woodwind, having that sensation could not be for one like hearing an oboe. And if one also lacked any concept of the sound of a woodwind, what it would be like for one to have that sensation would then be correspondingly more generic. If one lacked even the concept of a sensation's being of a sound as against being of some other type of stimulus,

having the sensation would for one be like merely having some indiscriminate sensory experience or other. This sequence makes it plausible that peeling away that weakest HOT would result, finally, in its no longer being like anything at all to have that sensation. Even though HOTs are just intentional states, and so have no qualitative properties, having HOTs does make the difference between whether there is or is not something it's like for one to have particular sensations.

Note

[1] One might argue that the new concepts pertain not to the distinguishing properties of our conscious sensory experiences, but rather to the perceptible properties of the perceived physical objects and processes, e.g. the wine or the musical performance. [...] But it's clear that in the cases just imagined we also focus introspectively on the distinguishing properties of our conscious sensory states. So those cases involve new concepts of the distinguishing properties of sensory states.

Multiple drafts and the stream of consciousness

Daniel C. Dennett

Source: Dennett, Daniel C. (1991) *Consciousness Explained*, London, Allen Lane (originally published by Little, Brown, and Co), pp.134–8. Copyright © 1992 Daniel Dennett. Reproduced with permission from Penguin Group, UK and Abner Stein.

1 Visual stimuli evoke trains of events in the cortex that gradually yield discriminations of greater and greater specificity. At different times and different places, various 'decisions' or 'judgments' are made; more literally, parts of the brain are caused to go into states that discriminate different features, e.g., first mere onset of stimulus, then location, then shape, later color (in a different pathway), later still (apparent) motion, and eventually object recognition. These localized discriminative states transmit effects to other places, contributing to further discriminations, and so forth [...]. The natural but naive question to ask is: Where does it all come together? The answer is: Nowhere. Some of these distributed contentful states soon die out, leaving no further traces. Others do leave traces, on subsequent verbal reports of experience and memory, on 'semantic readiness' and other varieties of perceptual set, on emotional state, behavioral proclivities, and so forth. Some of these effects – for instance, influences on subsequent verbal reports – are at least symp-tomatic of consciousness. But there is no one place in the brain through which all these causal trains must pass in order to deposit their content 'in consciousness'.

2 As soon as any such discrimination has been accomplished, it becomes available for eliciting some behavior, for instance a button-push (or a smile, or a comment), or for modulating some internal informational state. For instance, a discrimination of a picture of a dog might create a 'perceptual set' – making it temporarily easier to see dogs (or even just animals) in other pictures – or it might activate a particular semantic domain, making it temporarily more likely that you read the work 'bark' as a sound, not a covering for tree trunks. [...] [T]his multitrack process occurs over hundreds of milliseconds,

during which time various additions, incorporations, emendations, and overwritings of content can occur, in various orders. These yield, over the course of time, something *rather like* a narrative stream or sequence, which can be thought of as subject to continual editing by many processes distributed around in the brain, and continuing indefinitely into the future. Contents arise, get revised, contribute to the interpretation of other contents or to the modulation of behavior (verbal and otherwise), and in the process leave their traces in memory, which then eventually decay or get incorporated into or overwritten by later contents, wholly or in part. This skein of contents is only rather like a narrative because of its multiplicity; at any point in time there are multiple drafts of narrative fragments at various stages of editing in various places in the brain. While some of the contents in these drafts will make their brief contributions and fade without further effect – and some will make no contribution at all – others will persist to play a variety of roles in the further modulation of internal state and behavior and a few will even persist to the point of making their presence known through press releases issued in the form of verbal behavior.

3   Probing this stream at various intervals produces different effects, precipitating different narratives – and these *are* narratives: single versions of a portion of 'the stream of consciousness'. If one delays the probe too long, the result is apt to be no narrative left at all. If one probes 'too early', one may gather data on how early a particular discrimination is achieved in the stream, but at the cost of disrupting the normal progression of the stream.

4   Is there an 'optimal time of probing'? On the plausible assumption that after a while such narratives degrade rather steadily through both fading of details and self-serving embellishment (what I ought to have said at the party tends to turn into what I did say at the party), one can justify probing as soon as possible after the stimulus sequence of interest. But one also wants to avoid interfering with the phenomenon by a premature probe. Since perception turns imperceptibly into memory, and 'immediate' interpretation turns imperceptibly into rational reconstruction, there is no single all-contexts summit on which to direct one's probes.

5   Just what we are conscious of within any particular time duration is not defined independently of the probes we use to precipitate a narrative about that period. Since these narratives are under continual revision, there is no single narrative that counts as the canonical version, the 'first edition' in which are laid down, for all time, the events that happened in the stream of

consciousness of the subject, all deviations from which must be corruptions of the text. But any narrative (or narrative fragment) that does get precipitated provides a 'time line', a subjective sequence of events from the point of view of an observer, that may then be compared with other time lines, in particular with the objective sequence of events occurring in the brain of that observer. [...] [T]hese two time lines *may* not superimpose themselves in orthogonal registration (lined up straight): even though the (mis-)discrimination of *red-turning-to-green* occurred in the brain *after* the discrimination of *green spot*, the *subjective* or *narrative* sequence is, of course, *red spot, then red-turning-to-green, and finally green spot*. So within the temporal smear of the point of view of the subject, there may be order differences that induce kinks.

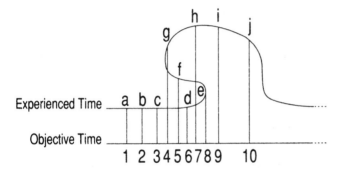

6   There is nothing metaphysically extravagant or challenging about this failure of registration. It is no more mysterious [...] than the realization that the individual scenes in movies are often shot out of sequence, or that when you read the sentence 'Bill arrived at the party after Sally, but Jane came earlier than both of them', you learn of Bill's arrival before you learn of Jane's earlier arrival. The space and time of the representing is one frame of reference; the space and time of what the representing represents is another. But this metaphysically innocuous fact does nevertheless ground a fundamental metaphysical category: When a portion of the world comes in this way to compose a skein of narratives, that portion of the world is an observer. That is what it is for there to be an observer in the world, a something it is like something to be. [...]

7   You have probably experienced the phenomenon of driving for miles while engrossed in conversation (or in silent soliloquy) and then discovering that you have utterly no memory of the road, the traffic, your car-driving activities. It is as if someone else had been driving. Many theorists (myself included, I admit [...]) have cherished this as a favorite case of 'unconscious

perception and intelligent action'. But were you *really* unconscious of all those passing cars, stop lights, bends in the road at the time? You were paying attention to other things, but surely *if you had been probed* about what you had *just* seen at various moments on the drive, you would have had at least some sketchy details to report. The 'unconscious driving' phenomenon is better seen as a case of rolling consciousness with swift memory loss.

8   Are you constantly conscious of the clock ticking? If it suddenly stops, you notice this, and you can say right away what it is that has stopped; the ticks 'you weren't conscious of' up to the moment they stopped and 'would never have been conscious of' if they hadn't stopped are now clearly in your consciousness. An even more striking case is the phenomenon of being able to count, retrospectively in experience memory, the chimes of the clock which you only noticed was striking after four or five chimes. But how could you so clearly *remember hearing* something you hadn't been conscious of in the first place? The question betrays a commitment to the Cartesian model; there are no fixed facts about the stream of consciousness independent of particular probes.

Index